I Did That

Paul Bailey

Published in Great Britain by
Paul Bailey

Paul Bailey Copyright © 20 The right of *Paul Bailey* to be identified as author of this work has been asserted in accordance with sections 77 and 78 of the Copyright, Designs and Patents Act, 1988.

ISBN: 978-1-80558-557-2

Preface

'Get Up Stand Up – Bob Marley'

The Greek philosopher Aristotle wrote, "Give me a child until he is seven, and I will show you the man." 'I Did That' provides an abridged version into the personal and professional life of Master, Mister, Police Constable, Detective Constable then on retirement after 30 years police service, back to Mister Paul Bailey. Many titles there but the same person throughout, as opined by Aristotle.

Growing up in inner-city Manchester in the 70s and 80s was never going to be easy. But add to that the external influences of peer pressure and, at that time, overt racism and bigotry, which more often than not went unchallenged. It wouldn't be unreasonable to say you had two options: fight or flight.

Fight, and that could lead to more trouble, flight, and the problem never goes away. Some choice!

Paul reflects on his formative years as a strong-willed black kid living in a multicultural district, attending grammar school, and playing sports which he excelled at. He's unapologetically him. He neither seeks pity nor praise. He did what he continued to do from his early years and throughout his life. You could say it's his unique selling point, loved by some, loathed by others.

Television police procedurals are full of uncompromising hard-nosed detectives who as characters we take to our hearts and hope they triumph.

Real-life policing is not so glamorous and those who get up and stand up are few and far between and often targeted for speaking out. Some people talk the talk but rarely walk the walk. Once the final page has been read you can decide which camp Paul is in. People of a certain age may remember the fictional police programme Dixon of Dock Green. Some say the halcyon days of policing. Younger readers will be more familiar with Line of Duty, which centres on police corruption, a subject Paul regularly tackled when he or others were subjected to it, much to the chagrin of senior officers.

Warning: An uncomfortable truth alert!

Despite the overwhelming majority of police officers being hardworking and operating at different levels of ability, the sad fact is that not only do some cops have to deal with thieves, robbers, miscreants and bigots on the streets, but they're often present in police stations up and down the country. The latter often wearing uniforms, or not if they're detectives, yielding great power, which is regularly abused.

'I Did That' only goes so far in some aspects, this book is Paul's personal journey, his story told in his own unique way. No quarter is asked, and none is given. It provides a microcosm of his 30-year career, which started as a uniform probationary constable dealing with bread-and-butter crimes and ended as a detective investigating the most serious crimes and interviewing some of the most dangerous and infamous criminals, many of whom will die in a variety of penal institutions.

As you read through this work, you're encouraged to research some of the names, incidents and court judgments to get a flavour of what can only be mentioned in the briefest of terms. Who knows, if there's an appetite, then a sequel could follow.

Greater Manchester Police is currently experiencing some turbulence it's hoped it will overcome it.

Contents

In the Beginning 1

Interlude 21

When One Door Closes Another One Opens 22

This Changes Everything 50

New Agenda 66

Coming in From the Cold 72

Interlude 81

You Know What's Up 82

Work It 96

I Walk A Lonely Road 108

It Will Never Be the Same Again 123

The Rot Starts 132

Ding, Ding Round Four 138

Revenge Is A Dish Best Served Cold 154

Lights-Camera-Action 171

If You Can't Beat Them, Cheat 180

Interlude 211

History Repeating 213

Everything That Has A Beginning 231

I Did That

In the Beginning

1989.

[Keep on Movin' - Soul II Soul]

It was a clear, bright December day. I recall that although the ground was moist, there was not a cloud in the sky. It was crisp. All of the deciduous trees in the park had shed their leaves, revealing the bare wood beneath. As I walked to my parents' house in Old Trafford, a journey that I had made thousands of times, I felt uneasy, hesitant even worried about my journey's end because today was different. Today was different to all of the days that I had experienced up until this point in my life; my life had changed. I walked to my parents' house to announce that I had joined Greater Manchester Police as a police constable.

I appreciate that for most in Britain in 1989, this should have been and would have been a joyous occasion celebrated and remembered. A day that would be full of tears of joy and remembered fondly in years to come. I didn't think any of that was going to happen. There may have been tears, but not tears of joy. As a black man living in inner city Manchester in the 1980s, joining the police wasn't exactly the first career choice. Joining the police probably would not have made the average black man's top ten career choices, top one hundred even. Black people weren't exactly banging on the door of the police station to sign up; they still aren't.

Becoming a police officer was a difficult thing to do when you are black. It was in 1989, and it is today.

I got to the front door of my parents' Victorian terrace. Even though I had moved out a couple of years earlier it still felt as though I was going home. I walked into the lounge and without hesitation declared that I had joined the police as a cop; clearly, the adrenalin had kicked in. My father did not say a word. He remained sitting in the armchair that he always sat in. My mother, unsure about what I was telling her, enquired if I meant that I intended to join the police. Unfortunately, her hearing had not failed her, "No, Mum, I'm not applying. I have been accepted".

My parents were processing it – it felt like an eternity.

I realised that there was no going back now. Life for me would never be the same again.

It would be years before I appreciated how my decision had impacted the lives of my family. When I look back at this day now over thirty years later, I understand that my journey to the police had started much earlier.

1978.

[Staying' Alive – Bee Gees]

I went to Seymour Park Primary and Junior School in Old Trafford.

In the nineteen sixties and seventies, Old Trafford was made up of several diverse communities and would certainly be described as multi-cultural by any standard. There was a large African-Caribbean community made up of the Windrush generation and their families of first-generation black British children. I was one of those. There was also a large white Irish community, a significant white Polish community and a decreasing white English community who were disappearing south to the suburbs as fast as they could sell their houses. In addition, there were significant Asian communities, primarily Indian or of Indian descent; however, people from

I Did That

Pakistan or of Pakistani heritage were arriving in the area in ever-increasing numbers. Even in the seventies, I was not shy at speaking my mind or calling out inequality. I recall that one day in class during another Eurocentric brainwashing lesson, I asked the teacher why we were always being told about white people and white history? I questioned why the lessons did not reflect the life that I could see before my eyes living in such a multicultural area; in short, what about my history? She was clearly dumbfounded and unable to justify the whitewashed curriculum. I'd like to think that she thought, "Aww, what a pleasant, inquisitive little boy," experience tells me that her inner voice was saying something very different.

Anyway, my school report of July 1978 read:

Other Subjects – *'Paul takes a keen interest in everything and is prepared to ask questions. He works hard and achieves good results, though often his work is badly presented - he has good reasoning'*. There's nothing like a backhanded compliment.

My Mum has one of those old-fashioned photograph albums, the one with sticky cardboard and clear plastic leaves intended to protect the image. That 1978 school report sits in that album. Maybe my mum knew something I didn't, or maybe she just liked the fact that I had no fear, even at an early age, of taking on the establishment.

What she probably did not know was the disparity that existed in schooling. I was always told that being forthright would be my undoing and that I should learn to fit in, or I would amount to nothing. This was the very low bar that was presented to young black children like me in the seventies, the establishment not being foolish enough to commit this view to paper to be immortalised in my mum's fifty-year-old photo album. My response to being told that I would achieve nothing unless I acquiesced, "We'll see about that".

One thing that couldn't be denied was my sporting ability, even that 1978 school report commented, simply - 'High standard in games.' The lack of any further description and the begrudging tone of this comment rings as loudly in 2020 as it did in 1978.

Departing from the cricket-loving tradition of the Caribbean, the sport of choice was football. Football seemed to be the only sport that people watched back then. As there were only three channels on the TV, it was hard to avoid football programmes, especially at the weekend.

Viv Anderson and Laurie Cunningham were the first black players that I recall seeing. Pioneering, skilful and racially abused for the colour of their skin. That didn't stop me. I played football whenever I could. Seymour Park had a football team made up of all-black players. This must have been very scary for white folk. What was even scarier was how good we were. I cruised along in the school team before I knew it, I had been picked to play for the area team. Stretford Boys under 11's team was drawn from junior schools throughout the Stretford area.

The team consisted of black boys from inner-city schools and white boys from further south of the borough which was predominantly white. Gavin Morris, Wayne Collins and Steve Black also played for Stretford Boys.

I had gone to school with Gavin from reception class through primary and junior school. He wasn't as tall as I was, but he was pretty fast and undoubtedly determined. Wayne and Steve were also from Old Trafford, naturally. Wayne is my cousin, Steve lived only a short distance away. They went to Old Trafford Junior School.

Seymour Park's arch-rivals. This inter-school rivalry was quickly forgotten when we pulled on a Stretford Boys top. The team was awesome and gained great success. All the time I harboured dreams of becoming the next Viv Anderson, but better. It would take another forty years before the importance of seeing black role models achieving success would be fully accepted by British society. Black children of 2020 would be horrified at the thought of 'Love Thy Neighbour' or 'Alf Garnett.'

1980.

[Master Blaster Jammin – Stevie Wonder]

The natural progression for black children where I grew up was they leave junior school for the local comprehensive.

My older brother Andrew was one of the few who had passed the Eleven Plus (11+) exam, and therefore, by 1980, he had been at Stretford Grammar School for boys for a few years. Surely, two black boys from the same household could not pass the exam. Remember how low the level of expectation was? Think again. I'm sure my junior schoolteacher thought that I had passed the exam just to spite her. Gavin also passed, so we were on our way.

At first, it felt a little strange donning a different uniform to the majority of the children who lived in my area, but that soon wore off. There was a group of us who walked from Old Trafford to Stretford Grammar School For Boys a couple of miles away.

There was Jimmy Donegan, a white boy of Irish descent. When I look back at Jimmy, he was the one white lad hanging out with a group of black lads in 1980. He was pretty cool, really, a Rockstar.

Donovan 'Danny' James, he was ultra-cool. He was like a mini-Teddy Pendergrass. Gavin 'Gavman' Morris, I've told you about him.

Chris 'Kingpin' King; Chris' parents were also from Jamaica and knew my parents well. He went to Old Trafford Junior School but wasn't much of a footballer, he was really good at something else – that will come later. We walked every day in all weather and became a tight-knit unit. 1980 was a bumper year for black boys passing the 11+.

There were two other black boys in our year, Dexter Dunn and Greg Husbands. Although they were not part of our unit, so to speak, we all looked out for each other.

I continued to play football. Stretford Boys had transformed into Stretfordian Juniors.

Mark O'Hara, despite his name, was a black boy from Old Trafford of Jamaican descent, he played alongside Steve, Wayne and I. Bizarrely, Gavin had chosen to play for a different team called Meadowside.

The 1980s was when racism undoubtedly aired its ugly head for me. On the pitch, we'd hear monkey chants and abusive comments from opponents and spectators, often the parents of our opponents. This abuse increased if our opponents were losing. We won – a lot. It was the first time that I identified 'The Switch.'

The Switch:

> If you imagine a wall, six feet three inches tall, black, impenetrable, thirty feet away. Throughout my life, there have been numerous people, far too many to recall, who have thrown objects at that wall, much to the wall's annoyance, but without any reaction from it. Then imagine that that wall has an invisible switch. People could throw objects at that wall their whole lives without any reaction, but if they hit the switch – well it's on, and it cannot be turned off. I am the wall.

There is a scene in Forrest Gump that perfectly demonstrates 'The Switch.' Forrest goes to a Black Panther party in Washington, DC. There, Jenny is struck across the face by her current boyfriend,

Wesley. Forrest immediately becomes solely focused on Jenny's attacker, his senses sifting out anything else not immediately connected to Wesley. In a blink of an eye, Forrest subdued Wesley with a blaze of punches. In this scenario, who is to blame, Wesley or Forrest Gump? In the movies, Forrest is heralded as a hero. Real life is quite different, especially when you are black.

It was at Stretford Grammar that I met Plutos 'Plute' Vourliotis. He was the oldest child of Greek/Cypriot parents; Plute loved basketball, and so did Kingpin. Remember that 'High Standard in Games' school report? It turned out that I had a penchant for any sport with a ball. More than that, I was pretty good at all of them.

This trio of Plute, Kingpin, and I were the ingredients for probably the best school basketball team that Manchester had ever seen.

Plute was the tallest; he had a large garden and driveway at home. His father had erected a basketball hoop on the driveway that Plute used morning, noon and night. As a result, he developed an outside long-range shot that was beautiful to watch and deadly accurate.

Kingpin was maybe an inch or so smaller than Plute. His mid-range game was stylish and charismatic. He wasn't afraid to go into the paint; the result was either two more points to the total or a trip to the foul line. Kingpin was ultra-confident, taking free throws.

Then there was me, the smallest of the trio and the epitome of 'Survival of the Fittest'. Let me explain: the trans-Atlantic slave trade saw the forced relocation, kidnap, imprisonment, rape, torture and murder of enslaved Africans taken predominantly from the West coast of Africa and transported to the North and South American continents, including the Caribbean. In the case of my ancestors, Jamaica.

Firstly, the slavers only took the fittest Africans, those likely to make the trip and disembark at the other end. What would be the point of sailing across the Atlantic only to arrive with no cargo? Secondly, only the fittest were able to survive the harsh working environment whether it be picking cotton or harvesting sugar cane, by hand. The result was a breed of super athletic African-Caribbean/ African–American people who excelled in sports. This is one theory anyway; another is that there were and are few outlets for black children to excel. Sports and music were acceptable pathways that black children followed in numbers.

In any event my game was simple: total domination of my opponent. High-tempo, high-energy basketball at both ends of the court. We crushed other teams, sometimes trying to stop them from scoring a single point. From the start of the game, we would be all over the other team. We had a set play from the opening tip-off. Plute would jump. Failing disaster, he would win the jump ball, pushing the ball forward to Kingpin, who was standing in the opponent's half with his back to their basket. I would set off in motion as soon as the ball went up. By the time Kingpin caught the ball it was a simple sideways pass to me now moving at full speed. I would then dunk the ball (Boom) before our opponents realised what had happened. If they didn't think they were going to lose, they did now.

Upon enrolment at Stretford Grammar, the school was divided into sub-units called 'Houses' that competed against each other in sports. Stretford Grammar's four houses were named after famous American astronauts Armstrong, Collins, Glenn and Lovell. Plute, Kingpin and I were in Glenn, inter-house basketball was like shelling peas.

It was undeniable that our trio was very special. Our sports teacher, Mr Patterson, loved coaching a school basketball team like ours. He arranged matches against older students. We played older teams as a way to make the competition interesting - for us. We played against my brother's varsity basketball team. Varsity teams weren't really a thing in Britain at that time, but you understand the analogy.

Andrew was three years ahead of me. The result was the same: an embarrassing crushing defeat - for them. The school's teachers had the good sense not to take us on, fearing their fate would be the same as everyone else.

Sport took up most of my time, I represented the school in football, basketball, cricket and even table tennis. Football was the only sport marred by racism.

1981.

[One in Ten – UB40]

The Windrush generation had found a home in many inner-city areas of Britain, including Manchester's Moss Side. Migrants from the Caribbean had settled in the area for over thirty years by the early nineteen eighties.

In July 1981, Moss Side was the scene of mass rioting that started at Moss Side Police Station, moving to the surrounding streets the following days. Racial tension and mass unemployment were described as key factors for the riot. Old Trafford bordered Moss Side. To the casual observer, there was little difference between the two areas. The Ayres Road area of Old Trafford saw its share of rioting and property damage.

The relationship between the police and the African-Caribbean community had been strained at best. In 1981, divorce proceedings were announced. I recall seeing the destruction in the aftermath of the riots. Selected shops along Ayres Road had been targeted, their windows smashed, stock destroyed or stolen. Moss Side shopping precinct looked like a war zone, as did Princess Road.

After the riots, for the first time in my life, I noticed that the local police tried to be friendly with the African-Caribbean community. If a local cop saw us playing football or just hanging around, he - cops were invariably male and white - would try to positively engage with us. This was the first time that the police were OK, I even thought about joining the police quietly to myself. The newly acquired police coolness after the riots didn't last, as the police quickly reverted to type, searching black people for no reason and being aloof.

1982.

[Get Loose – Evelyn King]

By 1982, the fourth TV channel appeared on our screens, imaginatively called Channel 4. The advent of this new channel meant that I was able to watch the National Basketball League live on TV.

I continued to play as many sports as I could but felt my interest in football was waning. A pivotal moment for me was when I saw other players nowhere near as talented as I was progressing to trials with established football league clubs. It wasn't just me. There was a perception that other black players were side-lined whilst white lads progressed. I must applaud the black players who made it to the top flight.

By 1982, Viv Anderson and Laurie Cunningham had been joined by Cyrille Regis, Ricky Hill, Mark Chamberlain and Luther Blissett.

During a club match, one of my opponents hit 'The Switch'. There was always trash-talking during competitive sports, a n d name-calling wasn't uncommon, however, in addition to the usual insults this guy fouled me literally every time I got the ball, it was personal.

The last foul was cynical and obvious. I bounced up off the ground, and before he or I knew it, he was on his arse with the referee blowing his whistle furiously. I was sent off – he stayed on the pitch. It didn't seem fair, but fairness had nothing to do with it. The establishment hadn't finished with me yet. I was banned from representing the school in any sport. I couldn't even play sports during PE. It was clear that the school were trying to make an example of me; they were going to teach me a lesson. I had never seen such a sanction imposed on a schoolboy. Oh well, it's always nice to be the first.

During PE, instead of going to the gym, I had to report to the headmaster's office. I sat in the hallway outside of his office for the length of the lesson. Sometimes, he would send me to a classroom to pass on a message. I'm not sure if this was necessary or if it was intended to humiliate me further. What the teachers didn't know was that it made me cool in the eyes of some of the other boys. I was the proverbial 'Bad Boy' so bad that the headmaster himself was called in to tame me. He couldn't do that - No one could. Although I missed playing sports, the lack of it didn't affect me anywhere near as much as I thought it would. My view was fuck them. Perhaps this was written all over my face as the ban soon came to an end. This teeny sanction wasn't enough to break me – please.

Football seemed to fizzle out after this for me. I played basketball more than anything else for the remainder of my time at school. Our school team went from strength to strength. Plute, Kingpin and I were picked up by local teams. I went to the Manchester Giants junior team. They went to Manchester United's equivalent. To this day, I do not know how that happened. Basketball got more and more airplay on the TV. I watched pros like Pete Mullings, Kevin Penny, Keith Ramsey and Dave Gardner playing on the national stage.

The remainder of my time in school certainly wasn't a bed of roses. Racism kept rearing its ugly head. I recall that one boy took a real dislike to me. He wasn't someone who I had taken notice of, not for the whole time that I had been there. One day, he decided that his time to shine had come. In the schoolyard, he grabbed a hold of me by my shirt and told me that he wanted a fight. He called me a 'Wellie-faced nigger.' He had clearly revealed his intent to his entourage beforehand as they were standing by. I'm not sure if it was their intention to watch or take part. If it was the second option, then this would have been a mistake. I told him to let go of me, which led to him pulling me forward towards him. That was it, within seconds he literally had a bloody nose. The disappointment of his entourage was palpable. What I didn't know was that a teacher had watched the incident from an upstairs window, slyly reporting the incident to the headmaster. It wasn't lost on me that the headmaster's involvement could lead to a more severe sanction being meted out to me. Suspension perhaps, expulsion even, was that the aim? I found myself in front of the headmaster again. I was learning valuable lessons in how to survive the privileged and closeted ranks of the white middle class.

By the next day, the other boy's parents were baying for blood, my blood. Their darling boy was sporting two black eyes. Someone had to pay for that. Unfortunately, their darling boy did not tell them that he had planned and started the fight. He also missed out the 'wellie-faced nigger' part. I was quite within my rights to act in the way that I did. When the full facts of the incident were revealed, I was completely exonerated. I told my mum about the fight, and all she asked was, "Did you win?" "Yes, mum." She then carried on with her day. No one came near me again, nor did anyone utter the word, nigger, in my presence anyway.

'I got no respect for a man who won't hit back. You kill my dog; you better hide your cat' - Muhammad Ali.

[Well done to all of those black children who survived football in the 1970s and 1980s, who survived an environment that was unapologetically racist and unforgiving. I must also applaud Wayne Collins for his perseverance; Wayne made it to professional football, having an eleven-year professional career playing for Crewe Alexandra, Sheffield Wednesday, Fulham and Stockport County]

1989.

[Fight the Power – Public Enemy]

By 1989, I had played for several basketball teams, both as an amateur and professionally. These teams included Manchester Giants and Manchester United. I had had the opportunity to play with players that I had seen years earlier on TV. I had even played for an emerging Bury team with Ed Bona and Terry Crosby. It was during this period, whilst playing for Joe Forber, that I met a young John Amaechi.

I recall seeing John for the first time during a practice session. He was huge. I immediately thought that he was built more for rugby than basketball. I am sure that John would be the first to agree that he came to the game late. He lacked coordination, and the ball did not sit comfortably with him. His size worked to his advantage, being about six feet ten inches tall, but at this stage of his career, he had a long way to go. I was not sure that basketball was going to be for him. I could not have been more wrong. John went on to play basketball in the United States, at college level for Vanderbilt and Penn State. He also played in the NBA with the Cleveland Cavaliers, Orlando Magic and the Utah Jazz. John was awarded an OBE in 2011 for his services to sport and the voluntary sector. [In later life John and I would reunite playing in an over forties' tournament in the UK].

Brian Dobson was a serving police officer at Brownley Road Police Station and an Assistant Manager for Manchester Giants. He worked alongside Jeff Jones, both of whom I played for. Brian was a fan of my high-energy, high-tempo game. Since school, I had honed my game. Defensively, I was able to defend the strongest of big men. No opponent was safe shooting the ball if I were any closer than three steps away. Offensively, I could score in bunches quickly and play above the rim at both ends. Clearly, Brian was impressed with that. Brian had reignited my earlier thought of joining the police. I had sought to apply at eighteen years old, but the joining age for GMP was 21. After that, I lost interest.

For a number of years, our home games were played at Stretford Sports Centre. Ironically, the Sports Centre was directly across the road from my old grammar school and the gym where I started off playing. I couldn't turn into the sports centre car park without glancing over at my old school and school gym. There were days when I would have three of four dunks in the game and as many blocked shots. This type of play pleased the crowd and normally got a reaction out of them. One of those who watched those games was Martin Harding.

Martin Harding was a black police inspector and, apparently, a fan of basketball. Not only had this black man joined the police, but they had promoted him. I suppose that others would have been immediately impressed by this. His achievement within the police was lost on me at first, but not for long.

We got talking, and he broached the subject of me joining the police. Kevin Penny had joined sometime earlier and still managed to play professional basketball. The precedent had been set. This worked in Martin's favour. Martin was well aware of the enormity of what he was asking me. He was black, after all.

My personal interactions with the police were mostly negative – a few games of football with the neighbourhood beat bobby after the riots in 1981 that had sparked my interest in the police, but that felt like a thousand police stop checks ago by the time I was twenty years old. The police were not seen as the friends of the black man. Quite the opposite. I had been stop-checked so many times that I took to carrying my driving documents with me so that when I was stopped driving by the police, an inevitability back then, I could get it over as soon as possible without the need to produce my documents at a police station. I didn't have to drive a car to be stopped by the police.

I recall walking through Seymour Park when I was approached by two uniformed cops, who, without any introduction, pulled the bag that I was carrying away from me before roughly and aggressively searching me and my bag. Obviously, they found nothing illegal or wrong. They left as quickly as they arrived. This was just one of many searches that I suffered, but these two cops left a lasting impression on me, a negative one.

The only time that I saw black people comfortable in the company or at least in close proximity to the police was when my father and I went to see the West Indies cricket team play England at Old Trafford. All the West Indian supporters would congregate in the same stand, turning the terrace into a carnival. It seemed to be the only time that the inhibitions of my father's generation were left at home. The police there openly supported England, and every black person supported the West Indies.

I found myself fighting the conflict of whether to follow through with joining the police, as I had considered before, or to once and for all decide never to join. On one side, it was clear to me that the police weren't there to protect me or people like me. Where I grew up you did not call the police even if you had been a victim of the crime. The general view was, why call the police? They would treat you roughly, disbelieve you and only make matters worse. Why else were they called 'Pigs,' 'The Filth,' or 'Babylon?' None of these words were intended as terms of endearment. On the other side, I had a serving police officer, a black serving police inspector no less, asking me to sign up.

Basketball did not have the same public appeal as, say, football, cricket or even rugby. Only the top British professionals and the

American stars earned enough money to live comfortably on. I, therefore, worked in the insurance industry in addition to playing national league basketball. I worked for a well-known company in Didsbury, Manchester. I was the only black person there, of course, so everyone in the company knew me. I was able to work full time in my office role Monday to Friday and still play basketball during the evenings and weekends.

One day, before the conversation with Martin, I was working at my desk when I received a call from reception. The receptionist told me that two detectives wanted to speak to me. I put my suit jacket on and walked to reception trying to maintain a persona of calm. There were two white male police detectives sitting at a table waiting for my arrival. They immediately stated that they were investigating a murder. My initial thought was I had not witnessed a murder, so why were they here? Then the scene turned dark as they said that I lived nearby and had left the country shortly after the murder had occurred. Wait a minute, was I a suspect? - You have got to be fucking kidding me. I had no idea who had been murdered, how they had been murdered, or why. I certainly had not been involved in a murder - in any way.

At the time, I lived in a block of flats on Upper Chorlton Road on the Old Trafford Moss Side border, murders weren't exactly a rarity. The police had gone to the trouble to check who had left the country after the murder had occurred and came up with me. What was I supposed to be, an international hitman who went to the trouble of leaving the country only to return days later because I loved insurance so much? Were these clowns for real? Yes, I had left the country, but I had left with the entire Manchester Giants basketball team to play in a tournament in Holland.

I was furious. These Keystone Cops had got it badly wrong and decided to embarrass me and themselves at my place of work. I could see the other people in reception pretending to busy themselves with other tasks whilst clearly trying to gain a better position to hear my conversation. I pointed out the error in the police assertions, made it clear that I had no information that could possibly help their enquiries, and politely asked them to fuck off. In my mind, I was transported briefly back to that school corridor outside of the headmaster's office. I know that place now as 'The corridor.'

I moved to Northenden, nearer to work, had an easier commute and, most importantly, had a lower murder rate. This wouldn't be the last time that the police suspected that I had done something that I had entirely no knowledge of.

I was conflicted with the police. Deep down, I didn't trust them and had been on the receiving end of their blatant racist attitudes and racial stereotyping. This view was common for black people at the time; conversely, white people seemed to love the police rolling out the bunting whenever they arrived. A clear dichotomy of views of the police. Clearly, Martin's powers of persuasion were better than I thought. Looking back now, the fact that he was a serving police inspector, a black inspector, won the day. I was going to join the police.

Martin came around to my house in Northenden to talk me through the process. I lived in a shared house. He was opened-mouthed when he saw women mingling around wearing very little, he had turned up in full uniform that piqued their interest. Martin joked that I would have to move out of this house as the police would never allow me to stay.

[Wonderwall – Oasis]

There were a number of different stages to the joining process. There were interviews, written, and physical exams that were spaced weeks or months apart. It was during this process that I met a man called Chris Barnes. Chris was a keen Rugby player but made his living as a tiler. He lived in Chorlton and was a Manchester City fan, a

Manchester City super fan, and this was at a time when City were rubbish. We instantly got on and became friends; I didn't know it at the time, but we would become lifelong friends. Fate works in different ways. Every time I progressed to the next part of the process, Chris was given the same date.

At the fitness test, Chris turned up in old, torn sportswear, whilst I turned up dripping in the latest gear. I enjoyed the free sportswear that came with playing national league basketball. I was in peak condition, so passing the fitness test was easy. Fortunately for Chris, it was a fitness test and not a fashion test. He also passed.

I continued to play national league basketball and even had time to play for other teams. The local youth club in Old Trafford wanted to turn a team out for a tournament primarily for inner-city clubs. I said I'd play but had forgotten that I had committed to the event when the day came around. It was early morning when I heard banging on the front door of my house in Northenden. My bedroom was at the front of the house on the first floor, but I wasn't there – nope, I was curled up with one of the women that I lived with whose room was downstairs. I hadn't been asleep long; it had been a long night. I could hear Kingpin outside. He knew where my room was, so I couldn't look out of the downstairs window bollock naked, could I? I had to sneak upstairs past the front door then I presented myself at my bedroom window. Happy that my ruse had been successful, I then bounded back down the stairs to the front door. Kingpin looked at me, "What have you been doing? I've been throwing stones at your window for ages". My reply was not convincing as he gave me that look, the look that a parent gives their child when they have caught them being naughty. In my case, it was 'In flagrante delicto'. I got dressed, and off we went.

I got through all the stages really quickly and without much incident. I would later learn that other people took years to get through the process. What on earth were they doing? I would have lost interest if the process had not been so rapid. The day of my final interview came around. I can honestly say that I was not nervous, probably because joining the police was not 'the be all and end all' for me. The panel sat there, protected behind their desk. They asked the obvious mind-numbing questions, "Mr Bailey, why do you want to join the police?" I didn't think "Martin Harding talked me into it." was the right answer, so came up with some bunkum. Whatever I said worked because that was it, I was in – but not so fast.

Back then, you had to have a medical assessment on the same day as the final interview, well, I did anyway. I wore a pair of shorts whilst my height, weight et cetera was assessed. They were aware of my fitness test score of 181 out of 205, an easy pass. Secretly, I was not happy with that score and wanted to improve upon it. Then everything hit the brakes. The nurse, at least I think she was a nurse, stated that I was too heavy for her chart. Too heavy, I was six feet three and 'ripped' without any fat on me. You could wash a week's worth of your delicates on my abs. Did I mention my fitness test score? Evidently, the chart was another indication of the one-dimensional view of the world that the police had. I am sure that thousands of white people fitted perfectly into this one-size-fits-all all chart. However, an athletic African-Caribbean might just struggle even if they have not got an ounce of fat on them.

This is not a small or isolated issue. If the process is unfair and discriminates, whether that is by design or not, then the police service would never reflect the communities that they are supposed to serve. [Eurocentrism is a belief system that positions Europe as the central force in shaping world history, promoting universal values and representing progress and development]

In 1989, this was an indication of discrimination or unequal treatment based on the membership of a particular ethnic group (typically one that is a minority or marginalised) arising from systems, structures, or expectations that have become established within an institution or organisation. There were other examples of this type of discrimination within the recruitment, some of which GMP did not have control over. If you accept that black people as a minority group in Britain are overrepresented in the criminal justice system, then the likely outcome is that they will know, be associated with, or be related to another black person who has a criminal record. If this association becomes a bar to the applicant joining the police, then black people will be sifted out at the application process. Surely, someone would recognise this and perhaps think of a name for it.

Coming back to my story, the nurse said that she was sorry but I couldn't join; she just needed this to be signed off by the doctor. I can't say that I was disappointed. It was like being offered a meal that you didn't genuinely fancy, only to be told that someone else had eaten it.

I went straight in to see the doctor, who looked at my file, looked up at me, stood there, and, without any further deliberation, declared that I had passed.

I'd best go and tell my parents then.

Interlude

1960's.

[This Is a Man's World – James Brown]

It was the late 1960s; by this time, my mother and father had two small children. Andrew, my older brother and Marcia, our sister, who was the oldest.

One day, out of the blue, a young man appeared at the front door. The young man was accompanied by a much younger girl, a child, who turned out to be his daughter. My mother was surprised by the visit and even more surprised when she realised that the young man was my father's son from a relationship well before my mother and father ever met. No one ever said that the 1960s was uneventful.

Paul Bailey

When One Door Closes Another One Opens

1990.

[This Is How We Do It – Montell Jordan]

My start date was in January 1990. By January, I had had the opportunity to tell Andrew and Marcia of my decision to join the police, Greater Manchester Police. Their reaction was equally frosty. Marcia was merciless in her piss-taking. At every opportunity, she would comment about the pigs. Despite this, I got the feeling that she supported my decision even if she did not agree with it. My mum appeared to have come to terms with my decision. There was no hiding the fact that she did not agree with me joining and would be counting the days until I left. My father had still not commented. I respected his silence. I told my closest friends, who were generally supportive, some hiding their apprehension about me becoming a police officer better than others. I was under no illusion that the news would filter around Old Trafford in its own time.

I was to report to Sedgley Park on 15th January 1990. Sedgley Park was and still is GMP's training school. I had not heard of the place before joining up, so I did not know what to expect.

Arriving at the front gate, I had the feeling that you get when you strap yourself into a roller-coaster, waiting for it to climb over the crest of the first fall. Surprisingly, I was not the only black person who started as a constable on that day. There was a black man of mixed heritage who looked relieved when he realised that he wasn't the only one. His joy was short-lived. The students were separated into classes. The two black guys were separated.

We were allocated classrooms where we were given details of our postings. Each recruit would be assigned to a borough of Greater Manchester, called divisions. Today, they're called districts. These boroughs would be our permanent postings once we had left the training school. I was assigned to the Trafford Division (M) and would be working from Stretford Police Station.

Soon, everyone in Old Trafford would know that I joined the police. I knew that being assigned to the division or borough where I grew up was a possibility, so I silently listened to my posting and said nothing. I was not sure if this was a test of my nerve or if this was a genuine posting with no ulterior motive attached to it. I knew where Stretford Police Station was, literally across the road from my old grammar school. The police station complex backed onto Stretford Sports Centre. At least I'd be able to find it.

Tracy Cobb had also been posted to the M Division, her collar number was 7825, mine 7826. I had not joined the police to make friends. To be truthful, I was still trying to work out why I had joined. As new recruits, we were going to spend four weeks in force, a mixture of classwork and being an observer with serving constables in our respective divisions. After this initial period, we would be going to Bruche Police Training Centre for ten weeks of intensive training, followed by a further five weeks later on.

By the second day at Sedgley Park my intake of recruits were coming to terms with wearing their police uniforms for the first time. They were checking each other out, no doubt, to see who looked best. Not everyone was donning their new uniforms. My uniform didn't fit. I needed a long pair of trousers, but for my inside leg measurement, the waists of the uniform trousers were all too big - way too big. Who had these trousers been designed for? Had Luciano Pavarotti been a GMP police officer? Was the circus in town? The irony of my medical assessment was not lost on me. They had told me that I was too heavy using their Eurocentric 'boys in blue' chart. Then, the uniform turned out to be so big that the best use for the trousers turned out to be as a hand glider, a parachute or a tent. The poor apparel turned out to be the only remarkable thing that happened in the first week, with the exception of me signing up for the police pension scheme.

Walking into Stretford Police Station for the first time as a police officer was a strange feeling. I now had a uniform that fit. My shoes were polished, and I was ready to go.

I recall attending my first road traffic accident, called RTA's, at the time. It was on Chester Road in Stretford near to the former public hall that had originally been a public library given by John Rylands. I was in the company of a traffic cop who drove his Ford Capri at breakneck speed once he received the call. When we arrived, I saw a motorcyclist lying in the northbound carriageway. It wasn't immediately apparent, but when I got closer to him, I saw that he was lying on his back. His legs had been broken backwards, which meant that his back was resting on his own legs. The motorcyclist was conscious; the paramedics had given him a mask. I suppose it was delivering some sort of sedative to him before he was lifted off his own legs. Ok, that was the worst thing that I had seen firsthand. It was clear that the driver of a car had emerged from a side road into the path of the motorcycle that had the right of way on the main road. The motorcyclist collided with the side of the car, the impact catapulting him forward to the position where he lay. Surprisingly, this did not bother me the way that I might have thought. Maybe I did have the stomach for this sort of thing.

I continued to accompany different constables and observed many different incidents. I was surprised at the monotony of the work and the range of reasons that people called the police. Most of the time, we seem to be marriage counsellors. The dreariness was short-lived.

I Did That

One day, I was walking along the main corridor at Stretford Police Station in full uniform. Partway along the corridor was an entrance door that led to the custody office and cell area. As I walked towards the entrance, a black man emerged from the custody office, I recognised him as a local man from the Old Trafford area but did not know his name. I could see instantly that he had just been released from police custody. He was in the process of pushing his belt through the loops on his trousers. Belts and laces were taken from people in custody to prevent them from hurting themselves. He saw me, and his mood and face instantly changed. He called me by my second name and said that I should not have joined the police. He tried to be careful but made it clear that me joining the police was not a good idea. He asked if I still lived in Old Trafford and said that houses burn down, I didn't but he was referring to my parent's house. He was undoubtedly making a threat that he clumsily tried to conceal, but the threat was clear.

Not another corridor scorched into my memory. I did not realise that this interaction was witnessed by a superintendent, who was in the corridor at the time, who later called me into his office and asked me what the incident was all about. I told him that I was from Old Trafford originally, and that could cause problems for me moving forward, especially as I was assigned Old Trafford as a foot-beat. That was it I was transferred to the south of the borough, South Trafford. After Bruche, I would be working from Sale Police Station. I also moved into the hostel at Stretford Police Station. I was assigned room 13. Good job that I was not superstitious.

By February, my first stint at Belmarsh Bruche had started. Bruche was a regional police training centre that took recruits from forces all over the north of England and even the Isle of Man. Being residential, we all had been assigned individual rooms within the dormitories that were separated by gender. Recruits were not allowed to leave the premises. This made it feel more like a prison than a school to me. If the 'no leaving' rule was bad, during the evenings, there was 'quiet time' when you were expected to work from your room or work out at the gym. This antiquated system was an indication that the police were living in the past. Was it ready for people who looked and thought like me? We would see.

I quickly learned that police officers fell into certain types (This is the 1990s):

> 'The Nepotist' – They cannot help telling you that their daddy was a cop and his daddy before him. They expect everything to be delivered to them on a plate irrespective of their ability and always think that they are superior to everyone else.
>
> 'The Nationalist' – Pro Britain and anti-everyone-else. Anyone who does not bleed red, white and blue is a terrorist. They think that their view of Britain is right and anyone who departs from any part of this view is 'one of them.'
>
> 'The Worker' – This is the average guy who just wants to do the job. The police officer who tries to do the right thing but sometimes allows self-preservation to win over morality or ethics. The ranks of the worker have sometimes been infiltrated by incompetents who are there for nothing more than the money.
>
> 'The Narcissist' – They are self-obsessed with a grandiose view of their importance. They seek and crave attention like no other and will burn anyone to promote their agenda. Under normal circumstances, they should be avoided like the plague.
>
> 'The Wannabe' – They feel better moving around in packs and telling bad jokes. They see the police as a legal way to have the power to do whatever they want and get away with it. If you are a minority or if 'The Wannabe' takes a dislike to you then watch out. Fortunately, The Wannabe' isn't as

clever as they think, they are clumsy and easy to defeat.

And finally;

'The Serpico' – They will do the job the right way regardless of the consequences to their aspirations. They have an unshakeable code that will not be broken and show empathy to any who deserves it. The Serpico naturally develops an in-built lie detector and, after time develops the ability to see into the future.

It is possible to be a hybrid of these types, The Narcissist-Wannabe' being particularly unpleasant. Conversely, some types cannot be mixed. There is no such thing as The Serpico-Narcissist.

On 28th February 1990, I was sitting in a classroom before the start of the day's session. PC David Pankhurst, a Lancashire Constabulary recruit and relative of Emmeline Pankhurst, was reading a paper. Believing that I would be interested in anything basketball, he summarised an article that he had read. He said Tony Penny died last night. I immediately got up and ran out of the classroom. As it was 1990 with no internet to speak of, social media had not been invented and wouldn't be for years – mobile phones were few and far between. I ran to the payphone. I called Kingpin at home. Kingpin said that during last night's game, he was sitting next to Tony on the bench when he felt Tony leaning onto him. Believing that Tony was messing about, Kingpin turned to push him away but quickly realised that Tony was having a medical episode. Tony collapsed and died - he was 23 years old. Tony was Kevin Penny's brother and former Central Connecticut State University basketball star. I knew him and had scrimmaged with him a number of times. I was unaware that Tony had any heart conditions, but I later learned that he had been diagnosed with hypertrophic cardiomyopathy.

The last time that I saw Tony was in Manchester city centre. We approached Cross Street walking towards each other from different directions. As we crossed in the middle of the carriageway, we fist-bumped each other and continued on our way.

I knew Kevin very well and had played with him for some time. Kevin was also a serving police constable with GMP. I returned to class that was already underway, I can't actually remember what the lesson was about. David Pankhurst came up to me afterwards to apologise for the way that he delivered what was essentially a death message. I told him not to worry about it. He didn't know that I knew Tony or that my reaction would be what it was. I had all the time in the world for David after that.

The course curriculum was displayed on the class wall. Each week was laid out in sections that corresponded with chapters in our course handout. One day, I noticed that there was a section on race and diversity intended for a week quite early in the syllabus. Later that day, I turned to that section in the course handout even though the race and diversity section was weeks away. I was horrified by the tone and content of this book, which included stereotypical assumptions about the hierarchy of black or African-Caribbean families and racist tropes about the makeup of these families. It even made assumptions about why black people would not look another person in the eye. It was total nonsense. The tropes were not limited to the course books. There were two black police officers from different forces at Bruche at the same time. Each recruit was given a nickname decided upon by the class. Yes, I know that this is an obvious recipe for disaster but bear with me. These nicknames were displayed on sweatshirts that everyone wore. One of these black PCs was called 'The Brick' and the other one 'The Brick 2,' a reference to black people being unable to swim.

[These racist tropes littered the police service. Sometime later, in the West Midlands, a friend of mine became the new boss of a section. One of the Asian PCs was referred to as 'Stan' by the rest of the section. My friend followed suit, initially calling the Asian PC

Stan until he got to know all of the staff that he was to supervise. He found out that the Asian PC was not called Stan at all. He had a name that fitted with his heritage. He asked this PC privately why his colleagues called him Stan, and the reply was, "Because they can't call me a Paki," this nickname ended that day].

The week when the race and diversity section would be discussed came and went without our class dealing with that section of the syllabus. I remained quiet as I knew that we had skipped it because of my presence. When our class eventually came around to this section of the syllabus many in the class revealed what they thought about race and racial issues. They said things like the police service was lowering standards to allow black people in. Black people had a greater propensity for violence and criminality, the whole nine yards. They were emboldened by one another and believed that the 'Safe Working Environment' of the classroom would protect them. I remained silent as I wanted to see what individuals thought. One of the course trainers' levels of discomfort got the better of him, and he engaged me directly, stating that he was conscious that I hadn't said anything. So, I pointed out how racist the whole thing was and reminded them that I had taken the same tests that they had, thrashing them in some.

One evening I was asked to go to class as a visitor had come to see me. It wasn't GMP's murder squad again, was it? No, it was someone representing the people who had produced the course handout. They got the same speech as my class – the result was that the section was going to be rewritten.

The archaic practices included recruits having drill practice. Somebody had to explain that one to me. To this day, I do not know why recruits spent so much time marching around the parade ground. For me, it was totally pointless unless the British police intended to invade somewhere. The drill Sergeant was a stickler for being clean-shaven and for shiny boots. The process of polishing a boot to a glass finish was called bulling and was bullshit. Someone had to explain that one, also, I suffered drill. It was pointless.

At my passing out parade, they had some official guy smartly dressed in military uniform inspecting the recruits. He saw me and walked straight over. "Where are you from?" he said, "Manchester," I replied, no "Where are you really from?" There it is right there. I had joined the police service, sworn my intent to serve the Queen in the office of constable and within a moment, I was reduced to an immigrant, someone who wasn't really British, I must be from somewhere else, right? My reply was, "Old Trafford." He got the point a scuttled on. Fortunately for me, someone caught that very moment on camera, immortalising it on an 8-mm film. At the end of the ceremony, David Pankhurst said, "Paul, I think that these people are here for you." I looked around, my mum had turned up with my sister and had been watching. I gave a copy of the photograph to my mum who kept it by her bedside for years.

Bruche taught me the law and procedure, but it did not teach me how to police, not really.

[In 2003, The BBC released a programme entitled 'The Secret Policeman.' In the programme, an investigative journalist called Mark Daly infiltrated Greater Manchester Police by joining GMP as a recruit. He spent months undercover at Bruche. He filmed racist behaviour among some recruits and trainers. The centre closed to police training in 2006].

My first stint on division at Sale was a gradual learning curve. I was being tutored by an Area officer, I knew them as a neighbourhood beat cops before joining the police.

Area officers patrolled on foot generally. Part of their role was to gain the respect and trust of the people in their areas and hopefully make them more effective and, with this, more successful. Because I walked with my tutor, the volume of work was slower than that of a section officer/ patrol officer who drove a patrol car and responded to incidents over the police radio. The slower pace gave me a good grounding.

On Fridays and Saturdays, area officers would work an evening shift responding to mainly public order incidents. This meant that the officers would drive around in a signed police personnel carrier, a PSU, that was nicknamed the 'battle bus'. I thought that this was a crass name as it suggested that the occupants were up for a fight. One evening I was working with other area officers patrolling in the personnel carrier. There were five or six constables and a sergeant riding shotgun (next to the driver). One cop was particularly vocal that evening, continuing to use racial epithets. Nigger, wog and coon were not far removed from the police vocabulary, but few dared to cross the line by saying these words out loud. The racial epithets went on for a while. As I was still a new officer on probation, I restrained myself from making comments which may have offended others in the vehicle, even though I was being offended myself.

I brought his racial outburst to an end by stating that if he continued, I would have to take him outside. He got the message. The sergeant realising that this officer had crossed the line, or maybe he realised that the line had been re-drawn now that I was there, told the officer to "shut the fuck up". He never came out with any of that crap in my presence again. Not what they had in mind when they nicknamed the PSU the 'battle bus.' I mentioned this incident in my constable's development plan. I described it without committing career suicide but at the same time ensuring that I would be taken seriously from then on. I wrote:

> 'During a spell on the area van or PSU, the topic of racism and colour showed its ugly face. Several comments with regard to many nations, including Africa and Jamaica, were made. I had to refrain from making comments which may offend others even though I was being offended by what was

being said. I also tried to qualify anything I said by giving an example.'

I would later learn, from a heavily redacted copy of a report, that this incident was taken to a much higher level. The Chief Superintendent of the M Division wrote;

'PC Bailey is a black man, I think of West Indian origin.

He is an athletic person and I understand an outstanding basketball player having represented the force and the British Police recently. I have spoken to this young man on several occasions. Originally, he resided in Old Trafford and experienced some problems with residents who took exception to his chosen profession.... To be fair to PC Bailey, he came forward with those problems, and it was arranged that he would be placed in the hostel at Stretford. He has settled down well.

I have noted a recent self-assessment report where he commented while working on the area van, which at weekends is used as a mini PSU for the Division, that a white officer, namely... made offensive and racist remarks.... On the two nights PC Bailey was engaged on the area van, his duties terminated at Altrincham Police Station. He did not have personal transport to return to the police hostel at Stretford. On both nights... took PC Bailey to Stretford in his own car, passing through... where he lives. This gesture tends to indicate that there was no malice in...remark...I now recommend that this matter be allowed to rest.'

This report demonstrates how racism was dealt within 1990. The officer who made the racist comments gave me a lift home, so there's no malice against me. Now go out there and police the streets that are filled with Africans and Jamaicans.

At the time, I did wonder what I was doing in an organisation like GMP. I decided to stay in the police because of one overriding thought: if my parents could survive the racism that they experienced when they arrived in Britain, I could survive this.

[Holding Out For A Hero – Bonnie Tyler]

My first day on independent patrol was a day shift. There was only a short walk from the police station to the main shopping street in Sale town centre. I did not have any nerves. I just wanted to get out there on my own. Back then, there was a practice of winding recruits up. Established officers would think of increasingly imaginative ways to get one over the next officer through the door. They saw it as a rite of passage. As I turned onto the main shopping street, an ageing woman collapsed in front of me. I thought that this was a wind-up at first, looking around expecting to see members of my relief laughing, but no. It suddenly dawned on me that this was real, and I stood there in full uniform. Members of the public looking to me to sort this out. Luckily, I wasn't the only emergency worker there. A man quickly identified himself as a paramedic and did what he did best. The woman had had a mild medical episode that she quickly recovered from - phew.

My shift Inspector was not short on tradition or pomp and ceremony. He wanted foot patrol officers to be exactly that and wanted evidence that his staff were not shirking their duties. He would carry out location checks in the middle of the night. Without warning, each officer would be called on the police radio and asked for their exact location. We knew that he would be on someone's beat, and the possibility of him saying, "I'll see you there in 60 seconds," was real. No one wanted to be caught out. The Inspector would also ask us random questions like "What is the colour of the door at Boots?" if we got this right, there would always be a follow-up question, "The back door?" – shit! I continued to work at a high rate. I had to stay ahead of him.

My arrest rate was high, not in response to any quotas, just as a result of me wanting to do my job well. I particularly enjoyed self-generated arrests, arrests which were not an outcome of being sent to an incident. I knew that this dimmed the spotlight on me and raised eyebrows. I was under no illusion that, as a black officer, I needed to work twice as hard to receive half the recognition. White officers could be average, poor even, and not be hassled. Being a bad, black officer was not an option, certainly not for me.

Some things have certainly happened for a reason and have taught me lessons that would turn out to serve me well as my career progressed. During the first year of my service, I moved into the house of Janet Graham. I had known her for some time and had regarded her as a friend. She was a Police Constable in GMP. On 31st August, Janet and I had what was reported as a domestic incident after Janet had asked me to leave:

> 'However, whilst he was removing his property from the flat, they were involved in a heated argument – during which his radio was damaged. In fact, he claims that she threw the radio out of the front door and that the damage was caused on impact with the ground. PC Bailey reported this matter to me at 3.40pm on 5th September at Stockport Police Station. However, he did not wish to make a formal complaint about the damage, and only reported it as means of seeking civil redress...'

I was out of Janet's and back at the police Hostel in Stretford.

It wasn't long before I was given a driving course and assigned a car beat. By now, I was working with a good of friend of mine, Chris Barnes. He had started with GMP the month after I had, not only had he been posted to the Trafford division, but he had been posted to Sale on the same relief. He was a thoughtful officer who capitalised on his common sense, quick wit and relaxed approach to difficult situations. Chris gained the nickname 'Chester.' I understood that he had been named after an English table tennis champion called George 'Chester' Barnes. Chris liked the nickname and would refer to himself as Chester. There was a certain irony in this name, as Chris was terrible at table tennis. He was a trier, though. We all loved that.

I had been assigned the Racecourse Estate, a council estate located in Sale. It was seen by some officers as a difficult place to work because of its reputation connected to drugs, gangs and general criminality. A small group of people would run amok, disrupting the lives of the majority law-abiding population. There were now worse things on the estate than drugs and gangs – me. I spent as much time on the estate as possible so that I could acclimatise to the area. I also wanted to know the faces and the players. I would speak regularly to the sub-division warrants officer to find out who was wanted and what for. Executing these warrants were easy arrests. I couldn't understand why everyone wasn't doing this. I would also ensure that I knew who was disqualified from driving. There are two main roads leading into the estate. I would park my patrol car at the junction of one of these roads, which afforded me a view of the drivers of cars turning onto the estate. If I saw a disqualified driver driving a vehicle, then they were arrested. These arrests sometimes led to me identifying other offences that they had committed. I was never a traffic-minded officer or overly concerned with minor traffic offences, but using the information gained from the local intelligence office, I was able to identify people who were driving around without insurance or without other driving documents. I would stop these vehicles if I saw them being driven. During these stop checks, the drivers would invariably say that they had documents, just not with them, so I would issue a form for them to produce their documents at a police station. They wouldn't be able to produce these documents of course, and therefore subsequently found themselves disqualified. As a disqualified driver, if they continued to drive, they risked being arrested and having their vehicle impounded. The impound fees could be worse than being summonsed for an offence. During the night, I would park my patrol car on a side road before walking around the estate. It was amazing to see who was mooching around up to no good when they couldn't hear your car engine. There were times when I could make two arrests for completely different and unconnected incidents on the same day.

Chris and I would back each other up all the time. On one occasion, he backed me up to a violent public order incident on the estate. We arrived in separate vehicles to a street fight involving several men, some of whom had knives. We managed to subdue the group and made some arrests. We worked well together and became the best of friends. I recall being assaulted by a man who turned out to have several drugs on him. I called for assistance, something that was unusual for me. My call for assistance must have caused concern as officers from North Trafford turned up also, even though they were on a different radio channel. I got the better of the man and arrested him. He turned out to be an associate of the men arrested by Chris and me at the violent public order incident and had supported them at the subsequent court hearings.

[Disco Science – Mirwais]

One lovely summer night, I was sitting on the bonnet of my patrol vehicle parked in a school car park. I was with another officer who was also sitting on the patrol vehicle's bonnet and a dog handler who was sitting on the bonnet of his van. The peace was disturbed by a squeaking sound. The squeak was repetitive and rhythmic. All three of us remained still as the squeak got louder and louder. A man then appeared in the car park pushing a wheelbarrow full of electrical equipment. Not really the time for shopping or for moving house. He saw the three of us sitting on our patrol vehicles and instantly set off running across the school field. The dog handler casually walked to the rear of his van, releasing his German Shepherd, who pursued the wheelbarrow pusher across the field, a scene worthy of the film

Snatch. The dog caught the wheelbarrow pusher quickly, he volunteered to show us where he had stolen the items from. I went to the door of the house pointed out by the wheelbarrow pusher who was now in custody and in the rear of the police vehicle. Waking the household up with a knock, the door of the house was opened by a giant of a man that even I had to look up to. I had to convince the householder that he had been burgled at first, but when we finally inspected his home and he realised that he had indeed been burgled, I had to be at my best to stop him getting to the wheelbarrow pusher, who was still sat in the rear of the police vehicle immediately outside. Anyway, as it turned out, Mr wheelbarrow pusher was the brother of the man who had assaulted me. Funny how things turn out, isn't it? At least they wouldn't be lonely during their stay at Her Majesty's pleasure.

After leaving Bruche I played basketball for the force team who played in the local Manchester league. This really was the golden age of basketball in Britain, as this league was surprisingly competitive. Many of the teams had older, more established players who had once played professionally in the national league. They may have lost a step from their playing highs but were still formidable opponents. They generally played with a group of much younger, keener, fitter and faster men some of whom were destined for careers in basketball and generally much greater things. Kevin Penny also played for the force team, as did Pete Mullings who had joined the police in the months before I did. Pete was a monster of a man, I mean this with the utmost respect, love and admiration for him. He was the strongest man that I had encountered. There were many contenders for that throne. Prior to joining the police, I would sometimes weight-train with Pete as it was important to maintain our upper body strength to remain competitive on a national stage. The gym was equipped with a bench press machine. This machine allows a person to lie on their back and safely press weights up to about

100kgs without the fear of the weight falling on them. Using free weights, a person could just keep adding more weight to the bar. The bench press machine did not allow for this, in theory, anyway. Pete could bench press the maximum weight of the machine. If that were not impressive enough, he could bench press the machine's maximum weight with me sitting on top of it. He was a strong man. It wasn't only Pete's strength; he had an awesome inside game and a very reliable mid-range jump shot. I never saw that shot blocked. He always looked like he was moving in slow motion when he played. If you saw him play from the sidelines, you couldn't help but think that you would get the better of Pete on the court because he looked so slow. The reality was very different and sometimes painful. During a game, Pete accidentally knocked an opponent's teeth out whilst challenging for the ball. I never got that close to Pete on the court after that.

Keith Ramsey also joined GMP in the months after I had, anyone would think that GMP was building a national league team. Keith was around my height and had a long-range shot that needed to be respected at all times. He looked for the three-ball all the time as it was a high-percentage shot for him. If you think of Steph Curry today, Keith shot the three-ball in the same way decades earlier. He didn't go into the paint much, but he didn't have to. Keith's basketball IQ was very high.

Nick Power had joined GMP a few months before I had. He was a six-foot-six lefty who loved to shoot from the elbow of the three-throw line. He was a natural baller who liked to block shots. Paul Ogden joined GMP years before the rest of us. He was a prolific scorer liking to shoot his quick-release shot from the top of the key. Paul was definitely the best passer of the ball that I had ever played with. He could pass the ball through the eye of a needle without looking. Ivan Hewitt joined in the autumn of 1990. Ivan was a very close friend of mine before joining the police. We played for Manchester Giants junior team together at a time that Vince

Brookings was taking the sport to a new level. Watching Brookings play was an inspiration to me. Truly the first guy I saw who played above the rim. Anyway, Ivan had a super leap on him also, not Air Jordan high but high enough. He did not seem to pursue a career in basketball in his later teens for reasons known only to him, however, once in GMP as a constable, his desire for the game seemed to be revitalised. Ivan lived around the corner from me in Old Trafford. Through our teenage years, we would be regulars on the Manchester party scene. There were other members of the team who although not mentioned by name here but were equally important to us.

Brian Dobson was the GMP team coach. He played me at point guard, historically this position was filled by the smallest player on each team. Brian bucked that trend. He had seen that for the last couple of seasons of my national league career, before joining the police, I had played point completely shutting down players like Ronaldo Lawrence or effortlessly feeding the ball to Terry Crosby. From point, I could control the tempo of the game being young enough and fit enough to run the legs off our opponents. Then by the second half, our opponents were normally dead on their feet. With great players like Kevin, Pete and Keith to do the bulk of the scoring life in this league was easy for us, we were very successful.

Each year, the Police Athletic Association held a national police basketball tournament. The PAA tournament would be hosted by different forces around the United Kingdom. The force that hosted the tournament would get automatic entry as did the holders from the year before. GMP had a strong team but our overall victory in the tournament was not assured. Merseyside police had been having a recruitment campaign of their own.

Dave Gardner, who played for Manchester Giants and who already had several full England international caps to his name, had joined Merseyside along with Welsh full international Simon

Coombs. These two would later be joined by ex-Manchester Giants players Mike McLaughlin and Jason Ray. Merseyside were coached by Peter Vaux who was also the head coach the Great Britain's Police national team. It appeared that I would be still playing national league basketball after all. On this national stage, I brought out my 'A' game. Offensively GMP had great firepower with Kevin, Pete, Paul and Keith, complemented by Nick and others. Playing from point I saw that my role was to control the backcourt and overpower teams down the stretch. I had certain go-to plays especially defensively.

'The chase down block' – When an opponent gets ahead of the defence, they find themselves with an open lay-up. In this situation, they rarely look back. I would chase them down and once they released the ball, I would pin it against the backboard before scooping it under my arm. Nowadays players are acutely aware of the chase down block as Lebron James has claimed this defensive tactic as his own. You will hardly see a player attempting a lay-up without looking around themselves like a gazelle being hunted on the Serengeti.

'The weak side block' – When an opponent shoots the ball, they are normally more concerned with the person guarding them than anyone else on the court. Once they had started to release the ball, I would move from the weak side of the court and reject their shot. I would look to throw the ball as far off the court as I could, even if I could catch the ball and retain possession. The reason why I did this was more psychological than tactical, retaining the ball was the obvious tactical option. If a player saw their shot flying into the stands, they would think twice before trying the same shot again. Psychologically, their shot altered and they were more likely to miss. I suppose I was making life easier for myself down the stretch.

'The pickpocket' – When defending the opposing guard who was dribbling the ball, I would wait for them to look away. Once the ball left their hand, I would change direction quickly trying to get to the ball before it bounced and returned to their possession. If successful, I would naturally be moving towards their basket, with the opposing guard normally being the last line of defence. Under these circumstances I would have an open uncontested shot. Dunking the ball in this scenario was particularly satisfying.

All three of these moves would get a positive reaction from the crowd. Other players would massively outscore me during games but it is these highlight plays that people remembered after the game ended. During the first few years that I played in the national tournament, the final was between Merseyside and GMP, we won them all. With respect to the other teams that competed in these early years, they were playing off for third place or just enjoying a weekend away. Brian Dobson 'Dobbo' was the assistant coach for the Great Britain team, he knew Peter Vaux 'Vauxy' well. Dobbo and Vauxy weren't building national league teams, they were building a national team.

In March 1991, a black American man called Rodney King was beaten by Los Angeles Police Department Officers during his arrest for allegedly driving under the influence of alcohol. After a high-speed chase, Mr King was filmed by a member of the public being beaten by the officers. The footage was covered by the media and appeared on our screens in the United Kingdom. Despite relating to the police in the United States of America, police everywhere were seen as a danger and a threat to the black man. As a serving police officer at the time, I found myself defending my decision to join the police within the black community. The police were seen as 'beasts' and I was worst of all as I had chosen to join the beast. My white counterparts in GMP were not subjected to this type of criticism or scorn. The majority view within GMP at the time was that he was evading arrest and deserved what he got. I did not share this view.

I was working hard and playing hard. Being proactive in policing and getting the job done did have its disadvantages. I was picking up complaints. It was without question that most of these complaints were vexatious. It became apparent to me that black officers were more likely to be complained about and that those complaints were more likely to be pursued. These complaints were not only internal grievances, but complaints made by members of the public who appeared to be more willing to complain about a black officer than a white officer. Pete Mullings had also been posted to South Trafford. He worked on a different relief to me, but we still saw each other in passing or if our shifts overlapped. He was the only person that I was aware of who was attracting more complaints than I was. Two black officers, same experience. I was once called in by an inspector who stated that she had received a complaint that I had looked at a woman the wrong way. Seriously, I treated that one with the contempt it deserved.

Each sub-division had a Criminal Investigation Department headed by a Detective Chief Inspector. I was asked to report to the DCI for South Trafford. When requests like these were made the natural reaction is 'here we go.' I walked into the DCI's office and took a seat. He told me that a Terminator 2 poster – Arnold Schwarzenegger was big in the nineties - had been received at the police station. Written on the reverse of the poster was my name and a threat. The threat stated that I needed to back off. I was unable to see the poster as it was going to be sent off for testing. To his credit, the DCI took threats to officers seriously and was displeased that something like this could happen. I was not worried about the poster at all. No self-respecting criminal would lower themselves to this. No, they would just get on with it. I found it hard to believe that anyone would be so stupid to announce their intention to commit a crime. What was I going to be 'terminated'? give me a break. I had more respect for the black man in the corridor at Stretford, at least he said it to my face albeit disguised. I am sure that others would not have shared my view of the poster and the writer's intent. I knew one thing - I wasn't going anywhere. No one was ever traced in relation to this incident. Will I be able to look at Arnold

Schwarzenegger holding a pump-action shotgun on the back of a motorbike again?

[911 Is A Joke – Public Enemy]

I may have been picking up more complaints than I would have liked but I was picking up commendations also. Chris and I were commended for catching a burglar having anticipated the offender's escape route and having hatched a plan of what we were going to do in the event of an automatic alarm being activated in a particular area. The commendation read;

> <u>Chief Superintendent's Commendation</u>
> I commend PC 1118 Barnes and PC 7826 Bailey, whose local knowledge and quick response to a report of a burglary led to the arrest and subsequent imprisonment of the offender.

I did not need to be on duty to detect crimes. One day whilst visiting my parents' house in Old Trafford I noticed a young black youth struggling with a moped, he was with another black youth. The first youth looked as though he was trying to carry the moped instead of wheeling it. They avoided the road preferring the alleyways at the side or rear of the terraced houses. It looked odd, very odd. I approached the youths, and the second youth disappeared. On doing so I saw that there was a wheel lock still fitted to the moped preventing one of the wheels from turning, this explained why he was trying to carry the moped instead of pushing it. I spoke to the youth telling him that I was a police officer and asking him what he was doing. He claimed that the moped was his, an explanation that did not pass the smell test. I detained the youth shouting to my mother who brought me a cordless phone. I called the police explaining what had happened to them, that I had detained someone and to impress upon them that I was an off-duty police officer. My detention of the youth started to attract attention. A number of people approached me as I had taken hold of the youth to prevent him from escaping. Before long, a crowd had formed around me. I was verbally abused and threatened by the crowd for detaining the youth. It was clear that some of the people thought that I was a traitor for detaining one of 'Our own' and that I was showing out for the white police. There were attempts to pull the youth from my grip, but this only increased my resolve. The police response was not what I would call rapid. I expected the police to be there in the blink of an eye, nope. I was left there for a long time in the middle of a baying crowd. What chance did the community of Old Trafford have if this was how the police responded to incidents? When the police finally arrived, I could not hide my displeasure. This incident should have been responded to immediately. I was written up for a commendation it read;

> <u>Chief Superintendent's Commendation</u>
> For his actions, whilst off duty. Police Constable 'M' 7826 Paul Bailey is commended.
>
> The officer arrested a youth for the theft of a motorcycle. The officer had to endure both verbal abuse and threats of violence for 30 minutes prior to the arrival of assistance. Police Constable Bailey's actions were highly commendable.

[The youth I had arrested and the second youth that I had seen him with initially turned out to be brothers. Both of them would have their lives cut short, one of them being shot dead in what was described in the media as a 'gangland feud,' In the mid-1990's. Hand-to-hand violence is one thing, being strapped another. I may have been in more danger than I thought].

It took until 2020 for my mother to tell me that after my arrest of the youth, word had spread to her that her home was going to be burnt. She did not tell me this at the time or throughout my subsequent career as she did not see the point of adding pressure to me. She believed that I was under enough pressure as it was. The

Windrush Generation, truly remarkable.

In December 1991, I received a memo from the Assistant Chief Constable of the training department. The memo was dated 16th December 1991 said;

> 'I have the pleasure in informing you that following the successful completion of your probationary period on the 'M' division you are now confirmed in the office of Constable.'

Chief Constable.

By January 1992, I had been recognised by people outside of the police service as someone who could influence young black people in the community. After all, it was a black police officer, Police Inspector Martin Harding, who had finally convinced me to join the police. It was not beyond the bounds of imagination that, as a serving police officer myself I would have influence or be able to reach young black people who were travelling this difficult road behind me. The Manchester Mentor Project aimed to motivate black students to fulfil their potential by matching them with successful black mentors from the world of business, the professions, the arts and local industry. It was the first time that I had been recognised in this way for anything that was not sport related. I was contacted by the Project Co-ordinator who wrote;

> 'Your name has been put forward as someone who would be interested in making a positive and unique contribution to the future of black communities in this country by offering yourself as a role model for black students who are just starting in life. Your own experience would be invaluable in helping such students by giving relevant careers guidance and personal support.'

I was so enthused by this invitation and the deeper meaning behind it. My life thus far was filled with white teachers and educators who constantly told me that I couldn't or who were more interested in fulfilling their white syllabuses rather than seeing me as the individual that I was, the free thinker who would stand up for what I believed in even if it did not meet with white approval or fit in with the majority view. It wasn't only this that struck me. My work inside the police had been noticed outside of the police and had been a topic of discussion. I began to realise that if I put myself out there, I would attract attention whether I wanted to or not. As the request was made for me in my role as a Police Officer, I thought it wise to ask permission to take part. There is an old saying, 'It is better to ask for forgiveness than to ask for permission,' I should have heeded this prophetic advice. On 10th March 1992, the Chief Superintendent 'M' Division wrote;

> 'I enclose documentation my constable M7826 Paul Anthony Bailey has received from …Roye, the Project Co-ordinator.
>
> I have ascertained from Constable Bailey that the approach was made by way of telephone from Roye, who had heard of this officer's good work in the community.
>
> You will note that the project is funded by the Department of the Environment through the Urban Programme.
>
> I have informed Constable Bailey I have no objection, in principle, to him assisting the project and he has informed me he is willing to do so. However, I ask for clearance via your office before him taking the matter further.'

It strikes me, looking back now, at the hurdles placed in front of me. This was a government-run and funded initiative that had identified me as a positive role model for young black students, yet the police service was so autocratic that I had to apply to take part. Not only that, a person at the rank of Chief Superintendent thought that they should seek clearance first. My participation in this initiative for black students and the black community was being stalled. If this initiative was for another group, one that did not contain the word 'Black,' then would my participation in it be debated at force level? The Assistant Chief Constable 'U' Department wrote to the Chief Superintendent 'M' Division on 16th March 1992.

> The Manchester Mentor Project – Constable 'M' 7826 Bailey
>
> 'Thank you for your memorandum of 10th March 1992 on the above-named officer.
>
> Approval is given for the Manchester Mentor Project – a report on Constable Bailey's experience would be of interest, for the benefit of 'UP'

So, authorisation was given on the proviso that the training unit in GMP could benefit. The report says nothing about the benefit to black students, or for the wider black community. It was a privilege to have even been considered for a project like this. Over the years I would speak to many young children from all walks of life about my experiences in life and in the police. I also spoke to them about the difficult road ahead of them and how to navigate this road avoiding the pitfalls.

It was a Monday, I was working an afternoon shift that started like any other. Before long I had made an arrest, looking back now I cannot even remember what the arrest was for. I knew that I was going to be tied up for a while processing my prisoner at Altrincham Police Station, so I decided to go to the Canadian Charcoal Pit, a fast-food restaurant, to get a bite to eat. When I returned to the police station, I was told that there was a call for me in the custody office. Chris Cropper, the custody sergeant, looked despondent when I walked around the counter to pick up the receiver; I will never forget the look on his face. Andrew was on the other end of the phone, my heart dropped. Without any hesitation, he told me – our father had died. Sgt Cropper placed his hand on my shoulder. He already knew what I was going to be told, in fact, another patrol sergeant was already on his way to collect me as they did not want me to drive the patrol car. The drive to my parent's house was solemn. I went to register my father's death, cerebral haemorrhage and myocardial infarction. A few days after my father's death, I received a call from my sergeant, who was apologetic for disturbing me, but he said that he was being pressured from above. He wanted to know when I would be returning to work. I said, "Can I bury my father first?"

[Still – Dr. Dre]

In April 1992, three LAPD officers were acquitted of using excessive force in the arrest of Rodney King. The jury failed to reach a verdict for the fourth officer. The Los Angeles Riots started after the verdicts were announced. The riots were played out on the UK media, revealing a dichotomy of views segregated along racial lines. The view was held by some of my white counterparts within GMP that the riots were nothing more than criminality, dismissing the underlying issues that had led to the riots starting in the first place. Issues such as police brutality towards the black community and discrimination within the criminal justice system. There would need to be a serious sea of change in the United Kingdom if we're ever going to see the change within the police service that we needed.

The GMP basketball team continued to be successful at a national level. A report of 11th May 1992 read;

'Over the weekend of 25th and 26th April 1992, the 1992 P.A.A. Basketball Championships were hosted by Lancashire Constabulary at Blackpool.

The GMP Basketball Section are the current champions having won this title 3 years running in 1989, 1990, and 1991. The following were involved:

Inspector X Harding PC B 4370 Penny PC C 2004 Ramsey PC D 2021 Dobson PC F 4575 Hewitt PC M 6862 Mullings PC M 7573 Power PC M 7826 Bailey PC Q 1345 Ogden Other officers listed

Over the course of the championship weekend, the section defeated South Wales, Constabulary and the Sussex Constabulary to reach the quarter-final. At this stage, they defeated Central Scotland. In the semi-final they defeated the Strathclyde Police to place us in our fifth consecutive final, the opposing team being Merseyside Police. After a close-fought game, played before Mr Johnson, the Chief Constable of Lancashire, Mr Evans, the Chief Constable of Devon and Cornwall and other distinguished guests, the section finished winners by 3 points with a final score of 80 – 77.

This was a fourth consecutive championship which is unequalled in the history of P.A.A Basketball.

PC 'M' 7826 Bailey was voted as one of the top five players of the tournament, PC 'C' 2004 Ramsey was nominated by Mr John Evans as the Man of the Match in the final.

I feel that this performance is worthy of recognition, and I ask that a copy of this report be passed to:

The Chief Constable.

The Chairman of the Sports and Social Committee The Chief Superintendent 'C' Division.

The Chief Superintendent 'M' Division.'

This Changes Everything

1993.

[The Chain – Fleetwood Mac]

By 1993, I had established myself as a competent police officer who did not suffer fools gladly. During several one-to-one meetings with my supervisors, it had been suggested that I take the sergeants examination as a means of progressing in the service. I got the impression that they thought that I would get bored and look for something else, possibly outside of the police. I had resisted my supervisors' attempts to coerce me into taking the exam for a few different reasons. First and foremost, I had no interest in taking it. I saw the role of the sergeant as primarily checking other people's work. I had no interest in that, certainly not at my age or length of service. In addition, I was not sure how long I would remain a police officer. There had been a number of issues that made me question my continued service as a police officer. The culture of the police was not what I had thought, plus I saw the differential treatment depending on who you were. Part of me did think that my 1978 school report had led me on a path inexorably to the police but that did not mean that I had to stay. Granted, I was now a married man with a family so my responsibilities were mounting but still, this didn't mean that I had to stay. Finally, I watched those in the promotion system or who had been promoted and with a few notable exceptions they were locked in, they towed the party line fearful to say or do anything that would upset their march upwards or cause their fall. Even if the party line was wrong, corrupt or complete bullshit, they would still follow it. I wasn't prepared to give up my individuality, I cherished it too much.

One day, I received a call over the radio to go in and see Inspector Handforth. When I arrived, he was waiting for me, here we go again. I wondered what I was walking into. He told me that the DCI was very impressed with me. He was impressed with my written reports and saw that my name appeared on the arrest list regularly. Inspector Handforth went on to say that if I were to apply to go into the CID it would be looked at favourably. I had not planned on applying for the CID, not this soon anyway, but hearing this I'd be a fool not to. I applied and was accepted.

On 22nd April 1993, Stephen Lawrence was murdered in a racially motivated attack whilst waiting with his friend, Duwayne Brooks, for a bus in Eltham, London. The case reverberated around the nation due to the police handling of the investigation, the handling of the suspects and their handling of the witness to the unprovoked attack. It was difficult not to have heard about this murder even in 1993. The fallout from this murder and its subsequent investigation would change the face of policing and legislation forever.

In May 1993, the British police basketball team travelled to Athens to play in Championnat D'Europe Des Polices, the European police basketball tournament. Pete, Kevin, Keith and I had been selected for the British police team. Brian Dobson and Dave Edge would complete the GMP contingent. Dave Gardner, Simon Coombs and Mike McLaughlin were selected from Merseyside; Peter Vaux was the coach. The team was made up of other players from West Midlands, The Metropolitan Police and two Scottish forces. Sir John Evans, I'm not sure if he had been knighted in 1993, was the head of the British delegation.

It wasn't a great start to the trip, the plane looked rusty to me. I am not a nervous flyer, not in the slightest, but rusting planes weren't my thing. When we landed in Athens the coach waiting for us was rusty – was everything bloody rusty? The journey on the coach seemed to take a lifetime, finally, we arrived at the hotel. I went to my room that I would be sharing with Andy Nicholson, a West Midlands police officer clearly on the fast track to become a senior officer one day. I could see the airport from the hotel. Why had the coach taken so long? We were in Greece let the games begin.

I had played in great stadiums around Britain and Europe but this stadium was something else. It was huge with seating rising high into the rafters on all four sides. It felt like the Colosseum in Rome, "We were here to entertain".

Our first game and I think the first game of the tournament was against Garda Síochána, the national police service of the Republic of Ireland. This was international basketball, there were no mugs here. I played point guard and at the start of the game, I was presented with a direct path to the basket. One of the Garda players tried to block my path and I suppose block my shot, he misjudged how high I could jump. I rose much higher than he thought dunking the ball over him. Adding insult to injury, he was struck in the face on my way up which resulted in him sustaining a swollen face and a black eye. He would not be able to play on. The audience exalted; other teams shifted uncomfortably in their seats – Great Britain had arrived. We won the game.

The team went out to a bar, come on we were in Greece it would be rude not to. I saw the Garda player who I had collided with. We had a drink, and he laughed "I'm here all week, I don't have to worry about playing now". We ended up in a bar that was packed full of people, the drink was flowing. I don't know how it started but Pete was arm-wrestling with anyone who would challenge him. The cost of defeat was that the vanquished had to buy the victor a drink. Pete won - a lot - and was getting more and more drunk. The atmosphere was brilliant, more people took Pete on losing one after the next. I am not sure some of them even thought they were going to win, they just wanted to be part of the crack. The rest of us were buying our own drinks.

In 1993, Greece's currency was the drachma I don't know why but the drachma seemed to go further then. Pete was pissed, after a while he said that he was going to call it a night and go back to the hotel. I saw an opportunity. I quietly spoke to Pete trying not to draw attention to myself; I had a proposition. I saw little point in Pete abdicating his arm-wrestling crown especially if that meant that no one would not be benefitting from the free drinks that came with his undefeated status. If he was turning in for the night he may as well arm-wrestle me, letting me win of course, then I would become the new king and inherit his fortunes. Amazingly, Pete agreed, he really was drunk. I waited for a while before openly throwing my hat into the ring. This bar was becoming increasingly busy with tourists and Athenians alike. They saw my challenge and quickly fought for the best position to see battle commence. Pete and I sat down facing each other. We interlinked our hands, "3-2-1 go". If Pete didn't go along with the plan this would be a short contest resulting in him ripping my arm off. He put on a good show so that the fix wasn't obvious, then I pressed his hand to the table. Quiet fell across the bar, the crowd's disbelief told me how much they had thought of my chances before the bout started. Ok, left hands now "3-2-1 go" I pressed Pete's hand to the table even faster this time around, victorious. I revelled in my newly acquired status as champion, Pete bid farewell. I was then approached by a man saying "You are obviously a very strong man, very strong, can I buy you a drink?" Was he trying to chat me up? I made my apologies stating that it was late and I had to get some sleep. My ruse had netted me no drinks but at least it had earned me an admirer.

Whilst relaxing by the pool, Andy Nicholson fell asleep on a sun lounger. Pete crept up to him with the guile of a big cat stalking its prey. He then called for those people in the pool to get out or to move to one side. In one full movement, he picked up the sun lounger with Andy on it before throwing the sun lounger and Andy into the pool.

Not the way anyone wanted to be woken, Andy thrashed around in the pool initially then he just calmly climbed out. A couple of us recovered Andy's lilo, sorry, recovered the sun lounger from the pool whilst still in fits of laughter. Pete said Andy would be a Chief Constable one day and he'd always wanted to throw a chief in a pool.

The Greek national team had their personal array of national league players. They weren't known to me personally but I understood that at least some of them had played for teams like Panathinaikos. Everyone knew when the Greeks had a game, the auditorium would be filled with spectators and seemingly every police officer in Athens. The crowd would not be disappointed, their team was awesome. The British team made it to the semi-finals where we would meet the Greek team. It was disconcerting to see the referees arrive at the auditorium with the Greek team in their team bus, maybe they were doing their part to reduce their carbon emissions by travelling in the same vehicle. It was 1993, no one cared about carbon footprints. The game started, and it was on. Pete produced his statement of intent early on when he cut baseline under the basket emerging on the other side with a thunderous windmill dunk. I swear the ground shuddered. The game was close and fiercely competitive but, despite our best efforts, the Greek team won. We came third, which was a brilliant result, but I think that we were good enough to win the tournament outright.

When I returned to work, I was called into the police station to see a Chief Inspector. He said that he understood that I had been away playing for Great Britain and that we had come third, receiving a European bronze medal. He had my annual leave request form on the desk, I had to apply for leave before flying to Athens. He tore the form up in front of me exclaiming that no one representing their country should have to take their own annual leave.

[Right Here – SWV]

I Did That

After a week-long induction course at Sedgley Park, I started at Altrincham CID. The CID office bizarrely was not in the police station but located in a converted double-fronted Edwardian house on Barrington Road. This meant that patrol officers had to make a special trip if they wanted to speak with a detective.

My tutor was an older, very experienced detective who had clearly seen it all in his time. There was no rush in him, I don't mean that as a criticism, he was steady. I did not find the work overly taxing, at the same time I saw a different side to the police that I did not know existed when I was in uniform. As a patrol officer, I was concerned with my area, a small pond so to speak. Now not only had the whole division opened to me, but the force also. I discovered branches and departments that I either had not known existed or had heard of but had no reason to contact. Now that I was investigating more serious offences, I had regular contact with these departments upping my ability and police IQ. I also found that people responded differently to me when I said, DC Bailey. Patrol officers would be relieved when I turned up at a scene even though three months earlier, I had been pushing a patrol car just like them.

It was not all armed robberies and serious sexual offences. At the time detectives had to re-visit domestic burglaries and follow up on less serious offences such as vehicle crime. I was following up on one of these less serious volume crime cases when I called at an address in the very plush South Trafford area. Hale, Hale Barns, Bowdon, and Altrincham were filled with very expensive houses and eye-wateringly expensive cars. The contact for this crime was Vivian Anderson. I called at the address speaking to a very pleasant woman at the door. After identifying myself as a detective, I asked for Vivian Anderson, she smiled and shouted Viv. Yep – my childhood hero Viv Anderson came to the door.

[Internal voice – "Stay professional Paul"] Bringing this short story to a close, Viv and I had tea and biscuits and great conversation. This was remarkable because I didn't drink tea.

There weren't many black police officers in GMP in the nineties. The Trafford division had a few, but generally not many and certainly not reflective of Greater Manchester's population as a whole. It was around this time that I became increasingly frustrated with the disparity between black officers and their white counterparts. The lack of equality of opportunity in the police was marked. The handful of black officers on the Trafford division were all in the lower ranks. One worked in a plain clothes unit primarily investigating drug offences, the rest, except for myself, were uniformed constables. From my research, this situation did not improve looking at the force as a whole. It was during this time that I met the most wonderful woman, Karin Mulligan.

Karin is probably the most remarkable person that I met in GMP. She was a black policewoman, full marks for that one straight off the bat. Surviving and excelling in a white, male and racist organisation should be applauded. Karin was much more than someone who hid in the shadows hoping that the spotlight wouldn't fall on them or acquiesced to the white majority view. No, she took the police on with her outstanding intellect, her calm, her foresight and most of all her courage. We were like-minded individuals who came together for a purpose that we believed in wholeheartedly and would fight for, no matter who else was in that fight.

Karin was the sister of Martin Harding; it was not lost on me the influence that this family had had on me. At first black officers including Karin and I began to meet socially as a support network. We shared common experiences both prior to joining the police and inside of the police. We saw little point in suffering in isolation. Having people who knew and who had experienced what you had was a relief and a source of strength. Our meetings were away from police premises. If black police officers were seen to be holding meetings, then this would be met with suspicion. Of course, it would, why else would black police officers be meeting other than to plot some type of coup? The irony of the suspicion surrounding black organisations can be traced back to colonial Britain. During the trans-Atlantic slave trade, the British would strip enslaved Africans of their names and language. Slave owners did not want their slaves speaking to each other in a foreign tongue, a tongue that they could not understand. So, the original languages spoken by the enslaved Africans were lost. The result was that the slaveholders would be aware if the slaves were planning anything. The suspicion of black groups was the police's problem, not ours.

The second issue we faced was the vitriolic response to any group or movement that had the word black in it. GMP had many other groups. Try this exercise, The Association of Chief Police Officers, is this threatening or a cause for concern? Now try this, The Association for Black Chief Police Officers, is this more or less threatening? This immediate revulsion to anything black existed during the civil rights movement in the 1960s, in the police service in the 1990s and during the Black Lives Matter movement in the 2020s. Try the exercise again, The Christian Police Association versus The Black Christian Police Association. We faced a massive uphill struggle. My involvement with this movement did not go unnoticed. Surely there would be a reaction.

After my probationary period in the CID, my tutor confirmed that I had met the grade and had passed the course. The next step was to be assigned a permanent posting as a detective. I went to see the DCI who for the second time looked as though he was carrying a burden. He congratulated me on passing my trainee detective course and confirmed that he agreed with my tutor's assessment of me. However, there were no permanent postings available at that time. I would have to return to uniform duties and wait for a posting. He was waiting for a reaction from me, I didn't let that happen. I just thanked him for his time and left. It was the Detective Chief Inspector who had seen my potential and presented me with a path into the CID, now there was no spot for me. I did not have to ponder what had changed, I knew what had changed. I was being taught a lesson for being vocal about equality for black police officers in GMP. The organisation was not stupid enough to say this outright but what had happened to me did not pass the smell test.

I returned to uniform duties now being assigned to the van. The van was normally double-crewed as it attended potentially violent incidents or incidents where it was anticipated that more than one police officer would be needed. It was also used to transport prisoners having the call signs MM03 or MM04. I worked with PC Dave Searson. Dave was an ex-Royal Marine and a real comedian. He wasn't one of those people we have all met in our time who believe that they are funny when they really weren't, Dave was funny. He wanted to progress to become a traffic officer and looking for a path to achieve this ambition, I leant towards crime avoiding anything traffic-related, so as a team we worked well. I'd take on all the crime enquiries or investigations and he would take on all of the traffic-related matters. Dave's reputation as a joker followed him around. When a picture of Uncle Fester was discovered pinned to the front of Chris Barnes' file Dave was the prime suspect, even if there was no evidence to prove that it was him. Chris enjoyed the joke so much that he kept the picture of Uncle Fester for a long time after the prank.

One night, I paraded at Altrincham Police station to start my shift. We all sat in the parade room waiting for the parade to begin. When the sergeant entered the room, he was accompanied by Richard Brunstrom, a superintendent who had moved to the Trafford division in the early nineties. Superintendent Brunstrom was going to work with a patrol during the night. The practice of senior officers working on the ground with ordinary patrol officers was relatively new back then. It was seen as a win, a win for the senior officer who would be seen mucking in with the troops, they would be able to say that they were still in touch with the streets and not forgetting Public Relations. Public relations is the practice of deliberately managing the release of information to affect public perception. The art of self-promotion was in its infancy but would become a corrupt monster in years to come. I had never seen such a quiet parade, I'm not sure if everyone decided to be on their best behaviour for fear of being reprimanded or if they were consumed with secretly praying not to be teamed up with the super.

I was MM03 that night, I had this sneaking feeling that Superintendent Brunstrom and I were going to be buddies for the next eight hours. "Paul if you take Mr Brunstrom out," those words rang in my ears when the sergeant announced the plan for the night. The other constables in the room could not hide their glee at not being chosen. I had several conversations with them with my eyes. This was about to be the longest shift of my career. After the parade, I gathered my things, not forgetting my hat, Mr Brunstrom and I got into the van and drove out of the police station. Maybe a hundred or so yards along the road fate would deliver me an escape. I arrested a man for being drunk and disorderly and acting against public decency and therefore would now be tied up for a while. When I announced that I had arrested someone so quickly I could feel the disbelief of my colleagues being transmitted through the radio waves. I have no doubt that there were shouts of 'lucky bastard' across South Trafford. Like I say, you make your own luck. Mr Brunstrom, whilst impressed by my arrest, now had to be teamed up with someone else.

I was plodding along waiting for a position in the CID. I suspected that I would be left waiting so that I had time to reflect on my stance on equality. It was during this time that I became a tutor constable. The tutor constables course lasted for two weeks. The course trainers' assessment of me concluded;

> Constable Bailey has an open relaxed style, and in my opinion, exhibits substantial potential as a tutor. For his students to gain full benefit from such talents and experience he should, whilst retaining his commendable, concise style, give all and any information which may assist the

probationers without acting as a filter to evidence his student may need to develop.

I have no hesitation in recommending Constable Bailey for a Tutor Constable's Certificate.

I tutored a succession of recruits, one of my trainees was PC Neville Nelson 'Nev'. Nev was a black officer of mixed heritage who had worked for GMP as a member of the support staff before becoming a Police Constable. Nev had great potential and was willing to get stuck in, he wasn't standoffish. We were referred to as 'The Soul Patrol' by some. This was not a new term, as when Mike Crooks and I had teamed up years earlier we were called the soul patrol also. I suppose Nev and I should have been The Soul Patrol II. Nev came with 'street smarts' that enhanced his ability as a police officer. Having been a member of the police staff before joining the regulars Nev understood the mechanics of the police and more importantly its politics. He hit the ground running. The days passed quickly with Nev, we would move from one incident to the next with relative ease. I showed him how to generate his own work and how to be a proactive officer instead of one of those officers who only ever attended incidents that they were sent to and nothing else.

During a shift, we came across a parked car that contained a couple who were engaged in a romantic embrace. It was not unusual for police patrols to come across this sort of thing, what was unusual was that it was broad daylight with the car not exactly tucked away on a remote country road. Nev was riding shotgun and positioned nearest to the parked car. He wound down the passenger window speaking to the couple who had now realised that the police had pulled up next to them. Nev said "What are you doing", the couple flummoxed by the question as it was obvious what they were up to, looked at Nev as though they had come across a simpleton. Nev's attempt at tact on this occasion led to an awkward and extremely funny moment. We quickly told the couple to move on as I could not contain my laughter any longer. Nev was a great recruit, he worked hard, generated lots of arrests, and became an astute investigator. I wanted to equip him as much as I could as the road black officers travel is a difficult one. I was now mentoring inside the police a substantial step forward for me.

The unfounded complaints kept coming. I lived in a middle-class suburb that although it came under the management of Wigan Borough Council was nearer to Manchester than Wigan. I arrived at the Altrincham Police Station one morning to be served regulation papers by a Detective Superintendent. When the police commence a formal investigation into a police officer's conduct, that officer should be served with regulation papers. The papers firstly inform the officer that they are under investigation and also outline the details of each allegation. The papers served to me that morning contained several allegations from a neighbour who claimed, amongst other things, that I had 'beaten up' one of his sons and tried to hit another with my car. In addition, the allegations claimed that I had 'abused' my authority causing the man and a close neighbour and friend of his to be confined to their houses fearing stepping outside. The allegations were total nonsense of course. A step down from being suspected of murder but serious enough, potentially career-ending, maybe even a term of imprisonment if proven.

The complaints were vexatious and so from my view – not another complaint of being afraid of the big nasty black man. One of the boys in question had kicked a ball at my wife's car whilst she was driving it with her window rolled down. He was told to stop. To prevent them from using the close as a football pitch I parked my car outside of my house, instead of on my driveway, that annoyed the complainants. As for the older son who looked like an adult. I had never touched him; the allegations were ludicrous. Rather than entertain this bullshit, I told the Professional Standards Branch, known as the 'Y' Department then, to interview a group of neighbours who would confirm that these complaints were nonsense and that the complainants were a nightmare to live near. I made the Y work as I already had camcorder footage of the complainants that disproved their allegations. When realising that the footage existed the air escaped from the Y department balloons. Better luck next time. he disparity and severity of how black police officers were treated in relation to their white counterparts would become a prickly issue for GMP in years to come, I could feel it, it was inevitable.

I was treading water, at least that is what my then Inspector said to me when I was transferred into the Plain Clothes Unit. I had not applied for this position as I was still waiting for a permanent detective posting. I was not going to put myself at the mercy of GMP. If the organisation was waiting for me to change my position on race, then they were going to have a long wait. It was clear that there was a view that I was wasted in uniform. Plainclothes is a proactive unit that was primarily concerned with investigating drug offences but would also investigate volume crime if a particular problem or crime trend had been identified. Unlike being a police patrol working on a section, plainclothes officers had a freer remit, they were not expected to hump the radio clearing calls.

The unit was staffed by police officers with a knack for proactive investigation. I worked with a great group of officers including Mike Young and Paul Hitchen, who proudly wore the nickname 'The Butcher'. There were many rumours about how Paul had got that name, the most intriguing being that they called him 'The Butcher' because he had plenty of meat, which wouldn't do his reputation any harm. Paul didn't give away the true origin of the name but liked being referred to as such. I had an aversion to calling people by a nickname of an unknown origin, knowing that he did not mind The Butcher' he was. Besides, I acquired the nickname 'Pearl'. The Black Pearl is a fictional ship in the Pirates of the Caribbean film genre that is believed to be "nigh uncatchable." This would have been a great explanation if the Pirates of the Caribbean films existed in the mid-nineties. Simply pearls are gems and expensive.

The plainclothes unit worked its own shift pattern. This suited my family and gave me a better work-life balance. The unit soon developed a reputation for quality investigations and prosecutions. It was a joy coming into work again, I had an affinity for the work. I had spent my life before the police trying to stop people from offering me drugs. In addition, people didn't generally look at me and think 'he's a cop,' quite the opposite. I had spent my career having to prove that I was a cop.

Let me demonstrate how the public perception of what a police officer looks like affects the lives of black police officers. I was conducting a stop and search of a white person near to Altrincham sports centre. Whilst conducting the stop, I heard a call, over the police radio, for a street robbery in progress on the road that I was on. I couldn't see the robbery but had detained someone for a search so couldn't do anything more. Police patrols rushed to the scene of the robbery only to find that the report was about me. A call had been received that a black man was robbing a white man, society's prejudices in full view.

It was during this time that I met a man called Charles Critchlow. Charles was a black constable of Barbadian heritage who had joined GMP in 1990. He too had become vocal about equality of opportunity for black police officers and staff. He also wanted the police service to do more for the Black and minority ethnic communities. Never described as a thief-taker, he was more of a community champion than a feared investigator. The black police movement gradually gained momentum with more and more people attending meetings. The people attending the meetings weren't just black but also of Asian heritage. Asian police officers and staff suffered much of the same type of discrimination as black officers. The racial stereotyping and lack of career opportunities for Asian staff reflected that of black officers of African or African-Caribbean background.

Charles Maduemezia was a black officer of African heritage, the son of a tribal chief. I became friends with Charlie Mad, a shortening of his name and nothing else, who became interested in the level of discrimination within the police. The group was growing, and I was gaining the friendship of more people. I became friends with an Asian police officer called Nita Jhangi. Nita taught me about the values that were important to her and her culture. As an Asian woman she faced double discrimination. Karin became a mentor to Nita and other black, Asian or minority ethnic women who fought discrimination on more than one level. Karin was outstanding, guiding us through the police and nurturing talent that was not appreciated by the Eurocentric force in which we all served.

As the Black police movement grew, meeting in pubs, libraries and each-others houses, became less and less practical. Karin tried to gain permission for our meetings to take place on police premises. This request was denied. Karin arranged a meeting with a GMP command officer at the then GMP headquarters located at Chester House in Old Trafford. I was to attend the meeting also. When I arrived at police headquarters, I was denied entry to the building. As a serving GMP police officer, I was not allowed into police headquarters to discuss issues relating to black staff with the command of GMP. Black staff were being treated as one would treat a stray dog. I now used the term black to reflect people of African, African-Caribbean and Asian backgrounds. The approval for The Manchester Mentor was brought into sharp focus for me. When it came to issues for serving black staff, the command simply was not interested.

Two events that happened to me privately had origins in my earlier life. Whilst at the police station, I answered a phone call from a teacher at Stretford Grammar School. My old boy's school had been amalgamated with the girl's grammar school and was now located in newer premises in Stretford. The teacher introduced himself, he was enquiring about another officer who was not present at the time of the call. At the end of the conversation, I said to the teacher "You don't remember me, do you?" Not only had this teacher been at the boy's school during my time there but he had been my form teacher. I told him my name; this was followed by an earth-shatteringly long pause. I could feel the teacher processing all of the old boys who he had once taught. It came to him; I could hear his inner voice speaking to him. Not the boy who had been banned from sports, not the boy who he had described as anti-authoritarian. "You are a policeman," he said, shocked by my exposé. Yep, he did not expect that one, did he? What I had needed at school, was someone who believed in me not someone who years later would fall off their seat when told that I had become a Police Officer.

[Dear Mama – Tupac]

The second event was when human resources called me on a work extension stating that they had received a claim for child support from the Child Support Agency. At first, I thought it was someone winding me up but no he was deadly serious; his tone was monochrome. He told me the name of the claimant, my days in that shared house in Northenden had come back to bite me. I recalled sneaking passed the front door of the house to give the appearance that I had been in my bed. Kingpin hadn't been fooled, looks like I got away with nothing that day. She had moved out shortly afterwards I assumed to be with her boyfriend. I had moved out also as I was joining the police. As it turns out she went away and had a son. I drove the long way home that night. I told my wife what had happened that day and how I knew the woman. My wife grasped that all of this had happened before I had met her, but its spectre would remain. I naturally insisted on having a DNA test, the results were conclusive, I was the boy's father but I was not allowed to see him.

Paul Bailey

New Agenda

1997.

[New Agenda – Janet Jackson]

By 1997, the black police association was gaining momentum both locally in Greater Manchester and nationally. The Metropolitan Police launched a Black Police Association in 1994. GMP had yet to embrace its black staff or even engage with them in any meaningful way. On the contrary, Martin Harding, now a Chief Inspector and the highest-ranking black police officer in GMP took the force to an employment tribunal. Martin believed that he had been unfairly held back and passed over for promotion 56 times whilst his white counterparts jumped the queue. He claimed that he had been the victim of racial and sexual discrimination. Having filed a discrimination claim, the force had promoted him to Chief Inspector. Martin stated that during his 23-year career he had been a trainee detective after which he was promised the next CID vacancy, but that never happened, sounded all too familiar to me. Hearing the details of Martin's complaint, I couldn't help but reflect on my own experience within the CID. The police defended Martin's claims stating that their actions were not racist or sexist.

I was becoming known on a local stage as a person who was willing to fight for what I believed in. Damn the cost.

I continued to play basketball for GMP in the Manchester League and at the national championships. I played for the English police team and for the British police team. This meant that there were a number of times a year that I was away from home. I gained the unwanted but totally warranted reputation of 'A player' having a string of women on what I can only call holiday romances, 'basketball holiday romances' except there was no romance. At the end of the weekend, I would go home and that was the end of it. There came a time when it was a bad weekend for me if there wasn't at least one holiday romance. Basketball was almost becoming secondary. There also wasn't a tournament when I didn't go out clubbing, sometimes drinking to excess. I was not a big drinker at home, so I saw these few weekends a year as an opportunity to let my hair down, metaphorically speaking of course. I would like to say that the late nights didn't affect my performance, on the court, but inevitably there was a time when it did.

During a national championship, I hurriedly got dressed for an early game that we had. It had been a late, late night. Players normally wear warm-up uniforms over the team strip. The warm-up uniforms have press studs allowing the wearer to pull them off quickly. When the five-minute warning went off, I pulled off the warm-up top only to discover that I was naked underneath. Further inspection revealed that I was only wearing a jockstrap – oh shit. Fortunately, the hotel wasn't far away, a colleague went back to the hotel to retrieve my forgotten kit whilst I sat out at the start of the game.

I had been stopped many times by the police since I was a youth and a younger man. The area that I lived in now was not ethnically diverse at all, a far cry from the multi-cultural area that I grew up in. In fact, according to the 2001 census Wigan Borough, with a population of roughly 300,000 was 98.7% white; I doubt that these figures would reveal much change in the nineties.

I found that I was being stopped by police patrols regularly. They always said the same thing, "Just a routine vehicle check". There was obviously nothing routine about it. I was being targeted, and the reasons for these stops were unequivocally a result of racial profiling. These patrols would go out of their way to stop my vehicle, executing crazy U-turns when seeing me drive past them in the opposite direction. On occasion, they would say things like "Can I just check your spare wheel" not realising, at first anyway, that I was a cop and knew that there was no reason for them to be checking my spare wheel that was in the boot of my car, their ulterior motive being to see what was in the boot of my car, a backhanded and unlawful search. I'd naturally refused. I would not declare my status as a police officer unless I was specifically asked or if the police officer concerned was a total arse. Having my children in the car with me did not make any difference, I would be stopped all the same. It was not long before enough was enough. I made an appointment to see the Chief Superintendent for the Wigan Borough Julia Hodson. I explained to her the problem that I was having without sugarcoating it. She was polite and concluded the meeting by stating that she would look into it. The 'routine' vehicle checks stop after that.

May 1997, it was Championnat D'Europe Des Polices, part two. This time the tournament was to be held in Antwerp, Belgium. No rusty planes this time, it was a coach trip all the way Belgium. The trip was pretty cool, McDonald's with mayonnaise on your chips and a can of Stella Artois. My form was still good, I benefitted from the fact that many of the ex-national league players who became police officers were older than I was, so I still could outperform them athletically. I was playing enough basketball to compete even at an international level. I had been selected again without hesitation. There were a couple of additions and a few retirements from the game since Athens, but we were still a competitive team.

Other countries had learned the lessons of Greece and came fully loaded with their own crop of professional basketball stars turned police officers. Even if their warrant cards were not fully dry. The tournament was less remarkable than Athens. The stadium was a good-sized sports hall at best with light dusting of spectators at most games. The teams were more evenly matched as the tournament had become an alternative to the full European championships. The games were hard-fought but less memorable than Athens. We were good enough to make the semi-finals. We lost that game but were good enough to come third winning the third and fourth place play-off. A second European bronze medal for me, I would have preferred going one better but it was not to be.

My desire to reform GMP and make it an organisation that was equitable for all was not limited to issues that just related to black staff. In June 1997, the force exposed its police officers to C S Gas during training sessions. I objected to this for numerous reasons including that C S Gas was a noxious substance and carried a health risk, that medical examinations had not been given to staff before exposing them to the gas and that administering a noxious substance was an assault therefore, I refused. I was informed that if I were not exposed to the gas, I would fail the course and possibly be disciplined by the Chief Constable who at this time was David Wilmot. It was without question that the gas was debilitating for a person exposed to it but exposing staff to it did not make any sense, to me at least. I found the arguments that existed that officers needed to experience the effects of the gas to appreciate how to use it to be as foolish as they were misguided. Put it another way if I wanted to apply for a position in firearms would I need to be shot first? There would never be an expectation that firearms officers would need to take a bullet before being able to appreciate the effects that a round had on the human body, any suggestion would have been laughed out of any arena – surely. Yet in GMP at the time that expectation existed for C S Gas, a noxious and flammable substance. I could not believe that any police officer would accept this. My refusal was taken up to force command – police officers in GMP no longer have to be exposed to C S Gas to be trained in the use of the gas.

In July 1997, the then Home Secretary Jack Straw announced that there would be a public inquiry into the racist murder of Stephen Lawrence. The black teenager was murdered in an unprovoked racist attack in 1993. The inquiry was to identify lessons for the police dealing with racially motivated crimes. The inquiry was to be chaired by Sir William Macpherson, a retired High Court Judge.

In 1998, I challenged GMP over the way it paid its staff for rest day duties worked at Manchester United Football Club (It could have any club but, in my case, it was MUFC). I believed that the force was not paying the correct amount to officers in line with regulations. I was unconcerned with the impact that this may have had on the force as the regulations were there to be adhered to. Again, this went to command; the result, I received the correct payment and force-wide guidance was published to ensure common practice adhering to the regulations across the force. Again, all officers benefitted from my challenge to the force.

On 14th October 1998, David Wilmot acknowledged that GMP was infected by institutional racism at the public inquiry chaired by Sir William Macpherson. Mr Wilmot told the inquiry that we lived in a society that has institutional racism, and that Greater Manchester Police is no exception. He stated that we accept that we have a problem with some overt racism, and certainly that we have a problem with internalised racism. He was the first Chief Constable to have acknowledged institutional racism in his own force. Martin Harding was quoted in the media welcoming the admission made by David Wilmot he is quoted as saying:

> "I am delighted that he has now come forward and admitted that racism exists in GMP. Before anything could be done to improve the situation, it has to be admitted that there is a problem, and I'm pleased he's done that."

David Wilmot's comments may have been a revelation for some but not for black officers like me who had been highlighting the racism for years. I felt vindicated for all the times that I challenged racist behaviour and all the times that racism within GMP had been denied. Naively, I suppose, I hoped that Mr Wilmot's comments would be universally accepted within GMP at least and that Martin's comments about admissions being a precursor to remedy would be realised. The response was very different to my hopes. Every conversation that I had, not related to a particular investigation after this point seemed to be about racism and David Wilmot's comments. I found that I had to explain and justify David Wilmot's comments in a way that white people are never expected to. For example, no one expects the average German to explain the actions of Adolf Hitler so why were black officers expected to be an authority on what David Wilmot said?

The general reaction I found was denial and anger from my white counterparts. Some of the backlash was crass, sometimes mischievous but rarely considered. It was even more brutal than the reaction to the Black Lives Matter in 2020.

Paul Bailey

Coming in From the Cold

1999.

[So Good – Destiny's Child]

David Wilmot's admission of racism in GMP may have gained him plaudits from the media, from the community and even the parents of Stephen Lawrence, but the reality of his admission for serving black police officers in GMP, like me, was that we had to deal with the fallout, often in isolation.

The black police movement gained traction in the wake of the Chief Constable's admission. There was a change in the attitude of the command within GMP. Black staff who had previously been ignored, denied the use of police facilities, and in my case, even denied entry to police headquarters were now welcomed. We were no longer treated like stray dogs; the dog had been let into the house now coming in from the cold and could feed at the table. Black staff, who up to this stage had not been overt in their support of the black police movement, came forward. Undoubtedly, some of this support was because it was suddenly popular to do so when the movement was about to become successful. It did not matter to me why more black staff were joining the movement. If they were jumping on the bandwagon that was not the issue for me, I was more interested in the optics both internally and externally.

I had always realised that those who were merely jumping on bandwagon would soon jump off it when it no longer suited their purpose. In any event, these people were easy to spot, they were generally disingenuous and lacked any real knowledge about black history. At the same time, there were white staff who accepted the command team's embracing of the black police movement without complaining because of the realisation that they could do nothing about. They couldn't, as the Chief Constable had made the admission at a public inquiry, the whole of the United Kingdom was aware of that fact, there was no going back. Karin and I became the face of the black police movement in GMP. I learned from Karin whose experience, depth of knowledge and support was invaluable for me.

My time in the Plain Clothes unit had come to an end. I had worked in the unit for years and had enjoyed it immensely. By the time of my departure, I had worked on a number of drug investigations and proactive crime investigations. As a black officer, I took advantage of the fact that I could do things that others in the unit couldn't do, I could go places where they could not go, and people would tell me things that they wouldn't tell a white officer. The value of having a diverse police force had never been so obvious to me as my time in the plain clothes department. The unit had become both successful and desirable with the competition for places in the unit being fierce.

Due to a complaint, in another force, that the Criminal Investigation Department was an old boys club with access to it based on nepotism rather than ability, the CID trainee scheme changed within GMP. Applications to the CID were dealt with centrally rather than locally in the division. This meant that I had to reapply for a position that I had passed years earlier. I did so without hesitation as uniform work was behind me and I did not want to find myself in the same position that Martin Harding had done years earlier when he took the force to an employment tribunal. I passed the interview and would be sent to Stretford CID to start in February 1999.

On 1st February 1999, I started in the CID at Stretford, a place that I had been transferred from at the very start of my career due to the threat on my parents' house. There are clear differences between working in uniform in a given area and working in plain clothes. Uniform officers have no control over where they go and what they do. They respond to calls as they happen over the radio. CID officers are investigators who manage their own workload at a much slower pace. CID officers do not hump calls on the radio nor do they patrol in uniform. The work is totally different. I worked in the plain clothes department for years, and some of the protracted enquiries I conducted were in Old Trafford and more widely the North Trafford area. Working in the CID at Stretford did not have the same risk for me as working in uniform did, this fact should not even be debated.

[Kung Fu Fighting – Carl Douglas]

I found myself on an investigation in the company of DC Chris Gill 'Gilly.' Gilly was a tall white detective with a super sharp wit and a penchant for impersonating others with hilarious effects. He looked very unassuming, which worked to his advantage. Below that ordinary exterior was a trained fighter in some martial art that I struggle to remember now. During the investigation, we went to an address in South Trafford. The front door of the house was opened by an old grey man, dishevelled in appearance, who was lacking any front teeth. If you had seen him on a park bench drinking out of a bottle wrapped in a brown paper bag, he wouldn't have looked out of place. The old man took one look at me and said "Paul Bailey". He certainly had me at a disadvantage as I had no idea who he was. He beckoned Gilly and I into the house before disappearing. We looked at each other believing that we were in the company of some eccentric professor who had a time machine hidden in his garden shed. The old man emerged holding several old photographs; he had also put in his dentures that filled out his face giving him an appearance less scary than before. It turned out that this man was a retired teacher who used to work at Stretford Grammar School for

Boys. He was also the teacher who had reported me to the headmaster during the 'wellie-faced nigger' incident. He had with him old school photographs that he proudly showed to Gilly and I. Gilly was desperate to see if I was in any of these photographs, if I had then the piss-taking would have lasted for the rest of my career. Luckily, I was not in any of the photographs – the history lesson was over. On leaving the teacher's house he turned to me and said "Paul, well done." My trip down memory lane ended abruptly when Gilly and I got into our waiting police car, Gilly said "You went to fucking grammar school?"

24th February 1999, the Stephen Lawrence Inquiry Report was published. The report included 70 recommendations that police forces in the United Kingdom needed to adhere to. The recommendations included:

> Race relations legislation to apply to all officers.
>
> The public being encouraged to report racist incidents by making it possible to report them 24 hours a day, and not only at police stations.
>
> Dedicated Family Liaison Officers must exist in every police force at a local level.
>
> Any evidence of racist motivation is to be declared at all stages of the prosecution. No exclusions on the grounds of plea bargaining.
>
> Police forces should reflect the cultural and ethnic mix of the communities they serve.
>
> A Freedom of Information Act should apply to all areas of policing (with the exception of the 'substantial harm' test for withholding disclosure in exceptional circumstances).
>
> Government inspectors will have 'full and unfettered powers' to inspect police services. An investigation into the

> Metropolitan Police will begin immediately, with particular emphasis on unsolved murders and the handling of racist incidents.

And

> The government will establish performance indicators to monitor the handling of racist incidents, levels of satisfaction with the police service and ethnic minorities, training of family liaison officers, racial awareness training, stop and search procedures, recruitment of ethnic minorities and complaints about racism in police forces.

The force had to deal with all the recommendations arising from the Stephen Lawrence report and therefore needed to put together a team to push through the recommendations. This would in turn improve GMP and all the communities that GMP serve. The recommendations were, in my view, trying to save the soul of the police service. GMP needed people who they trusted to carry out this task without any fear and asked me to join that team. Obviously, I was not going to give up my career in the CID so, it was agreed that I would be seconded away from the CID at Stretford returning once the work on Lawrence had been completed. On 12th April 1999, I was seconded to Community Affairs at Chester House.

I continued to play basketball for the force, for Great Britain and became the captain of the English team. I had become one of the oldest players on the team with younger players being recruited to the police from local basketball leagues. These ex-local league players did not have the skill or the experience of retiring ex-national league players whose places they were taking. Great Britain's team suffered as a result. National teams from countries that historically had no chance against Great Britain suddenly became more competitive. I also had picked up an injury to my right elbow that eventually required surgery to fix. I continued with the holiday romances that I had seen as disposable pleasures rather than meaningful pursuits. All that changed when I met a woman from the North East who I will refer to as Miss X. She was beautiful and talented on course to much greater things.

My move from Stretford CID to Community Affairs happened without incident. I would return to the CID once the secondment came to an end. Although I had never worked in force headquarters before I was known there by more people than I expected. The fact that I had taken the force on previously, twice, had not gone unnoticed. GMP's response to the Lawrence Inquiry report was called Operation Catalyst. It was called this as the report was supposed to be the catalyst for change - time would tell. The team was made up of middle-ranking officers, headed by Detective Chief Inspector Dave Jones. Dave was an ambitious detective who was clearly on his way up. He didn't know me personally but after a short period of time, I made it clear that I was not there to make up the numbers. I wanted to get the job done. The team would later be joined by Karin who was an Inspector and familiar with this type of work.

Each member of the team was allocated different Lawrence recommendations that had been grouped by the department. For example, all the recommendations that affected Complaint and Discipline 'Y' Department, were grouped together and given to that department to review and respond to. The Department lead liaised with the OP Catalyst team member who would oversee their response. This meant that middle and senior managers were liaising with me who was a junior rank to them. I couldn't have cared less if this caused them a problem, if it did then they had to grin and bear it. I had stopped worrying about what people thought of me much earlier on in my service. I wasn't going to lose any sleep over their insecurities.

The OP Catalyst team also met with leading members of the community, or at least influential members of the community, to gain their support and help. This opened the door to me in other ways. The black staff movement in Manchester would also need contacts and support from the community. Suddenly I had a Rolodex full of contacts. In addition to this the media had an appetite for anything Lawrence related and was keen to understand the GMP response to the report. My forthright and fearless approach to the media was an absolute gift to them. If GMP had any illusions that I would tow the corporate line, then these hopes would have been quickly dashed. I told it how it was and became the media's darling as they could rely on me to answer questions honestly even if that answer was unflattering for GMP or its command. I appeared in the tabloid press numerous times and sometimes even made the front cover. I was then and I am now unapologetically black, the media couldn't get enough of me.

OP Catalyst had a public launch event that was held at GMP's Hough End Centre. During this event, I spoke in front of a packed audience firstly about the circumstance surrounding the racist murder of Stephen Lawrence, then about the police response that had been heavily criticised, and then about my personal experiences of the police both as a boy after the riots of 1981 through to the present day. A black woman sobbed as I spoke so was the depth of feeling for the black community that had been marginalised for so long. The event was well received by the media and OP Catalyst became a word that David Wilmot used – a lot. He was quoted in the media;

> "Discrimination is one of the most important issues facing the police service, and GMP, in the late 20th century. We are wholly committed to the principle of anti-discrimination and the need to treat people fairly according to their needs... GMP is already ahead in a lot of areas highlighted by the Lawrence Inquiry, such as murder reviews, but we continually seek to improve the confidence the community has in Greater Manchester Police and the service we offer."

I was going to hold GMP to that.

The meetings of black staff in GMP continued; during a

meeting, we decided upon a name. Greater Manchester Black and Asian Police Association. GM BAPA for short, but BAPA became the name that everyone used. The term black in the Black Police Association encompasses everyone from a black, Asian or minority ethnic background. In Manchester, we understood that, the name BAPA merely came from a vote from the staff who were present at the meeting on that day. During that meeting, there was also a vote for the person who would lead BAPA moving forward. I was voted in as the first Chair of BAPA with Karin Mulligan being voted in as the first Deputy Chair. I was privileged to have been voted in to become the first Chair, who wouldn't be? A question: Who was the second man in space? – exactly. After the enormity of being the Chair of a Staff Network subsided the reality kicked in, Karin and I have now painted huge targets on our backs, let us see what we can see.

The Launch of the Greater Manchester Black and Asian Police Association was in November 1999 at Manchester Town Hall. After the Lawrence Report being black in the police was either something to be revered or something to be hated, there did not seem to be a middle ground. The launch of BAPA was no exception. Naturally, as Chair, I spoke before the audience in the main chamber of town hall. All the people who had been voted in as part of BAPA's Executive Committee were present. The Executive Committee included Ivan Hewitt, Fay Wilson, Charles Maduemezia, Charles Crichlow and Martin Harding. Chief Constable David Wilmot and the Lord Mayor of Manchester were also present.

I had got word that a black journalist was going to attend the launch and challenge me. The thrust of her attack was that I was in fact the one who was racist and that the Black Police Association was also racist. I have seen black people do the bidding of white people before. This type of person has existed throughout history and is used to subjugate black people and black organisations. A successful attack like this on a fledgling association like BAPA would have been catastrophic. By sheer coincidence the journalist was sitting next to my wife who was white, blonde with blue eyes, you couldn't get any whiter than that. During the question-and-answer session, I went straight to the journalist to ask her question, a meaningless inquiry followed with no follow-up, how disappointing. Maybe she lost her nerve or maybe someone had pointed out who she was sitting next to. I was going to thrash her publicly instead I gave her a knowing look and sat down.

Interlude

[Heat – 50 Cent]

It was just another day, nothing remarkable, I had a day off during the week, so I was at home. I turned the television on. The local news came on, filling the room with sound. I heard the newscaster describe a firearms incident that had occurred overnight. Firearms had been discharged on a terraced street and at a particular house on that street in Old Trafford. The incident was described as a serious escalation of violence in the area. The fact that the incident had occurred in Old Trafford immediately caught my attention. I repositioned myself to get a look at the screen to see my parents' house on the news footage.

This was definitely a stop everything moment.

After picking my jaw up, I got into my car and drove directly to my parent's house. When I arrived, their terrace was inside the police cordon tape. There were police patrols and Scenes of Crime Officers everywhere. My pulse dropped slightly when I saw that it was the house opposite my parents that had been targeted. I knew the uniformed officer stood at the cordon and I spoke to him, "I need to get in my mum lives there," I said, "That's your mum's house?" he enquired, "Yep." The officer had tried to stop my mum from going into her house before I got there, to which she dressed him down and went in anyway. Upon seeing me arrive this made perfect sense to him.

You Know What's Up

2000.

[U Know What's Up – Donell Jones]

By January 2000, Operation Catalyst had been running for several months with varying results that depended on the department or branch the Catalyst Project Team were dealing with. Some department heads took great interest in the Lawrence Report and the recommendations that came from it and were keen to ensure they were implemented.

Others had little or no interest in Lawrence and had even less time to talk about race. This type of attitude was corrosive and unhelpful. I had little time to cajole people who did not want to be part of the transformation of the GMP and the wider police service. In short, I was not asking them to change, I was telling them. The OP Catalyst Project Team had been imbued with the power of the Chief Constable, this pissed off those resistant to change. In the same month, GMP appointed Dr Brian Holland, a white middle-aged man, as the force's first Race Advisor. Despite the Lawrence Inquiry, the public hearings and the work to employ the recommendations, the force had reverted to type by picking another white middle- aged man to sit at the helm. It was apparent to me that the force had learnt nothing, and I decided to give them a sharp kick up the arse.

Racism is a lived experience more than anything else. I doubted Dr Holland had any first-hand experience of any type of discrimination or its effects. In addition, his appointment would not add a diverse view to the senior management team of the force it would just be more of the same. 'If you always do what you have always done, you always get what you have always got.' I was not impressed by the force's constant use of his title Doctor; this may have impressed others but had the opposite effect on me. I immediately went onto the offensive which was very easy in this case as it seemed everyone outside of GMP was thinking exactly what I was.

The story ended up on the front page of a local paper with my picture next to that of Assistant Chief Constable Vince Sweeney. The story was also picked up by the national press giving it a wide exposure. ACC Vince Sweeney was a tall man who always looked to me like an officer in the armed services. I felt for him in this case as he looked like the guy who had been reluctantly pushed out of the front door into this head-on collision. Behind his rank, he was quite a nice guy. I remember him calling me into his office one day for a chat. It was just the two of us there when he told me a story. He said that when he was a young Lieutenant in the Navy [knew he was a military man], he quickly realised that he could not get anything done without the agreement of the Leading Seaman. He would give an order, and everyone would look to the Leading Seaman for his approval of the order. Rather than resist this he embraced the Leading Seaman as he realised that they should be working together. Whether that was a true story or not I understood the message. Vince finished by saying to me "You are more powerful than me Paul, they follow me because they have to, they follow you because they want to." I don't recall either of us ever having a crossed word after that moment.

It was not only Vince Sweeney who I had a one-to-one moment with. I had a meeting with Chief Constable David Wilmot. After Mr Wilmot's declaration of racism in GMP and the newly found love for all things black and the Black Police Association. I thought I would put him to the test. There is an old saying, "Don't tell me you love me, show me you love me.' During the meeting, I produced a BAPA 'Application for membership' form stating that Mr Wilmot could sign up as a display of his commitment to BAPA and the aims of the organisation. This was followed by a pregnant pause, but I had not intended to follow this offer up with anything. Mr Wilmot looked at me, we were like two poker players playing for the entire pot. Ok, I'll go again "I can get further forms for the command team if you wish". Mr Wilmot did not sign up but I believe that he saw in front of him a constable who would not kowtow to anyone.

Karin and I were targeted by the knuckle-dragging mob that was to be expected. Someone created a webpage that was dedicated to slagging me off with overtly racist comments. I wasn't happy with the picture they used – wasn't my best side. The website disappeared quickly. We were also targeted by someone who was sending offensive literature to prominent members of the black community. I've been there before [Terminator 2] but this time I was flattered that someone had taken the time to target me in this way – Thanks.

I underwent surgery on my elbow after which my arm was bandaged from my wrist to my bicep. I thought that the OP Catalyst work was so important that I came into work still wearing the bandage at a time that I should have been convalescing at home. In a meeting with ACC Sweeney, Vince pointed out that my bandage was bleeding. I had burst my stitches putting my recovery back somewhat.

My time at OP Catalyst had come to an end, it was time to return to Stretford CID. On my last day at headquarters, I was sitting in my office when I saw people in the open-plan area outside of my office stand up. There was a knock on my office door, ACC Sweeney then walked in. He said that he knew that it was my last day and he wanted to thank me for my efforts and to wish me well. We shook hands, he walked out. No one else visited me on my last day, I left headquarters feeling like a tenant that had been evicted from their house. I returned to a CID Trainee's Course which was more embarrassing for them than for me. I was there just to be confirmed with a permanent posting that should follow my six-month stint. Chris Barnes was at Stretford which made my time there more relaxing. He too was destined for a career in criminal investigation beyond Stretford CID. Chris and I maintained our friendship outside of work, I didn't do that with colleagues, outside of the BAPA, but Chris was different, we were friends.

At the end of the Trainee's Course when I had passed, for the second time, I was told that there were no places for me in the CID, for a second time. I was told I'd be working uniform patrol at Stretford - we'd see about that. I met with the Superintendent at Stretford, I found him to be a weasel of a man, who spoke condescendingly to anyone of a junior rank to him. I got the impression that he was pissed on power and thought to myself – has he seen a real criminal up close in his life? Bet he hadn't.

I wanted a transfer from Stretford for obvious reasons, uniform work came with an inherent danger not only for me but for my family who still lived in the area. There was a great deal of difference between working in an investigatory department like the CID and the uncontrolled environment of working uniform at Stretford. Throughout this meeting, it was clear to me that once again GMP, or certainly senior members within it, were going to have their pound of flesh out of me. Or so they thought - if you start a fight be prepared to get a bloody nose. He told me that I would have to write a report to transfer away. He confirmed that there was no record of why I had transferred away from uniform duties at Stretford before in 1990, there was. My argument was strong, so it was back to South Trafford. But they hadn't finished there.

Now they were going to mess me around with shift patterns. Trying to give the appearance of flexibility there was no doubt that they were going to stick it to me. One visit to the Superintendent at the Personnel Department and I'd be working a shift pattern that didn't inconvenience me. This was going to be my punishment, a clumsy and obvious attempt to make my life harder. I knew what was up and had the resources to punch back - hard.

After all of this had happened the Chief Superintendent 'M' Division wrote to me on 21st June 2001, he wrote:

> 'Divisional Commanders Good Work Minute,
>
> I would like to take this opportunity of congratulating you for all your hard work in securing the arrest and conviction of a man for aggravated burglary while you were a CID Trainee on the M Division. The man was sentenced to nine years imprisonment for offences against elderly persons who were traumatised by these events. I have awarded you a good work minute for your professionalism and determination and I would be pleased if you would put a copy of this memo and the attached item from Divisional Orders in your PDP. Once again well done!
>
> Chief Superintendent'

I was contacted by the Legal Services Department who were handling a case where the Chief Constable was being sued by a member of the public. He was alleging that he had been assaulted by the police whilst in their custody. As the result of this alleged assault, he claimed he had sustained serious injuries and therefore he wanted to be compensated financially, the amount claimed ran into tens of thousands of pounds.

What did this have to do with me? – that was exactly the question I wanted answering. To my alarm, the allegation was several years old by the time that it came to my attention. The specific allegation was that having been arrested and in police custody, a large black police officer, who was not concerned in the claimant's arrest or in the case against him, entered the claimant's cell and beat the hell out of him. Still – what does this have to do with me?

I had not been identified or named as the black officer responsible for this alleged unprovoked and serious assault. GMP hadn't even informed me of the case before the civil litigation that the claimant had now entered into. I was dumbfounded as to why I was now being told about the case and claim. As it turned out, an investigation had revealed I had arrested another person on the day in question and would likely have been in the custody office at the time when the claimant was in custody.

A meeting had been arranged with Counsel acting on behalf of the Chief Constable, I was asked to attend. I attended the meeting as intrigued as anyone. I had checked my pocket notebook, and I had indeed arrested someone on the day in question; I arrested a lot of people back then. The claimant's name meant nothing to me, in fact, I had never heard of him. My view of the claim was that it was flawed beyond belief. The idea that a police officer not connected to the claimant's arrest would obtain the claimant's cell key, enter the cell and for no reason beat the claimant up causing him severe injury was a 'flight of fancy.' Totally unbelievable as far as I was concerned. What was even more pernicious was the 'The big black police officer did it' part of the allegation. Was this allegation more believable to GMP, to Counsel and the court because the alleged offender was a big black man.

The case went to trial at Manchester County Court. Unlike criminal proceedings where witnesses yet to give evidence are not allowed in the court, civil rules allow all witnesses to sit in the court. This allows witnesses further down the list to hear the testimonies of witnesses who went before them. I sat in the court throughout the trial. It was clear that if the Civil Court found me responsible for this serious assault, there would be nothing preventing a criminal probe or misconduct hearing following on. I was not at court to defend the Chief Constable I was there to ensure that justice was done and protect my arse.

The claimant was naturally there with his Counsel. Not only had I never heard of him before but now I could confirm that I had never seen him before either. It came around to my evidence. I took the stand and was sworn in. My evidence was simple I did not remember the day in question as it was several years ago. I had my pocketbook that confirmed that I had arrested a person unconnected to the claimant and therefore I may have been around the custody office at the time of the claimant's detention. I also stated that I had not assaulted the claimant. Counsel for the claimant then went straight in with his attack. The thrust of the claimant's case was that if I could not remember the day in question or even recognise the claimant how did I know that I had not assaulted him? The response to this was quite simple because I had never entered the cell of a detained person and assaulted them.

The Judge had difficulty with the case and asked when the police officer, me, had been identified as the person responsible for the assault. I hadn't been, counsel claimed that the claimant had recognised me whilst sitting at the back of the courtroom! – truly unbelievable. The case was dismissed. This was another case where I had been wrongly accused of assault, the penalty of which could have been severe and life-changing for me.

Championnat D'Europe Des Polices, part three, this time in Bulgaria. I had again been selected to represent Great Britain in the European Championships. The team looked much different to Athens, or even Antwerp. I had the feeling that Bulgaria would be my last. We flew into Sofia, upon landing we queued at the exchange to buy Bulgaria's currency at the time, the Lev. The guy in front of me asked the cashier to exchange £500 pounds into Lev, the cashier dryly asked, "Are you staying here for six months?" Hearing that I exchanged £50; our meals and soft drinks were paid for anyway.

I Did That

We then had to catch a smaller plane to the coast so waited around for a while until the second plane was ready. On entering the plane our bags were heaped on metal shelves, on either side of the exit. The shelves in my garden shed looked sturdier. The plane's cabin was only big enough for our party, barely big enough. The rusty plane in Athens didn't seem so bad now.

Partway through the flight the tiny cockpit door opened. A man, who suspiciously looked like the pilot, walked along the aisle and into the rear compartment where our bags were. Minutes later, he appeared carrying snacks. I thought 'Don't worry about the snacks mate, concentrate on flying the fucking plane.' – I'm not a nervous flyer, really I'm not. We arrived safely, several days in Bulgaria with sun, sea and sand - great.

The Great Britain team were assigned a bodyguard, let's call him Vlad. Vlad was a tall strong looking man who looked like he had been made out of girders, iron girders. He had a chin that looked as though it had been perfectly chiselled from granite and black swept back hair. He always had his suit on, even on the beach. I don't believe that this was a fashion statement more of a necessity to hide his errrm... equipment, he was definitely strapped. The last sentence gives the wrong idea, sounds sexual even – in clear words, we thought he was hiding his firearm. Vlad was with us late into the night and amazingly he would be waiting for us in the morning, immaculately presented even down to his shoes being spotless. He apparently didn't need any sleep. He was awesome. I was frightened of him – I'm sure that I was not alone.

Colin Phillips the Chief Constable of Cumbria Constabulary was the head of the Great Britain party. He had been an Assistant Chief Constable in GMP and a useful basketball player himself in his time. Kirk Dawes, a West Midlands Police Detective, was now the manager of the team. Managers naturally lean towards the players they coach every day. I didn't believe that the new set-up of the team worked despite us still having some very capable players. We acquitted ourselves well during the tournament as did Kirk who should be commended for his efforts but fell short of a top-three spot. The games were shown on Bulgarian television such was the profile of the event. I would make sure that Bulgaria was not my epitaph.

A formal banquet was held for all the teams in a very contemporary-looking cellar. It was really very nice. There were endless bottles of fizz and other alcoholic drinks on tap so predictably the drinking games began. Colin Phillips played along and turned out to be invincible, I'm not sure that he even took a mouthful. Where he lacked in the sparkling wine consumption I more than made up for. The last thing I recall was dancing on a barrel wearing a sheepskin, not a sheepskin coat, an actual sheep's skin. I woke up in my room the next morning entirely naked apart from wearing one sock. At least the sock was on my foot.

We invited Vlad out for a meal at the end of the trip. We understood that he was married so asked him to bring his wife along. She was beautiful and humble. We had a Chinese banquet that was more 'hair of the dog' for me than anything else. Vlad said that apart from his wedding day this was the best night that he had had. Before leaving, I gave Vlad my tracksuit, it was new – I hadn't worn it. I thanked him and we shook hands.

I continued on as chair of BAPA building a staff network that was visible, challenging and most of all an authentic voice. There seemed little point creating a network that was just a mouthpiece for the Chief Constable, and that would do the force's bidding. This was an opportunity for real change and for people like me to stand up and be counted. I also helped other groups set up their staff networks. Sgt Julie Barnes Frank and I met and spoke regularly. Julie set up the Lesbian and Gay Staff Association in Greater Manchester now known as Pride. She drew from my experiences when I set up BAPA.

I also met other like-minded police officers around the country. Dr Leroy Logan was a black Detective Chief Inspector from the Metropolitan Police who had been instrumental in the Metropolitan Police Black Police Association. He was a Scientist before joining the Met and had had to deal with racism there in his own way. I always knew he was unshakable. If we were on a sinking ship then Leroy would be calmly looking for an escape route whilst others ran around screaming in panic and mayhem.

I also met a Metropolitan Police Superintendent called Dr Ali Dizaei. Ali was also a prime mover in the Met BPA and The National Black Police Association. Ali was British-Iranian and the son of a Deputy Police Commissioner in Tehran. He was a very different character to Leroy, he had a more direct approach, that I respected, and he left you in no doubt where you stood. I had spoken to Ali over the phone relating to the BPA matters. Only to find that he was under investigation by the Met. I understood that the Met investigation into Ali included allegations that he spied for Iran. It sounded like the plot of a cold war novel to me, and it still does. Ali would later file a claim for racial discrimination as a consequence of this investigation. This claim was settled out of court.

In May of 2001, following a period of racial tensions between white and Asian communities in the area, rioting took place in Oldham and Chadderton. The riots lasted over three days, being the first in a series of riots which saw similar conflicts in Leeds, Bradford, and Burnley. The riots in Oldham and Chadderton were very much a Greater Manchester problem. Bricks and projectiles were thrown at police lines. There were numerous injuries and damage to property. Despite the level of arson and violence, thankfully, there were no fatalities.

[Miami – Will Smith]

The United States of America also has a National Black Police Association. Founded in 1972, the association had aims that included working to improve the relationship between the police and minority communities and working towards reform in the areas of police corruption, brutality and racial discrimination.

In August 2001, I flew to Miami to attend the NBPA International Conference that would be held in the city. I arrived at Miami International Airport to be immediately disappointed; my bags had made it onto the wrong flight. It would be at least 24 hours before I would be reunited with my belongings. Looking as though I had just got off of a long flight and having no luggage with me, I hailed a cab and asked the taxi driver, who was black, to drive me to a hotel whose details I had on a scrap of paper. Upon hearing the address, the driver said "You mean the country club" in a predictable southern drawl. I detected a hint of disapproval or disbelief in his tone, my appearance did not help. He drove me to this fancy golf resort that had a gatehouse where visitors were screened. A security guard stopped the taxi speaking to the taxi driver who instantly pointed at me. I told the security guard my name who then checked it against a list that he was carrying. "Yes Sir, they will be waiting for you at reception." The taxi driver, now in shock, drove me to reception. As I paid him, I gave him a wink and then entered the building. Never judge a book by its cover.

There was quite a large British contingent at the conference, black police officers from other UK forces and even two Inspectors from Her Majesty's Inspectorate of Constabulary, Mike Franklyn and Maqsood Ahmad. The Brits naturally gravitated to each other, but they were all in a different building to me. Their rooms in that block were nice but could not compare to the suite I was in. Unlike other trips, I would be on my best behaviour, no waking up naked wearing one sock and having no memory of what happened.

The conference was way ahead of anything that we were doing in the UK at the time. It was evident that the NBPA-US was much more streamlined and organised. It wasn't just how logistically advanced the Americans were, it was the way that they thought about race and the police. The African-Caribbean communities in Britain had had a short but tumultuous relationship with the police. In the US, they had a long history of oppression of minorities from slavery, through the Jim Crow era, to the civil rights movements of the sixties. As a result, the NBPA-US were more aware of their history and knowledgeable of the issues that they were trying to influence. The passion of the Americans who had attended the conference also set them apart from the UK. UK conferences were like knitting bees in comparison. Black law enforcement personnel from over 17,000 agencies country-wide shared knowledge, information and experience on a level and in a way that I had never experienced before.

As clinical, confident and eye-opening as this conference was, I was enthused by the seminars and the powerful and carefully planned speeches. It wasn't all seminars and speeches. I went out socially with the American cops, more than once. A daytime trip to South Beach required sunglasses, the type that wraps around the side of your face, and not because it was sunny. The strip was everything that I had imagined it to be and more. At night, it transformed into a completely different place, becoming loud, neon and utterly cool. The Americans took me on a trip around Miami showing me all the sights, a trip to Casa Casuarina the house formerly owned by the late fashion designer Gianni Versace was particularly memorable. Being in the company of the police meant that you could get into anywhere, I followed on like a lost sheep drinking a Piña Colada.

The entire trip broadened my view and inspired me in a way that I could not have imagined when I set foot on the plane in Manchester. I needed to write a report on the trip upon my return to the UK. This report was more organisational than educational. The personal benefit lives with me to this day. On the way home at Miami International Airport, I was one of only two people taken out of the queue for an extended security search. Without the protection of my American police friends, I was returned to the reality of being a black man boarding a plane. I sat waiting to be x-rayed looking at the other passenger who had been selected. He was a minority, sweating, fidgeting and undoubtedly nervous.

In November 2001, I spoke before an estimated 500 people at the National Black Police Association (UK) Annual General Meeting. This was the second time that I spoke in the Manchester Town Hall. Before the conference, I researched the Hall and the ship that appears on the Coat of Arms for Manchester. Both had reminders of Britain's involvement in the trans-Atlantic slave trade. Before speaking, I downloaded a picture of a slave whose back was covered in scars caused by being whipped, the lash is as unforgiving as it is brutal. I told the man controlling the overhead projector to display the image a couple of minutes into my speech. When this huge image was displayed in the hall there were gasps.

The ceiling of the Great Hall is divided into panels bearing the coat of arms of the countries and towns with which Manchester traded at the height of its commercial power. One of those panels contained the coat of arms for South Africa, during Apartheid this South African panel of the ceiling had been covered. The end of Apartheid saw the panel revealed once again. I also spoke about the rioting that had occurred in Manchester earlier that year, comparing the riots to Apartheid and then introducing the ceiling in the very room that we were sitting in. Hard truths need to be spoken, however uncomfortable they were for some of the audience. The press rushed to me after the speeches ended but I thought it better to leave the public relations to somebody else.

At the end of my tenure as Chair, I thought I would be free to concentrate on my career as a detective. I had been posted to Altrincham CID, where I had started my career in criminal investigation years earlier. Looking back, I do not begrudge the intervening years between my first posting to CID and my eventual permanent posting to that department. Those years had given me the best grounding that I could wish for and would serve me well in the future.

In June 2002, I was seconded to the murder of a man by the name of Simon Dawson who had been stabbed to death in Clifton, Salford. This murder investigation would take months to investigate and eventually led to me making a permanent move to the Force Major Incident Team.

Work It

2003.

[Breaking The Habit – Linkin Park]

By 2003, it was clear to me that my basketball career was coming to an end. I was in my mid-thirties and had been playing the sport for over twenty years. All of that running, jumping and constantly changing direction had taken its toll on my fingers, arms, knees and back. By this time, I had fully recovered from the surgery that I had on my right elbow, I could feel that my time in this extremely athletic game was short. In 2002, I won the PAA Championships and the Inter-Association Championship which had conquered the demons of not winning a medal in Bulgaria. I had a long and successful career both outside of the police and inside. I had seen and done things many could only ever dream of and gained lifelong friends. I knew that it was time to call it a day on my basketball career, throughout one international basketball weekend.

I shared a room with a new player who was a Constable in the Metropolitan Police Service, they called him 'Dusty' for some reason. Anyway, over the two-night weekend, I had not slept in the hotel room at all. I essentially used the hotel as sports changing room. At the end of the weekend when we were about to check out of the hotel Dusty said to me "You are the nicest guy I never roomed with."

I had become the coach of the GMP women's basketball team. I'm not sure how that happened but it was great fun. At the start of my time as coach, it did occur to me that 'The hens have given the fox the keys to the chicken coop.' The team was made up of a great set of women who may not have been the most gifted basketball players, but they worked together and as a unit were hard to break down. I had learned 'Never shit where you eat'.

Within GMP a department called the Force Major Incident Team or FMIT was set up. The department would investigate the most serious crimes such as murder. I had worked on major crime since 2002 and applied for a permanent posting to FMIT. My application was successful, this called an end to my deployment to the Trafford Division. Soon, GMP would change the department's name to the Major Incident Team or MIT for short. MIT initially had 8 syndicates that were based at different geographical locations around Greater Manchester County. The syndicates were simply numbered 1 to 8.

In April 2003, the house Gina Adair and her children were staying in was shot at by gunmen. It was reported in the media that loyalist paramilitaries were responsible for this attack on the residential terrace house in Bolton, Greater Manchester. Gina Adair was the exiled wife of loyalist paramilitary leader Johnny Adair who had the nickname 'Mad Dog Adair'. Johnny Adair was reportedly charged with directing terrorism in 1995. He was also linked to a band which openly espoused the National Front. The attack on the home of Gina Adair came before the creation of the North West Counter Terrorism Unit so the investigation of the attack fell initially to MIT.

I was teamed up with a Police Detective who I will call Detective A. Detective A and I were the liaison officers for Gina Adair and her family. I understood this role as it was one of the recommendations in the Stephen Lawrence Report. I met with her, her family and associates many times. I would always sit in the same seat that was positioned in an alcove. From this position, the chair, and its occupant, were shielded from the road by the brick chimney breast. Before long, as soon as I walked into the house anyone sitting in this seat would get up. The Adairs realised why I always sat there. 'My mama didn't raise no fool'.

I did notice during our visits that Gina would be made up as if she were going on a night out. One day, whilst Detective A and I were at Gina's house I received a personal call, I took the call outside of the house leaving Detective A inside the house with Gina and her female friend. When I returned Detective A immediately left, leaving me with Gina and her friend. Gina said to me "Are you having women problems then?" I felt the walls close in. I made a stumbling reply hoping for Detective A to return. When Detective A returned, we hastily finished the meeting. As soon as we left and got into the car, I made Detective A have it. "You fucking bastard you set me up," – "Sorry mate but when you left she asked – Is your man gay" Detective A continued "Anyway after the florist I thought that you could handle it." Let me put some context to the florist comment.

Detective A and I went to a sandwich shop near to a florist for our lunch. Whilst sitting in the car eating our sandwiches, we saw a florist tending to her flowers outside of the shop. She was a pleasant-looking woman. Without saying anything I got out of the car, went up to the florist and bought a single rose which I got the florist to gift wrap. I then gave the rose to the florist and left. In response to Gina's enquiry, no I'm not gay but painfully aware that a bullet in the head would fuck up my Afro.

In June 2003, Chloe Fahey, a five-year-old child was killed by her mother Aisling Murray. Ms Murray was a paranoid schizophrenic and had a history of mental illness. She had been released from medical care less than a month before the death of her daughter as she was not considered to be a risk. Around 4am on the 26th of June, police were called to Ms Murray's address after a report that screaming had been heard. The police broke in to find a horrific scene. The child's bedroom had been stripped of its fixtures and fittings. Even the wallpaper had been removed. The bed resembled an altar in the room, Chloe had been stabbed 52 times. I was assigned to this case in its initial phase as the exhibits officer. I had seen and heard of some gruesome things during my time as a police officer but none as shocking as this.

By way of example, several years earlier I had dealt with a fire at an ordinary house in Trafford. The occupant of the house had left food cooking in the kitchen, whilst away from the kitchen a fire had taken hold. When the occupant opened the kitchen door they were caught in a backdraft and sadly died from their injuries. I will never forget the scene, seeing this poor person lay there burnt to a crisp. The house had practically been destroyed internally by the fire. I accompanied the body that was taken away to the mortuary. When I arrived the Mortuary Assistant and I tried to remove the body from the body bag, but the body had retained so much heat that it stuck to the inside of the bag, the smell of seared flesh filled my nostrils. I quickly understood that once I had seen something I could not un-see it. A year or so later, I attended a report of a burglary. When I arrived at the house, I realised that it was where the person had died in the fire. The new owners were modernising the house and had their tools stolen. When I walked into the house, I got a flashback to the night of the fire.

In the Chloe Fahey case, a post-mortem was to be conducted during the evening of the first day. As exhibits officer, I was expected to attend the post-mortem. I was in the incident room organising the exhibits when I heard a discussion about me attending the post-mortem. The scene was horrific enough without a lifelong memory of the autopsy. The Deputy SIO then came into my office and to his credit said that I did not have to attend if I did not want to. I chose not to in this case but the memory of the incident lives with me forever. A senior detective was quoted in the media after Chloe's death;

"It was quite simply the most appalling scene I have ever witnessed".

This was the type of work I undertook in my first year of MIT. They are incidents that will forever live with me.

2004.

[One Call Away - Chingy]

By August of 2004, Karin Mulligan had been promoted to Chief Inspector and became the first black female police officer in Britain to achieve this rank. The lack of progression for black female officers was more the story for me.

Michael Todd had replaced Sir David Wilmot, who had retired a couple of years earlier, as Greater Manchester's Chief Constable. It was evident to me that his style of leadership was very different to his predecessor's. I found him to be transactional, with GMP becoming more focused on statistics than service. I feared any progress that may have been made under the leadership of David Wilmot would be lost or at best stifled by the change at the top of the organisation. David Wilmot had accepted GMP was infected by institutional racism, that was at least a start.

Karin took Michael Todd to an employment tribunal. Like Martin Harding before her, she believed that pursuing recourse through the courts was her best option. Her complaint was that of race and sexual discrimination, the double discrimination that officers like Karin faced and the very issue that Karin had mentored so many female police officers on. Karin had been investigated by the Professional Standards Branch 'Y' being officially 'Advised' for her behaviour at the conclusion. At tribunal, Karin claimed the investigation into her conduct had been instigated in part because of her sex or colour or both. I understood that few officers were willing to provide a statement supporting Karin. Making a statement against the Chief Constable comes with its own dangers, I was aware of that, but the fear of reprisals or being ostracised within GMP did not prevent me from providing a statement for Karin's legal team. I was determined to do the right thing. The media reported on Karin's tribunal seeing the hearing as a blow to the force following on from The Secret Policemen that had exposed racism by secretly filming officers at Bruche training centre. Eventually, Karin's case was settled out of court, it was reported in the media that the settlement included GMP paying £2000 to a charity, this sounded exactly like Karin to me. Even in the face of controversy Karin's settlement agreement would benefit others.

A police spokesman is reported to have said:

> "GMP and Chief Inspector Mulligan are pleased to announce that an agreement has been reached over the issues which led to the institution by Chief Inspector Mulligan of employment tribunal claims. Chief Inspector Mulligan is a highly regarded GMP officer. GMP and Chief Inspector Mulligan are committed to a continuing and fruitful working relationship."

That may have been the case but were GMP committed to a continuing fruitful relationship with those who made a statement on Karin's behalf?

In April 2004, a Sikh man called Kalvinder Singh was attacked at a fast-food restaurant in Cheetham Hill, Manchester. Mr Singh died from his injuries over two weeks after the assault, he was a father of two. I was part of the enquiry team that investigated this murder. On this occasion, I worked in the Major Incident Room or MIR. The MIR is the engine room of any large or major enquiry investigated by the police, in fact, the computer system which the police use is called Home Office Large Major Enquiry System or Holmes for short.

In January 2005, the body of a girl was found in Harpurhey. Later identified as 15-year-old Amanda Hardwick, Amanda had been strangled. Again, I worked in the MIR during this investigation. Michael Hardy would later be convicted of murdering the schoolgirl. Both the Kalvinder Singh and Mandy Hardwick murder investigations were investigated by MIT Syndicate 1.

It was also on this syndicate that I worked with Detective Chief Inspector Rebekah Sutcliffe. Rebekah struck me as someone who wanted to be the centre of attention. I found her to be self-absorbed and full of self-importance, she was a bully. Whilst conducting the most serious of investigations, what was important to Rebekah, was to take me and two other male detectives to task over the wearing of ties. If this sounds trivial well it was. Female members of staff were not openly challenged in the same way over their dress. I found her approach to be over the top and unnecessary. I thought that the other male detectives were collateral damage and that the real target of this treatment was me. I chose to wait. The syndicate was aware of my continued involvement in BAPA, I believe that Rebekah was no exception.

By way of contrast here are some of the assessments that my supervisor made in November 2004:

> 'DC Bailey proves on a daily basis how well organised he is, in the Kiely case he managed his time so well that he completed more work than was expected of him.
>
> DC Bailey is a committed police officer and committed to the values of the service, maintaining the very highest standards in his work.
>
> DC Bailey is never late for work and has an envied sickness record.
>
> DC Bailey is enthusiastic and passionate about his work and committed to investigating crime. To this end, he has volunteered for interview courses and unsociable duties.

> I have worked very closely with DC Bailey for many months and seen he is regularly consulted by other officers on a multitude of issues through his involvement in the Black and Asian Police Officers Association covering diversity and equality issues and, in his dealings, keeps his focus on force priorities. As a team member, he is well-liked and respected by his peers. He works well with others and indeed sets an example to other members of the team.
>
> DC Bailey is very computer literate and highly skilled in the use of the HOLMES system as demonstrated in the Singh incident when his role as reader demanded these skills. DC Bailey is flexible to all aspects of his work be it procedure or duties. He will change his plans and workload priorities to suit all eventualities.'

I was not willing to be spoken to in the way Rebekah did. On one occasion she was telling me about wearing a tie when she was sat there wearing a turtleneck jumper. I pointed this out to her and left. To make my point, one day I attended work in cultural African dress. This was perfectly acceptable as cultural dress was allowed at work. During the briefing, it was clear to me that she was seething but understood that I was aware of the force policy and was merely exercising it. There was no tie attached to my smart attire. Rebekah's conduct was, in my view, done with the tacit or explicit blessing of her supervisor, I was being targeted.

In 2005, Augustine Maduemezia was found murdered in his flat in Miles Platting, Manchester. Mr Maduemezia had suffered severe head and facial injuries. His flat had been ransacked and items stolen from the address. Augustine Maduemezia was the father of Charles Maduemezia who had become a good friend of mine. Charles had been one of the founder members of BAPA and served on the association's executive committee when I was Chair. I worked on the investigation into his father's murder in the initial stages. One of the offenders had eaten or at least tried to eat a Plantain

– pronounced 'Plantin' in the Caribbean. Plantains are native to Africa, the West Indies and India, and are cooking bananas. They have a high starch content that makes them unsuitable to be eaten raw. They look like large bananas but have thicker skin.

In this investigation, someone had attempted to eat the Plantain raw but spat it out as it was unpalatable to them. I explained to some of my colleagues what a plantain was. It was a very clear indication to me of the type of person who would have mistaken a Plantain in this way. I said that the offender will be white to my colleagues. There was a chorus of 'How can you know that Paul, a bit racist that isn't it' – the simple answer being 'No black person would ever think that they could eat a Plantain like a banana.' There is value in having a diverse police service with staff who come from diverse backgrounds, cultures and experiences.

Two men, David Flynn and Anthony Crilly, would eventually be convicted of Augustine's Maduemezia murder. After the verdict, Charles is quoted as saying;

> "Our father was a hardworking, proud, selfless man with the utmost integrity. We, as a family, are proud to say we strive to maintain these values. As you can imagine, it has been a very traumatic and difficult year since our father's life was taken."

July 2005, the force chose to send Ivan Hewitt and I to Toronto, Canada. The International Black Police Association conference was to be held there, and the force instructed that a scoping study be conducted prior to sending a full party of delegates to the event later that year. I suppose I was chosen as I had previously attended the conference in Miami and had compiled a comprehensive report when I returned. The instruction for us to travel had come from command at headquarters – of course it did. Ivan and I collected our tickets, packed our bags and we were off, well not quite. At Manchester Airport we were told that the flight had been delayed. The plane required a specialist part that meant that the flight would not take off until the following day. Naturally, the change of flight day and time pushed back the day that we would return to the UK. We informed GMP and our families. A night in a hotel at Manchester Airport isn't that bad, especially when the mini bar is free. A fabulous meal and a good night's sleep later we were again ready to go.

Our seats were at the front of the plane. For some reason, a group of nurses took us for Air Marshalls. After September 11th, 2001, plainclothes police officers had been flying covertly on aircraft to prevent further terrorist attacks. Ivan and I weren't Air Marshalls, but it was the first time that people thought I was a cop.

'There is a fine line between genius and insanity. I have erased this line.' - Oscar Levant

We landed in Toronto and were straight to work. We visited several units and departments within Toronto Police. We spoke with all the people involved in the planning and coordination of the upcoming NBPA International Conference. The meetings seemed to be one after the next, Ivan and I had arrived on a different date so the Canadians were trying to accommodate us as best they could. I realised that our host's itinerary had run out when they showed us around the shooting range and arranged for a trip to Niagara Falls. I thanked our hosts but declined a visit to Niagara as I thought that it should be a romantic trip rather than a police day out.

There were a couple of days before our return flight, Ivan had family in Canada, he could visit. I remembered that Miss X, now Dr X, was working in Seattle, USA – We were in Toronto, Canada. Whatever the distance, she was only one call away. I made that call and the tickets were booked. Ivan thought that I was 'insane' or a 'genius' one or the other, nevertheless, I put a few belongings into a rather small rucksack, and I was off.

Over two thousand miles and three time zones later I was in

Seattle. Dr X and I had not seen each other in a long while so had a lot to catch up on. Seattle was a fab cosmopolitan city with a great vibe. On my last day there, Dr X tried to book a table in a fancy restaurant but its popularity at that time meant that you needed to book in advance. So, she told the restaurant that she had just gotten engaged which did the trick. When she told me about it, I said "What are we going to do if they ask to see the ring?" I cannot believe we did this, but we went out and bought a diamond ring that was too big but looked the part. The jeweller put some type of band on the ring so it didn't fall off. We had not got engaged, of course not, but it was our cover story. That night at the restaurant, as soon as we sat down the waitress said "Congratulations – let me see the ring," Dr X gave me a wry smile and proudly showed off her new rock, "Oh it's beautiful" the waitress said. It was a tasty and the most expensive meal of my life, not the food, the gemstone part.

My return flight to the UK was from Toronto not to mention my luggage, which was in a Toronto hotel room. I didn't tell Ivan about the restaurant-ring escapade as that would have confirmed the insanity versus genius debate. Anyway, one last night out on the town with Ivan and then it was time to return home.

When I arrived back at work, having gained all of the information I needed to complete my report, I discovered Detective Superintendent Martin Bottomley was not happy that I had travelled to Toronto at all. I had little time for the man, I found him to be sly and definitely someone I thought could not be trusted. He line-managed Rebekah and in my view was party to, if not behind her conduct towards me. I was unconcerned by his mood as I had been sent to Canada by the command of the force. If he had an issue, he could take it up with them if he wished. I knew he wouldn't do that, just like he couldn't touch me when I complied with the dress code by wearing African cultural dress but, I understood that he wouldn't stop trying.

I applied to move away from Syndicate 1 finally being seconded to Syndicate 3 located across the force in Leigh. This suited me just fine.

I Walk A Lonely Road

2006.

[Boulevard of Broken Dreams – Green Day]

On the 12th March 2006, two young men, Richard Austin, aged 19, and Carlton Alveranga, aged 20, were shot and killed at the Brass Handles Pub in Salford. Both men having sustained their fatal injuries managed to run from the pub collapsing on a grassed area outside. Two other men had been shot inside the pub, but they would survive their injuries.

The shootings immediately hit national television news and the print media. The incident had been described by one media outlet as a wild-west style shoot-out. Early reports revealed that the two dead men were 'would-be assassins.' This was the worst shooting incident that I could recall in Manchester both as a resident of the city and as a police officer. Manchester had been renamed Gunchester by many, shootings like this did little to argue that the city did not deserve this unwanted title.

GMP needed a team to deal with one of the worst shootings that the city had ever seen. MIT syndicate 3 were assigned to investigate. The competent and skilled running of the Major Incident Room would be key to the investigation. I worked in the MIR as I was skilled and trusted in this environment. I was integral to the investigation into the Brass Handles shootings. The syndicate was led by Detective Superintendent Andy Tattersall, he was a seasoned Senior Investigation Officer, and well-regarded in GMP and around MIT. Whilst working on the Brass Handles Investigation Janet Graham now called Janet Hudson arrived on the syndicate. In the years since our last encounter, Janet had been promoted to the position of Detective Inspector and for a while worked on the syndicate with Detective Inspector Diane Taylor. Many years had passed since my last personal encounter with Janet, described as a 'domestic incident,' now here she was again popping up like an unwanted weed that just will not go away.

The volume of enquiries by the Brass Handles investigation meant that I had to work long hours during the week and at the weekend. I did this willingly. I had also made a formal complaint about the conduct of some of my supervisors on the syndicate, who had treated me unfairly and who had discriminated against me. By 12th December, I wrote the following email to Steven Heywood who was in Headquarters CID Command.

> Mr Heywood,
>
> I have today (at 0945 hours) received a copy of my appraisal from 8th September 2006. I saw and signed the appraisal in September 2006, at this time there had been no comments made in the counter signatory section. I have now found that the appraisal has been completed by DI Hudson (Not dated when completed) and filed at Bradford Park. The comments made by DI Hudson include,
>
> 'Upon my arrival, DC Bailey did not seem settled this has however improved over the past 6 months and he has now integrated himself within the syndicate'

And

> 'DC Bailey must continue to seek feedback in order to develop and ensure his response to feedback is positive' – to what exactly?

This came as a surprise to both DS Warren and I. The second comment does not make sense, there is no evidence or examples for either. DS Warren believed that it was not fair that I had not seen these comments before now hence the conversation this morning.

Clearly, I dispute the above comments made by DI Hudson and now do not agree with the appraisal as a whole. DS Warren's assessment of me was sparkling throughout he states,

'DC Bailey is an excellent and competent officer who has the ability to move between different roles within the Major Incident Team department, which is a great asset for both the individual and the department as a whole.'

It must be said that I have no issue with DS Warren who I believe has acted with integrity throughout. The timing of this is spectacularly unfortunate.

For obvious reasons, I have not taken this issue to Det. Supt. Bottomley, however, I will ensure that DCI Giles is made aware of the position.

DC Paul Bailey

The reason I spoke of the unfortunate timing was that my complaint had been passed by GMP to West Yorkshire Police, who were supposed to be investigating the issues I raised. It was clear to me that Janet was trying to undermine me with comments that had no merit and were not supported by any examples or evidence. Janet did not have the support of the other supervisors on Syndicate 3 either. It was useful to see what Janet had written because she had broken her cover and shown her hand. DCI Giles wrote in response;

'...During our meeting, DC Bailey was assured by

Superintendent Tattersall, and myself that we were more than happy with his performance and had no issues with his work...'

Three people would eventually be convicted for their part in Brass Handles 'Wild West' shooting; all would be convicted of conspiracy to murder. Connie Howarth, who had acted as a spotter for the would-be-assassins inside the pub. Bobby Spiers, the Secretary for Paul Massey's security firm PMS was convicted for engineering the murder plot. He had given himself an alibi by attending a Manchester United football match at Old Trafford. And, Ian McLeod who had driven Richard Austin and Carlton Alveranga to the Brass Handles to carry out the attack.

I was called in to see ACC Vince Sweeney who had received the West Yorkshire Police report on the complaints that I had made. In short, my complaints had not been substantiated, no surprise there, the police cannot be trusted to investigate the police. GMP had learned nothing from the Stephen Lawrence Report as the first force tasked with investigating the Metropolitan Police's handling of Stephen's murder gave the Met investigation a full bill of health. Until there was a truly independent body capable of competent investigations into the police service, complainants and communities alike would continue to be disappointed by the outcomes.

ACC Sweeney went through the findings in the report. At the end of the meeting, he said that he had yet to read the second report. Second report – what second report? West Yorkshire Police had compiled a second report that had been given the title 'Addendum.' Vince couldn't tell me anything more about it. It was a revelation to me that West Yorkshire Police had compiled a second report at all. Was the writing of this report in their terms of reference, why had they done this, and who instigated this second report?

I had been targeted, the victim had become the offender. There were shades of 'The big black man came into my cell and beat me up' in what was happening now. Karin called me after my meeting with ACC Sweeney, I told her that Vince had mentioned a second WYP report. I was furious that this report even existed, Karin in her usual calm and reassuring voice said, "You don't think Vince said that by accident do you." It suddenly dawned on me, had ACC Sweeney given me the heads-up about what was coming around the corner?

2007.

In February, I returned from another trip abroad. Syndicate 3 had moved bases from Leigh to Bolton Police Station. I paraded at the Major Incident Room as normal only to find DCI Russ Jackson and another officer waiting for me.

In December 2005, Martin Rankin was murdered at his home in Radcliffe. Mr Rankin was brutally attacked and sustained multiple injuries that were believed to have been inflicted by an axe and a hammer. He was found collapsed at the address before being taken to a hospital in Bury. He was later transferred to Hope Hospital in Salford where he remained in a coma until his death on New Year's Eve. Russ was the Senior Investigating Officer during the investigation into Martin Rankin's murder. I ran the MIR without the aid of the HOLMES computer. Instead, I ran the MIR using a paper management system. This was done occasionally when staff with the requisite skills to run such a system were available. Three men, including Ashley Marshall who was the son of Martin Rankin's partner, were convicted in this case. Ashley was convicted of murder and sentenced to life imprisonment. This was not the only case where I had worked with Russ Jackson.

Russ was not at Bolton Police Station to steal my services for another major incident, no, he was there to serve me with regulation papers. This was the heads-up that Vince Sweeney had given to me. I was going to be investigated for a whole host of things including attending work in a French Connection UK t-shirt, attending work in cultural dress and bullying DCI Rebekah Sutcliffe. It did not end there, I was also being moved out of MIT on 'restricted duties' to Moss Side. That was the last straw, I refused to be moved to Moss Side as this was intended to inconvenience me. What was even more sinister was that GMP was aware of the issues that I had had in neighbouring Old Trafford, now they were going to kick my teeth in by sending me somewhere that could have an even more detrimental effect on my family's well-being. This was going to be my punishment for making a complaint, I thought about the great fanfare that existed after David Wilmot had admitted that racism existed in GMP now I had a front-row seat to see that racism in action.

Realising that I was never going to Moss Side, Russ transferred me to Leigh CID, away from the inner city, GMP could have done that all along. None of the people who I had complained about were placed on restricted duties or moved away from MIT, but then they were all white. I had to remind myself about the Lawrence definition of institutional racism;

> Discrimination or unequal treatment on the basis of membership of a particular ethnic group (typically one that is a minority or marginalised), arising from systems, structures, or expectations that have become established within an institution or organisation.

I promised Russ that I'd be back in MIT one day – I like to keep my promises.

The following day as I walked into Leigh CID office for the first time, I thought about my school days when I had been banned from sports and prevented from representing the school. I recalled how that didn't harm me, it made me stronger and a bit of a hero to many in the school. This couldn't happen twice, could it?

The Detective Inspector at Leigh was called Steve Crimmins, an old-school detective who had forgotten more than most detectives would ever know. I understood that he was a consultant for the 'Life on Mars' television series but this was never confirmed to me by him. Steve struck me as a decent and ethical man. He sat me down in his office and said that he was thrilled to get such an experienced detective like me. Talk over, time to get to work.

I was asked to investigate and oversee the investigation into a large-scale disorder that had occurred in the borough. This investigation had been allocated to another detective who had become overwhelmed with the volume of work, the investigation was codenamed Operation Lever. In addition, I was allocated the usual workload that a divisional detective would carry. The CID office moved from Leigh to Wigan where it was known as Wigan CID. During my 2007 appraisals, my supervisors wrote;

> 'Whilst DC Bailey has been seconded from MIT, he has shown that he is a very experienced and competent detective, he has quickly settled into the role and become a popular member of the team. He has taken the lead in Operation Lever, directing the investigation and utilising his experience for the benefit of less experienced officers.'

And

> 'DC Bailey has settled down very quickly in the divisional CID office. He is reliable, confident and competent. He has become a valuable member of the crime operations.'

S. Crimmins.

By the end of 2007, my supervisors wrote;

> 'Since beginning his attachment to Wigan CID, DC Bailey has proved to be an invaluable asset to the reactive CID, he has taken the lead in several investigations including

Operation Lever, and in doing so imparted his experience to less experienced detectives and uniform colleagues alike. DC Bailey is currently undertaking a training programme with Detectives in the reactive CID to train them in the use of the Major Incident Paper Management system.'

And

'Since arriving in Wigan CID, DC Bailey has consistently produced work of a very high standard. His abilities as a detective are excellent and he has become an invaluable member of the CID team. He is a very professional detective and an excellent role model for junior officers.'

S Crimmins

In January 2008, Joan Holland, a pensioner who suffered from Alzheimer's, was found dead at her home in Wigan. Joan was incontinent and unable to take care of herself. James Holland, her husband of nearly fifty years, was her carer taking care of Joan at their home. When Joan's body was discovered she had suffered several injuries and there was evidence to suggest that the address had been cleaned before the emergency services arrival. James was arrested and I interviewed him with a colleague from Wigan CID. It was a difficult interview as James was a pensioner himself and frail, despite him hurling an object into the bin that was across the interview room. I changed the way that I asked questions of James using a 'Management of Conversation' style, James could recall the detail of his movements on the day of his wife's death but could not recall much detail about how she died. He would later plead guilty to manslaughter as The Crown accepted that he did not intend to kill or cause his wife serious harm.

By February, I was still being investigated by the Professional Standards Branch, the length of time that the investigation was taking suggested to me that it was either not going the way that they liked or they were trying to do a number on me.

On the 19th, John Rao, a man with a history of mental illness, stabbed his sister, Geeta Rao, aged 43 and his mother Leela Rao, aged 73 at Geeta's house in Wigan. Geeta died instantly, Leela survived initially but was paralysed in the attack. She died months later from pneumonia that was brought on as a result of the stabbing. Geeta's children were in the house at the time of the murders. Although now a Divisional Detective with this type of murder normally being investigated by MIT, I led the interview of John Rao. After a period where Mr Rao made no admissions, under my questioning, he admitted that he had planned to kill his family whilst travelling on a train from London to Wigan. He bought a knife before going to Geeta's house where he carried out the attacks. Part of my interview with John was quoted in the media, he said to me; "My intention was to murder them all because they had been ripping me off, lying to me and not being fair to me."

The rules governing employment tribunals are very strict. Claimants have three months to lodge a claim after the 'Discriminatory Act.' Due to the length of time that GMP was taking to investigate me, I had lodged more than one claim against the Chief Constable of GMP, who was Michael Todd at that time. I was also aware of a 2005 report, written by Deputy Assistant Commissioner – Professor John Grieve CBE QPM, about racial discrimination in Professional Standards following Karin's employment tribunal. Karin had given me her copy of the report for my use, without any restriction. In the opening summary Professor Grieve wrote;

> 'This review holds it as fundamental that serious allegations by one officer against another should be investigated and that all officers should cooperate. This review argues that the Greater Manchester Police experiences in the case of Chief Inspector Mulligan are of an inquiry spiralling into ever wider

and complex, ambiguous directions. This is regrettable, avoidable, and understandable.'

This was the first paragraph of the report at 1.1. Surely the Chief Constable's attention span lasted beyond six lines. The report continued;

'I find that the statutory subjective test of bias, judged on a case by case basis, was experienced by Chief Inspector Mulligan as "unnecessary and debilitating pressures on the individual(s) concerned" (Lancet (2002) page 4). I find this too, understandable but regrettable. The statutory test and the experience of numerous concerns raised by Chief Inspector Mulligan and not acted upon leads to a finding of incompetence, racism and sexism.'

The Chief Constable of GMP was given one of the three copies of the report. The report gave a series of recommendations intended to prevent Karin's experiences from happening to another black officer. It was not intended to be a playbook of what to do to the next black guy through the door, in this case, me. I planned to use the report in my claim against the Chief Constable. The report had been commissioned during Michael Todd's tenure, and he possessed it.

On March 12th, I was on holiday in Hong Kong when I found out that Michael Todd had died. He had been reported missing by Greater Manchester Police; his body was found in the Bwlch Glas area of Snowdon which is the highest mountain in Wales.

I had continued to be active within BAPA and had turned my attention to the issue of the police investigating the police. By 2004, The Independent Police Complaints Commission, responsible for overseeing the system for handling complaints made about police forces, had been introduced. However, their strict interpretation of a particular section of legislation meant that they would not accept any investigation made by a police officer regarding a police officer under the employment of the same police force or constabulary. This was an obvious issue that needed to be addressed. So, I addressed it, this email from Karin to ACC Terry Sweeney of April 2008 sums up what I did;

> 'Sir, You may be aware that since their inauguration the IPCC have applied a strict interpretation of Sec 22 of the Police Reform Act 2002, and refused to accept complaints made by police officers against other police officers within the same force.
>
> This stance caused particular difficulty for Minority Ethnic Staff in Forces that were unwilling and/or unable to investigate complaints of racial discrimination against colleagues appropriately. Complainants were then further disadvantaged by being denied the opportunity of an independent investigation or intervention. I am now pleased to report that the IPCC has now changed their position, a change that has been brought about solely by the work of DC 07826 Paul Bailey. Paul has worked tirelessly with the IPCC, supporting and advising locally and nationally with Nick Hardwick. I understand that the IPCC now acknowledge that their stance was institutionally racist. I have taken the liberty of attaching the IPCC's briefing note that will be of interest to you. The Force will need to review its policy and guidance in this area and consider any necessary amendments. I kindly ask you to consider meeting with Paul, not only to formally recognise the hard work and effort he has put into bringing about this change but, with a view to GMP now continuing his campaign, it is viewed that a legislative change to Sec 22 will be required. The 'Gentleman's Agreement' currently in place is not sufficient for any professional organisation.'

GMP did not contact me after Karin had told them what I had

done. GMP continued to use Sec 22 of the Police Reform Act to sift out complaints that did not suit them.

I remained on restricted duties – the irony of this restriction being that the longer that they took in their investigation the more that I became a Rockstar at Wigan CID. After a limited and begrudging disclosure from PSB, I was formally interviewed by them. The interview related to complaints, that came from GMP police officers, no section 22 of the Police Reform Act in force here. The interview was a car crash, for them.

Firstly, I refused to be interviewed unless I obtained a copy of the recording. If they refused, I had my recorder and would make my personal copy. After all, it was my interview. Secondly, I chose to remain silent until they had disclosed their case. I just sat quietly writing down their topic areas. The wheels really fell off when they disclosed that Janet Hudson (Graham) was one of their witnesses. The amended appraisal by her without my knowledge of MIT now made perfect sense. It got worse, her statement was simply not true in parts, that I could prove. Having highlighted the parts of her statement which were not true what did PSB do with Janet, nothing. What did Professor Grieve write?

> 'The statutory test and the experience of numerous concerns raised by Chief Inspector Mulligan and not acted upon leads to a finding of incompetence, racism and sexism.'

It did not matter to me what GMP did from this stage, I was going to kick their arse. I was represented by DC Aidan Kielty, who was the Police Federation Misconduct Lead. He was, unfortunately, unavailable for the interview. He did keep the recordings of my interview, he later told me that whenever he felt low, he played the interview to cheer him up.

The misconduct hearing was listed to take place at headquarters. The Panel consisted of ACC Justine Curran, and Superintendents

Alan Greene and Dave Hull. I was represented by a Solicitor and a Barrister. The PSB was represented by a Solicitor and Barrister and bizarrely the panel had their own legal representation. The stakes were very high. GMP produced a series of witnesses whose evidence hardly helped the PSB case. I was on trial at a misconduct hearing for not saying good morning to a person, wearing a French Connection UK t-shirt and coming to work in cultural dress – the wearing of cultural dress which was allowed under the force's own clothing policy. What did Professor Grieve write?

> 'This review argues that the Greater Manchester Police experiences in the case of Chief Inspector Mulligan are of an inquiry spiralling into ever wider and complex, ambiguous directions.'

The PSB's star witness was Rebekah Sutcliffe who gave evidence of how I bullied her. I have never heard of a Constable bullying a Chief Inspector. She described how I had come to work in African cultural dress that she used as evidence of her being bullied. I distinctly got the impression from Justine Curran's reactions to the PSB witnesses that she was team PSB. Having said that I thought that the PSB case was going nowhere when during one of the PSB witness' testimonies Superintendent David Hull threw his pen on the table, pushed his chair back crossing his legs and stopped taking any further notes. Detective Superintendent Andy Tattersall chose to give evidence on my behalf, his evidence was a glowing appraisal of me. The result was that none of the things that were alleged were worthy of a misconduct sanction. If the allegations were not worthy of a sanction then why had the case been brought at all? The answer was clear and Professor Grieve had articulated it beautifully. The investigation and trial had a cost to the taxpayer, easily, tens of thousands of pounds and possibly hundreds of thousands. GMP had had their go, now it was my turn.

My misconduct trial was reported in the press both locally and nationally. One paper even had a black male model posing in an

African gown, the model also wore a hat. The image of this model was nothing like the cultural dress that I wore. My outfit was much more tasteful and I didn't have a hat. Justine Curran became Chief Constable of Humberside Police. She retired in 2017 after being asked to reconsider her position when further "significant failings" were found in her force following an Inspection by Her Majesty's Inspectorate of Constabulary.

Rebekah Sutcliffe was promoted to the rank of Assistant Chief Constable in GMP. In 2016, she was disciplined, found guilty of gross misconduct and given a final written warning for behaving cruelly and hurtfully towards a junior colleague. Ms Sutcliffe revealed her breast during a rant with the junior officer, the incident was named 'Boobgate' on social media. She would later quit the force to take up employment elsewhere. The PSB's star witness who complained that I had bullied her had been convicted of bullying!

It was during my time at Wigan CID that I became friendly with a woman called Sue Young. Sue was the typing pool supervisor and a live wire. She was jokey, entertaining and casually flirted with me whenever our paths crossed. It was just mild-hearted fun, there was never anything behind it. I always get my typing back quickly, especially transcripts of recorded interviews that I had conducted. These transcripts sometimes took a little longer to be returned to the interviewing officer due to their length; this was an unintended but welcome consequence of our friendship. I always recall her saying, "Avert your eyes ladies," whenever I walked into the room.

On 6th October 2008, the coroner ruled that former Chief Constable Michael Todd had died from exposure 'When his mind was affected by alcohol, a sleeping drug and "confusion" due to his personal circumstances.'

On the 28th I received the following letter from Chief

Superintendent Lee Bruckshaw, the Divisional Commander for Wigan;

'Dear Paul,

> Divisional Commander's Good Work Minute - I am pleased to inform you that you have been awarded a Divisional Commander's Good Work Minute for your excellent work in relation to Operation Lever, which involved numerous actions, statements, CCTV and exhibits; your tenacity and diligence provided a high standard of service for the victims involved.
>
> Lee Bruckshaw Chief Superintendent'

It Will Never Be the Same Again

2009.

[Something Inside So Strong – Labi Siffre]

By 2009, Peter Fahy had been installed as the new Chief Constable of Greater Manchester Police. He was the fourth Chief Constable of my service and would turn out to be the Chief Constable that I had the most personal contact. He was now the respondent in my claims for discrimination and victimisation. I had lodged a total of three employment tribunal claims that were being dealt with by David Franey of Russell Jones and Walker Solicitors in Manchester.

I had been denied a return to MIT due to GMP stating they had a duty of care to staff involved in my case who still worked in that department. This sounded like a sanction to me.

Karin called me one day in January 2009 for one of our chats. We spoke to each other regularly on the phone so there was nothing out of the ordinary in her calling me. We spoke about different things for some time then Karin told me that she had been diagnosed with cancer. It was amazing how this one word changed my perspective of the world in an instant. Karin described that she had felt unwell after she ate anything, this progressed quickly to her being physically sick – throwing up after eating. She had consulted with a doctor and had been diagnosed with stomach cancer. I was amazed that Karin spoke about other things during the call. For me, the cancer diagnosis would have been all-consuming, I would not have been able to speak or think of anything else. For Karin, it was just one of many things happening in the world. She was a much better person than I ever was. Even in the face of this terrible diagnosis, there was no self-pity with Karin, there was no 'Why me' or any defeatism with her at all. I continued to speak to Karin over the next days, maybe weeks, it is all such a blur now. It turned out that Karin's cancer was terminal, with her being given only a short time to live, maybe twelve to twenty-four months. I could only imagine what Karin, her husband Kevin, her two children and the rest of her family were going through. I was completely floored by what was happening to my friend and mentor. Despite her prognosis, Karin had planned to complete the Race For Life event that was scheduled for May.

One day, I was in a supermarket aisle when Karin called. She opened the conversation with "Paul, how are you doing?" She was aware that I was in the midst of my employment tribunal – three employment tribunals and wanted to know if I was coping with the pressure. Karin, a woman with terminal cancer and a limited time to live asked me if I was OK. This brought tears to my eyes. I told her my tribunals were completely insignificant and asked her how she was doing. She said, "I just wanted to talk to you about something else." She was weary from talking about her cancer and how she was doing. At the very time that she should be the centre of attention, she wanted to talk about anything other than her. Karin said that she had no regrets in her life and that as far as GMP was concerned, there was only one thing outstanding, my tribunals. I promised her that I would finish it.

That was the last time that I ever spoke to Karin. Shortly afterwards, I learned that she had been admitted to Bury Hospice. I sent her a bunch of flowers via Interflora with my best wishes.

On Friday 27th March 2009, I was working an afternoon shift at Wigan CID when my mobile rang. I answered the call to hear Kevin Mulligan's voice, he was upset – I knew before he said anything more. Karin had died. Kevin was heartbroken but managed to get the words out, "Karin asked if you would carry her coffin." I gave some bumbling reply, but the answer was "I would be honoured to." Karin had been the first black woman to reach the rank of Chief Inspector in the country and at one time held the rank of temporary Superintendent. But the rank that she achieved in the police did nothing to reflect her ability, her bravery, her determination, her intellect and her compassion. President Barack Obama once said;

> "If ten years, twenty years down the road, there are a thousand or ten thousand young people who are now moving into positions of authority and power and in some ways have been shaped by our example in a positive way. That's a legacy that may exceed anything that we did." I hope that Karin's legacy is described in these terms. Karin's death was reported in the media. Kevin Mulligan is quoted;

> "Karin was firstly an amazing mother who loved her family enormously. She was also an exemplary police officer who challenged injustice and prejudice wherever she found it, thereby, earning the respect and admiration of many.
>
> She was compassionate and acted with great integrity. Myself, our children, family and friends loved her and will never forget her."

On the day of Karin's funeral, I wore the uniform of one of my colleagues at Wigan CID. My uniform had disappeared years earlier and GMP no longer had police tunics in stock. A special order would have taken too long to arrive and was impractical as I would only be using the tunic once – hopefully. Karin's family and friends filled the church car park in anticipation of the funeral cortege. Uniform and plain clothes officers were also at the church as Karin was to receive an honour guard. As the funeral cortege neared the six pallbearers, two of whom were Karin's brothers, lined up in preparation to receive the coffin. I could hear people quietly sobbing as the hearse came to a stop. The pallbearers lifted the coffin smoothly and slowly carried it into the church. The honour guard lined the entrance to the foyer as we slowly carried Karin past them and into the nave. I saw Leroy Logan in the church as I entered, he nodded in a sign of respect to his fallen colleague. He would later nod again towards me as a greeting. Chief Constable Peter Fahy was also at the funeral. If he did not know that Karin and I were friends or if he had any scepticism about how close we were then seeing me carrying her coffin, with her brothers answered everything. The service was a celebration of Karin's life, she had achieved so much in her forty-five years. Before long, it was over and Karin would make her final journey to the crematorium. She was gone but her memory will live inside us all forever.

I had tutored numerous uniform colleagues in my time, and I had now turned my attention to CID Trainees. Kath Andrews was a CID Trainee that I tutored at Wigan CID. Kath was one of those equestrian types who was as happy mucking out as she was arresting suspects of serious crimes. She had a common-sense approach to policing, that was reminiscent of Chris Barnes and was one of those people who only had to be shown something once. I cannot tell you how frustrating it was to see a trainee continually committing the same errors and not learning from their experiences. Kath was not one of those people. On one occasion, Kath and I entered the custody office to deal with a suspect. Upon seeing Kath, the Custody Sergeant stood to attention and saluted her. He held the salute for a moment and then continued with his work. I was gobsmacked, what had I just witnessed and what was going on? Kath was almost apologetic for the Sergeant's display. As soon as we were out of the custody office, I needed to be brought up to speed. As it turned out Kath was a direct descendent of General Daniel Edgar Sickles, an American civil war veteran who lost his leg at the Battle of Gettysburg in 1863. He was awarded the Medal of Honour for his actions. General Sickles was known for more than just being a civil war veteran. He gunned down his wife's lover, Philip Barton Key II, the son of Francis Scott Key who wrote the lyrics to the American national anthem. General Sickles' amputated leg is still on display at the National Museum of Health and Medicine at Walter Reed Army Medical Centre in Washington. Although Kath told me about her esteemed ancestor, she did not know which side he fought for – The abolitionist Union Army of the North or the slave-holding Confederate Army of the South. She seemed quite relieved when she realised that he was a Union soldier.

Tommy Fung was also a CID Trainee at Wigan. He was an oriental officer of Hong Kong heritage. He was a small compact man who was powerful both physically and mentally. He was bilingual that was not appreciated or utilised and had found himself constantly under the spotlight that so many minority ethnic officers suffered. He was not my trainee, but I found myself trying to mentor and assist Tommy whenever I got the opportunity. I recall one time when we were in a hospital mortuary checking the body of a man who had died earlier that day. I wanted to make sure that there were no obvious signs of trauma to the man who had died after a fall. He was a big man, Tommy had trouble rolling him onto his side so I could get a better look at his back and take photographs where appropriate. Tommy exclaimed "Why am I not holding the camera," The Mortuary Assistant feeling sorry for Tommy helped him turn the man onto his side. My reply "When you're a substantive Detective with a trainee then you can hold the camera." I liked Tommy and thought that his eventual departure from the trainee scheme was unfortunate.

On 23rd July 2009, I attended mediation that had been arranged between me and GMP. The mediation was concerning the three employment tribunal claims. The mediator was none other than Professor John Grieve himself. I had met John Grieve a few times prior to the meeting so I had no qualms about him being the mediator. But, it also occurred to me that the new Chief Constable was probably aware of the content of John Grieve's report, hence John being asked to mediate. GMP was represented by Assistant Chief Constable Garry Shewan, Solicitor Laura Shuttleworth was one of two solicitors assisting Garry. A 'Compromise Agreement' was reached, and the details of which were bound by a non-disclosure agreement. I will say that signing an NDA was a bad move as the contents of that agreement would have served me well in the future. There is, however, one part of the agreement that can be mentioned. ACC Shewan agreed, on behalf of the Chief Constable, to second me to the Regional Crime Unit.

It was over, I felt vindicated. I had taken on the might of GMP, again, and had stayed firm to the end. Karin would have been proud of me. The Chief's capitulation was like eating a tasty dish – I gorged on my success. After bringing all three claims to an end I contacted Kevin Mulligan and told him about my promise to Karin, I wanted him to know that I had kept that promise. The next step was the Reginal Crime Unit. My final assessments at Wigan CID read;

> 'DC Bailey is an excellent Detective and is an excellent team member who is passing on his expertise to his trainee who no doubt will turn into a good Detective as well.'

And

> 'DC Bailey has now left the 'L' Division. During his time here, he has been an asset to the CID and the division as a whole. His professionalism is exemplary and his willingness to share his skills and develop others will leave a lasting legacy on the division. I wish Paul the best in his new role.
>
> Detective Inspector Clare Devlin.'

Historically, black people do less well in any sport, exercise, or examination where the assessments are subjective. Black athletes excel in sports where there is a clear winner, and the winner can be seen by everyone. So, if we take athletics, track and field as an example, the winner in an event can be seen by the judges and spectators alike. The person who crosses the line first, jumps the highest, or the furthest or who throws the furthest is not in doubt. As soon as you add a subjective element to the assessment, then bias rears its ugly head. In the 1988 Korean Summer Olympics, Roy Jones Jr, lost a fight 3-2 on the judge's decision to South Korean Boxer Park Si-Hun despite Jones landing 86 punches to Parks 32. Put another way, do you think that Jesse Owens would have won 4 gold medals in the 1936 Berlin Summer Olympics if the decision of who won was up to the judges? I should have realised that when I entered into the compromise agreement with the Chief Constable of GMP.

I was told that I needed to pass a surveillance course and an advanced driving course before I could be seconded to the RCU. Both courses are subjective and therefore left me at the mercy of the Police Service. I had tutored many people in my time and was always aware that I could write up or write down my assessment of them however I pleased. I would never do that, but some would. On 4th September 2009, the Chief Constable's solicitor wrote to my solicitor outlining these additional requirements. These requirements had not been terms of the compromise agreement, my solicitor told the Chief Constable this in no uncertain terms. There is a reason why people from certain backgrounds do not trust the police, here is an example why. GMP tried to unilaterally change the terms of the agreement which left me exposed to the whim of anyone with a grudge, an axe to grind, or who wanted to make a name for themselves. GMP had learned nothing and required a new lesson – I was going to teach them.

On October 1st I was seconded to the Regional Intelligence Unit (RIU), not the Regional Crime Unit (RCU) as per the agreement that the Chief Constable had agreed to. The North West Regional Organised Crime Unit (NWROCU) was made up of three distinctly separate parts. The Intelligence and Crime units are two, the third being the Financial Investigation Unit (FIU). The work conducted by these units is carried out by individual forces but the NWROCU crossed force borders. That is it, it doesn't need to be any more dressed up than that. When I arrived at the RIU, the reception was initially frosty. It was apparent that people in the RIU knew of my route into the department and disapproved. I didn't give a shit about what they thought, they were there to do a job and so was I. I wasn't there to make friends – as long as they stayed out of my lane then we would get along just fine. I quickly realised that I was the only Detective Constable in the RIU. The other constables were all essentially Police Constables wearing plain clothes; who were they to judge me? I had worked in plain clothes for several years in force so was comfortable with the environment. I was also relieved to get away from GMP – for a while at least.

The whole point of moving to the region was to give me distance from GMP, from the three-year ordeal that I had endured and from the people. The RCU had more Detectives than the RIU but it also had a number of police constables. Detective Constable Darren Bailey was one of the Detectives in the RCU. Darren and I had worked together in Stretford CID years earlier and got to know each other well. He was a useful ally and would become very useful to me as time moved on.

At the beginning of October, I went on holiday to the Caribbean returning in the second week. During my time abroad, I felt short of breath which was unusual for me. I was used to being in peak fitness but now that I had given up competitive basketball and gained a few pounds I was not as nimble as I once was. I visited the doctor, who after his assessment, instructed me to go to the hospital – like immediately. Following the doctor's instructions, I collected a pump spray of 'Nitrolingual' from the pharmacist and called my wife, even though we had separated, her medical knowledge would be useful. She arrived at the surgery, took one look at the spray in my hand and said, "he thinks you are having a heart attack." "What? If he thinks

I'm having a heart attack, why am I not in the back of a fucking ambulance?" She drove me to the hospital where I found that I was not having a heart attack but was suffering from hypertension. I got a prescription, went home and was back in work the following morning.

With Karin's death still foremost in my mind, I decided that I needed to be at full fitness once again. I took to the streets running a few times per week. My weight and blood pressure dropped and my speed and stamina returned. Lucky to be alive, maybe – fighting back - definitely.

The Rot Starts

2010.

[Get Back Up – T.I]

I continued to work in the RIU and became familiar with how the unit worked. Forces submitted proposals for an investigation that were scored by the RIU. The Development Team, which was a team of officers within the RIU, carried out an initial scoping exercise reporting on the strengths of the proposed investigation and if full surveillance was required. The reason why I use the term surveillance, rather than investigation, was from my observations that was primarily what the RCU did. It was not the pure investigation of MIT or CID; it was more a question of committing huge resources to surveillance operations that could take months or years hoping that the targets were eventually caught doing something. The RCU at that time did not use HOLMES which was a nationwide system. Even if they had, for a while, I was the only detective who could operate HOLMES.

I went on a surveillance course; it was clear to me that the course instructor was intent on giving me a hard time. This came crumbling down when one of the female trainers said that she wanted to see me in animal print underwear. If the roles were reversed, I would have been ejected immediately. I waited for the last day of the course and when I heard the words "Sorry you have been unsuccessful" I got up, left and filed my course report including the sexual harassment. True to form the course instructor reversed his decision about another minority ethnic officer who had also been unsuccessful. He said on review he thought that the officer should have been given a pass. It served only to prove that subjective courses in the police are open to abuse, cronyism and corruption. All this was academic as it was not a requirement of my Compromise Agreement, I knew that and GMP knew I knew that. ACC Garry Shewan had committed this very point to an email to ACO Julia Rogers; "Paul knows this very well indeed." I continued to work in the RIU and on the Development Team that started to finalise investigations without the need for the RCU. I also wrote investigative plans for operations that did not need the time and expense that came with full surveillance. I was back in shape running several times a week and taking advantage of my time away from the horror that was GMP.

In April, Brian Dobson died at the age of sixty-nine. Brian had been well known around the basketball world. He had supported me and so many other players managing to get the best out of us. His love for the game was unquestionable. I was sad to hear of his passing. Jeff Jones, the head coach of Manchester Magic, is quoted;

> "He has done fantastic work, voluntarily, for basketball in Manchester for many years. The time, effort and dedication he has put into running our club and for the sport in the city down the years have been phenomenal."

I had played for Jeff Jones and knew him well, I wholeheartedly agreed with his eulogy to our friend Brian.

In August 2010, I was informed that DCI Janet Hudson was joining the RIU and would be my line manager – it felt like a calculated decision. This was menacing and ominous for me. It was clear that making a false statement in my misconduct investigation had not harmed her any. I wrote to ACC Garry Shewan who was the Chief Constables representative at the mediation and who had agreed on the terms of the compromise agreement on the Chief Constable's behalf. I wrote;

'…You will appreciate my frustration and annoyance when I learnt this week that DCI Janet Hudson was joining my department as my line supervisor. Janet and I have a potted history, most of it acrimonious. She has previously made a statement against me, parts of which were false, she ultimately was not called as a witness to any proceedings. This development undermines everything that was agreed last year.

May I also take this opportunity to raise a second issue with you…I have not been awarded commendations that I deserve in spite of my emails over a lengthy period.

I believe this to be another indication of the ill- treatment that I have suffered for so long.'

On the 30th September 2010, I had a meeting with ACC Garry Shewan and Helen Phillips who was the second solicitor accompanying Garry at the mediation. During the meeting, Garry denied that my move to the NWROCU had anything to do with keeping space between me and those who formed part of the failed misconduct case against me. He said that if I had requested a return to MIT during the mediation, he would have considered this. This was not true, fortunately, I was represented by a Solicitor during the mediation process who had kept notes of the mediation. In addition, David Franey had become Judge Franey of Manchester's Employment Tribunal Court. I contacted Judge Franey and obtained the notes for the meeting. I had also discovered that I had been nominated for a Queen's award and that the misconduct investigation had led to my removal from the Queen's Honours list. The following email, which I sent to Chief Constable Peter Fahy in November, best sums up the position;

'…You and I are both aware that this investigation led to my removal from the Queen's Honours List; whether this was the intention of the investigation is yet to be seen. Since then,

DCI Hudson has been moved to my department within the RIU as my Line Manager. DCI Hudson made a prosecution statement during the (sic) my misconduct investigation parts of which were false...

I raised this with ACC Shewan meeting with him and Helen Phillips on 30th September 2010. During the meeting, ACC Shewan's position was clear; that my move to the Regional was at my request, that it had nothing to do with keeping distance between me and those who formed part of the prosecution against me and that if I had requested a return to MIT during the mediation, he would have considered this. I was so appalled by this position that I requested a copy of Helen Philips' notes.

David Franey acted for me throughout the tribunal and mediation processes. For your information, he has been promoted to Judge since the time of the mediation.

Judge Franey has provided me with a copy of his notes made during the mediation.

The key point is that it was ACC Shewan who said that I could not be posted back to MIT now (because others had been harmed by this episode) but that it might be possible in the future. It was after this exchange that I said that I wanted to go to the RCS. I don't think that it is right to say that if I had requested an MIT posting it would have been considered – ACC Shewan ruled that out by what he said.

At best ACC Shewan has a poor memory. I believe that this is another example of the continued victimisation that I am the victim of.'

I am not naïve enough to believe that ACC Garry Shewan was

not acting with the authority of the Chief Constable. Not only had GMP broken the 'Compromise Agreement' – I had not been seconded to the Regional Crime Unit – and unilaterally tried to change the terms of agreement but were now trying to rewrite history.

The only person I had trusted in matters like these in GMP was Karin, she was gone, there was no one else to turn to so I needed to go it alone. Ultimately Janet stayed in the RIU and so did I, I wasn't going to be run out of there with my tail between my legs.

2011.

[Written In The Stars – Tinie Tempah]

There were two main events as far as 2011 and the RIU was concerned. The first was when Janet Hudson approached me in the office. What does Cruella want now? I thought to myself. Janet told me that Diane Taylor, who we had worked alongside in MIT on Syndicate 3 and who was Janet's mate, had been involved in the production of a new police television series called Scott and Bailey. "Bailey?" I inquired. Janet, which happened to be the first name of the other lead character, told me to watch it as it would be worth my while. Well, I couldn't wait to watch this programme when it aired. Food literally fell out of my open mouth watching that first series. Granted, DC Bailey was now a white woman but the similarities between screen Bailey and I were not lost on me. Other characters were loosely based on real-life detectives.

The second thing that happened was that Chief Superintendent Paul Richardson, who was the head of TITAN, the new name for the North West Regional Organised Crime Unit, changed the tenure of secondments to TITAN. Members of the RCU and the RIU secondments were now five years instead of two. Ok, I thought to myself my tenure is five years, more time away from the wolves in

GMP.

Ding, Ding Round Four

2012.

[Fighter – Christina Aguilera]

In 2012, BAPA had become a pastiche of its former self. The association had no standing in GMP amongst the black staff that it was supposed to represent, with command or with the rank and file. BAPA almost had no media footprint or significant following in the community. The Executive Committee called an extraordinary meeting where they turned to me to lead the association, once again, and to rebuild what I had once built from scratch. I was the first Chair of BAPA, I would lead it again. One of the first things I did as Chair was to arrange a meeting with Chief Constable Peter Fahy, I needed him to know that there had been a change in leadership – I wanted to look him in the eye when he found out. I also wanted the BAPA membership to have access to the support and advice that BAPA was once renowned for. Finally, the association's profile needed to be raised both inside and outside of GMP. BAPA needed to be an authentic voice within GMP and not a nodding dog to command.

I got to work by filling the executive with people who were going to work and who were not afraid to speak their minds. A contact of mine built a BAPA website, I then restarted the quarterly newsletters that had fallen by the wayside. I knew that the re-energising of BAPA would attract dissenters and people who would seek to destroy those inside it. BAPA wouldn't suffer the same fate as Black Wall Street, not under my tenure.

I Did That

In March 2012, Janet Hudson told me about a large money laundering investigation that TITAN had taken on. The investigation was to be run on GMP computer systems at Nexus House. I was to be sent on this investigation as I was the only officer who could handle the enormous volumes of documents that needed to be read and disclosed. The investigation was codenamed Operation Holly and was scheduled to run until September 2013. I joined OP Holly which turned out to be an investigation into various security companies in Greater Manchester including Paul Massey's security company PMS. This was the company that Bobby Spiers was Secretary of at the time of the Brass Handles murders. From the outset, I understood the enormity and importance of OP Holly, since I was integral to the Brass Handles investigation, I knew many of the players, and understood their history and association with each other.

After twenty-two years of service as a police officer in GMP I had reached the point of my career where I would be commended. The Long Service and Good Conduct Medal is a Queen's award for service to the crown. It wasn't the 'long service' part that interested me, it was the 'good conduct' part as that would signify I was of good standing in the GMP. I had earned it and I was going to make them hand the medal to me, however much it pained them. I accepted the invitation to the ceremony and then was asked to write my own citation. I refused to do this, as any citation about me written by me would be meaningless. I didn't even know that writing your own citation was a thing – well it was in GMP.

On the day of the ceremony Clare and I attended the Sir David Wilmot building at Sedgley Park. Chief Constable Peter Fahy was there to present the awards. I sat waiting to hear my citation. The citations for others were long, drawn out and thoroughly boring affairs, clearly, some cops enjoyed talking about themselves. Then it came to mine and before it genuinely started it was over. GMP had managed to find very little to speak of. This truly brought home the pretence of the whole thing for me. It was a big sham dressed up in bells and whistles. Fahy handed me my medal, I'm sure he loved that, and then I made sure that I got a few pictures with him so that I could remind him, GMP, or anyone else for that matter, that I had been awarded this 'Good Conduct' medal.

Dr Graham Smith from the University of Manchester published a study into Disproportionality in Police Professional Standards. The DIPPS report, which was published in July, found that BME officers were statistically over-represented in GMP counter-corruption intelligence and that the existence of procedural disproportionality in internally raised misconduct proceedings was compelling.

Professor Grieve reported on Professional Standards seven years earlier. The only thing that changed for me was that I was then subjected to the same treatment that Professor Grieve warned against and described as racist and sexist. Now, a second report highlighted further serious issues in Professional Standards.

During the Autumn of 2012, I visited South Africa with my partner, Clare. We initially flew to Cape Town where we spent a few days taking in the sights of this world-renowned city. Table Mountain and Camps Bay were high on our list of places to see. We also found time to visit Cape of Good Hope which is not only the southernmost tip of South Africa but is the Southern tip of the African continent or so we thought when we visited.

The real highlight for me was our visit to Robben Island and the prison where Nelson Mandela was incarcerated for 18 of his 27 years. Nelson Mandela's prison cell was the main attraction of the tour. It was remarkably clean, tidy and maintained. If the cell had been manicured for tourists' eyes what couldn't be embellished was its size. I would not have been able to lie down in that cell in any direction – 18 years in this cell seemed an impossibility. I was in awe of Mr Mandela even more than I was before making the trip. He had fought against the racist Apartheid regime that saw the white minority ruling the black majority and spent 27 years in prison for fighting for the rights of his black and brown countrymen. What more inspiration could I need?

We then flew to Johannesburg where we picked up a hire car and drove to Rorke's Drift in KwaZulu-Natal. There we stayed on a ranch that had an imperious view of the landscape beneath. From this base and with a local guide, we were able to visit the site of the Battle of Isandlwana in Nhloya. On 22nd January 1879, the Battle of Isandlwana was the first major encounter in the Anglo-Zulu war between the Zulu Kingdom and the British Empire. The battle ended in a decisive victory for the Zulu's but today we hear little about this battle that has been whitewashed from our consciousness. British history defaults to the Battle of Rorke's Drift which saw a successful British defence of the mission station at that location. You wouldn't think that the two battles happened on the same day – each Christmas we are treated to another re-run of Michael Caine and Stanley Baker. During the battle of Isandlwana, the Zulus killed native Africans who helped the invading British Army. They saw this as an absolute betrayal by their kin, an interesting view I thought.

We then went to Rorke's Drift where we toured the battle site. Our guide happened to be the local Chief who owned the land. Bizarrely, all he wanted for payment for his services was a Manchester City shirt.

At the end of this part of our holiday, we drove back to Johannesburg arriving in the evening. The hire car was a brand-new BMW 3 series saloon. When we arrived at the guest house we had pre-booked. The owner of the guest house, a middle-aged white woman, spoke to Clare, a young white woman. I was at the back of the car removing our bags from the boot. The guest house owner looked at Clare and said, "So you've come on your own?" Clare looked around at me, then back at the owner "No, Paul's there." The owner looked at me then at Clare and said, "That's OK" – to this day I do not know what she meant by 'That's OK,' the mind boggles. I was brought back to my passing out parade when the military man asked me where I was really from. In Johannesburg, I had been transformed into 'The Help.'

Over the next few days, the owner would randomly call in her black staff and lecture them in front of Clare and I. She would say things like "See, if you work hard enough you can be like him." She had a gift for insulting people. I do not know who was more embarrassed me or her staff. To cap it all the owner of the guest house was from Bury in Greater Manchester. South Africa hadn't moved on as much as I had hoped and had found a niche for bigoted Greater Manchester immigrants.

No trip to Johannesburg is complete without a trip to Soweto. The owner told us that we couldn't possibly go on our own as it was too dangerous. We ignored her and drove there without the help of the National Guard. I do not know what Soweto is like at night but during the day it was just a housing estate, there are rougher places in Manchester. We visited Nelson Mandela's home, now a visitor centre, and enjoyed the day without being mugged, assaulted, or otherwise bothered. Keep an open mind and don't be held back by the prejudice of others.

By November, Detective Sergeant Julie Barnes, a GMP detective who had worked on OP Holly from the outset, told me a letter had been sent to me informing me that I was no longer a member of TITAN. The letter had been sent by Chief Superintendent Caroline Ball the head of GMP's Organisational Learning–Workforce and Development Branch. The irony of the department's title again was not lost on me as I had seen little learning since David Wilmot's declaration that GMP was racist. Caroline Ball's letter would direct that I would remain on OP Holly but as a GMP officer. Notwithstanding the obvious differential treatment, GMP secondments were now five years – I had spent three years on

TITAN, the decision had other financial implications for me – here we go again. Not one other GMP officer would be treated in the way that I had, of course not, they were all white. TITAN leadership would later argue that I was never 'seconded' to TITAN I was merely 'attached.' Could there have been a more stupid thing to say; TITAN was effectively stating that GMP had breached the compromise agreement. This was yet another example of how the police service made things up as it went along.

I complained about my treatment to the temporary Assistant Chief Constable Zoe Sheard, Garry Shewan's Ex, who despite The Stephen Lawrence Inquiry Report, despite all the previous reports on Professional Standards by police personnel and academics alike and in spite of force policy, did not record my complaint as a Professional Standards matter nor did she pass it onto the Professional Standards Branch. I lodged employment tribunal number four.

2013.

[Hero – Jessie J]

I was at work when I received an email from a woman whose name I didn't recognise. The message asked if I was 'the' Paul Bailey who used to work at Wigan [CID]. Cautious about everything, I gently enquired about why I was being pursued. The woman was a colleague of Sue Young, Sue had been diagnosed with cancer and the prognosis was, once again, terminal. I hadn't seen or been in touch with Sue since leaving Wigan CID. Her colleagues were having a buffet at the police station as Sue would not be returning to work. "She would love to see you Paul," was all that she needed to say.

On the day of the buffet, I drove over to Wigan Police Station. It looked strange as departments and offices had moved around. My old seat in the CID office looked worn and shabby, showing its age. I greeted a few of Sue's colleagues who I recognised, I then waited for Sue to arrive. Sue was helped into the room, she stepped cautiously as though she was learning to walk for the first time. She looked ill but I could still see the Sue of old, the live wire with the sharp wit. I walked over to her a gave her a kiss and a long hug. This gave me a moment to compose myself. Sue did the rounds speaking to all the people who had come to see her. I then sat down with Sue and explained that I had not known that she was ill. Sue said, "That doesn't matter Paul, you're here now." I held Sue's hand for a while as we spoke. Not wishing to monopolise her time, I gave her a kiss and left. That was the last time that I saw Sue, she died on 24th September.

Now that I was solely working on OP Holly, I found myself with more time to concentrate on rebuilding BAPA. I wanted to fulfil the original spirit of the association, for it to become a place where people could seek support and help when they needed it.

It was in 2013, that I first met a woman called Heather Ramsey. Heather was a black member of the support staff who worked in the force's Legal Services Department. In 2011, during Black History Month, Heather had a tattoo placed on her upper arm. The tattoo was of a broken chain that crossed through the year 1807 – 1807 representing the year that slavery was abolished in Britain – well it was actually the year that the taking and transportation of slaves was abolished. Slavery would exist in British colonies in the Caribbean for another three decades. In 2013, GMP took the view that Heather's tattoo breached the force's dress code. Heather was not in a customer-facing position and was not the only person who had a visible tattoo in the department. She was the only black member of staff with a tattoo. Heather faced discipline so came to BAPA for assistance after Unison had failed to give her any meaningful representation. Upon hearing Heather's case, I realised that I had been in a similar position, I had been the guy taken to a full misconduct hearing for wearing cultural dress to work. The issue here was obvious to me. It was not about Heather having a tattoo, it was what that tattoo represented. It was clear that GMP, or at least a representative of GMP, took exception to Britain's sordid, wretched and racist history being on display on a black woman's arm. Not that the tattoo was offensive in any way, it wasn't, they just didn't want to see it or be reminded of it.

After submitting her formal grievance Heather was removed from her post, supposedly 'to avoid further victimisation.' So, having been the victim of discrimination Heather was the one who was removed – this all sounded too familiar. I supported Heather through the entire grievance process, the stress of the case led to Heather having a period off work on sick leave. Finally, Heather found it necessary to pursue GMP legally, I assisted her through this process attending every meeting with her. After eight hundred and eight days, the force caved in, and Heather got the outcome that she desired. Before reading what Heather said at the end of her case know this, Heather had the strength and the will to see her case through. All I did was hold her hand, metaphorically speaking, she did all the rest – all of it. This demonstrates the strength that we all have inside of us. Given the right helping hand, we can achieve anything. Heather wrote this when her case finally came to an end;

> 'Paul has been there with me every step of the way. Not telling me what to do, just listening and supporting me in whatever I wanted to do even when he has his own things to deal with. We need to support and trust each other.
>
> I learnt a lot in the past two years and I intend to keep learning so I can continue to support BAPA as an executive member and others as Paul did for me.'

I continued to challenge the force on issues and policy. It was apparent to me that the force did not only suffer from discrimination

– racism, but from cronyism. The more people I supported the more the core of GMP was exposed to me and that core was rotten. I brought my observations and concerns about the force to the then Police and Crime Commissioner Tony Lloyd. Nothing meaningful came from this.

One of the issues that I challenged GMP on was recruitment. The recruitment process failed to deliver the diversity that was sorely needed. I believed that tweaking the existing process was simply not good enough and that there needed to be a wholesale change in the mindset and the process. Without this change, GMP would not attract or recruit people from minority ethnic communities. I sat on numerous boards that looked solely at this issue and asked for the recruitment process to start on a blank piece of paper. One of the meetings that I attended was chaired by DCC Ian Hopkins. I would later sit on further boards that looked at the progression of BME staff particularly within the CID, major and serious crime investigations.

I also supported a Police Community Support Officer called Shazia Awan. Shazia was an Asian Muslim PCSO who spoke multiple languages and was well thought of in her community. Shazia found herself being disciplined by GMP for allegedly using the term 'coconut' about an Asian colleague. Professor Grieve's report of 2005, DIPPS of 2012 even Lawrence of 1998 all came flooding back to me in this case. GMP clambered to investigate minority ethnic officers yet never seemed to find any evidence in allegations made about white staff. I had complained about the conduct of white colleagues only to find myself subject of a misconduct investigation that came at a heavy cost to the British taxpayer. Even the media were now calling out GMP on its record.

A programme aired on television was scathing about GMP. It revealed that between 2005 and 2012 the force investigated 519 public complaints of racial discrimination upholding exactly zero, not a single complaint. I used an image from the programme in a BAPA Newsletter that I sent to our members.

I defended Shazia at her misconduct hearing, but The Chair of the hearing found Shazia guilty, she received a sanction of a final written warning. I saw first-hand how harrowing the whole ordeal was for her, she suffered three heart attacks and was hospitalised as a result. I visited Shazia as she convalesced, I was heartbroken to see how poorly she was. Her case appeared in the local media, on the front page, under the headline;

'Top PCSO fell seriously ill after battle with bosses over 'coconut' slur.'

Shazia speaking about PSB Detectives is quoted;

> '[they] failed to pursue reasonable lines of investigation that would have supported my position and proved I was not guilty of misconduct, while officers lacked integrity, impartiality, misled and lied to me.'

I was quoted in the article;

> 'Det Con Paul Bailey, of the Manchester-based Black and Asian Police Association, said: "I wasn't there when the original allegation was made, but I can say she has always completely denied these allegations and is dedicated to clearing her name and any injustice against her."

Shazia was committed to clearing her name and took GMP to an employment tribunal alleging racial discrimination. She was so committed that she acted as a 'litigant in person' throughout the trial as she could not afford to pay for qualified legal representation. So many others would have given up and walked away but Shazia didn't – I admired her for that and was proud of the dignified way that she conducted herself in the court. She was still suffering the effects of her illness and struggled to breathe or even lift her files at times but, carried on – a real fighter.

Shazia was not successful in the tribunal; she was never the same after this ordeal and eventually left GMP altogether. Before Shazia left GMP I explained to her that she was a winner in my eyes and the eyes of so many others. She had fought for what she believed was right and paid a very heavy price for that, not only financially but physically with her health suffering the way that it did. Regardless of the cost, Shazia showed a strength few have and even fewer muster. The moment she put the organisation on trial she was a winner as GMP, with its infinite resources and staff, was always in a spiral of diminishing returns. The senior command's narcissism blinds them to this fact. The publicity that this case attracted would inevitably be used as a reference and a precedent.

2014.

January 2014 saw another scandal for GMP. This time Chef Constable Peter Fahy asked. former Superintendent Martin Harding to review the force's recruitment policy to see how it reflected the community. Martin's review was unequivocal the executive summary stated;

> 'Evidence was uncovered that would suggest that GMP is still an institutionally racist, sexist, homophobic and disablist organisation.'

But after submitting the report Martin was asked to change the conclusion to;

> 'Barriers still exist for all protected groups under the Equality Act'

Naturally, the media were interested in this story which hit the front page. I was asked to comment on the story, I said;

> 'Det Con Bailey, of BAPA said: "This report highlights the lack of progress GMP has made since the Stephen Lawrence Inquiry. It's a sad reflection of where we are, 16 years later,

and instead of solving the problem we are trying to hide the truth not only inside the organisation but also in the communities of Greater Manchester."

Chief Constable Sir Peter Fahy defended the decision to change the report saying that he believed the original conclusions were 'unhelpful' and 'wrong'. He commissions the report and then rubbishes its findings because it is not what he wants to hear. I have never heard of anything so narcissistic or egotistical in my police career. He is then quoted in the article;

"Despite some significant effort in the past to attract diverse communities that we need, if we had continued using the same approaches to recruitment that we had historically taken then it would have taken us until 2093 to get there which clearly is unacceptable."

Instead of addressing the findings of the report he ordered, or finding evidence that contradicted the report's findings, he chose to alter the report thereby lying to the public. I have long used the word corruption when speaking about GMP. The definition of corruption is: *Dishonest or fraudulent conduct by those in power; The process by which a word or expression is changed from its original state to one regarded as erroneous or debased.*

The Chief Constable admitted being corrupt on the front page of the local paper and no one except me took him to task over it. The rot had well and truly set in.

In June 2014, I met with Her Majesty's Inspectorate of Constabulary. The HMIC's role is to independently assess police forces. I provided the HMIC with a dossier, and within that dossier, I raised numerous concerns; concerns of corruption and 'cronyism' within GMP. Concerns about favouritism being shown to 'old friends' without regard to their qualifications. Concerns that the Professional Standards Branch was dealing with black and minority ethnic officers disproportionately and that a number of these cases had resulted in Employment Tribunal proceedings being brought by the officers concerned. I included Martin Harding's report which had been altered. And that Detective Sergeant Julie Barnes, who had been supportive of me, had been the subject of covert monitoring. I believed that the monitoring of her mobile phone had been controlled by Assistant Chief Constable Dawn Copley.

In August, the HMIC provided a full copy of the dossier to Deputy Chief Constable Ian Hopkins who in turn passed the dossier to ACC Copley. It was apparent the source of the dossier was me. I believe around August, GMP commenced a covert investigation into my conduct, particularly of my activities in my role as Chair of BAPA. This included 'Lawful Business Monitoring' where my email account would be covertly captured for a period of over thirty months.

Saturday 16th August 2014.

Rhyan Wilson was an 18-year-old black teenager from Stretford. On 16th August an altercation between two women boiled over into a disturbance which led to Dannall Dunkley, a 36-year-old black man also from Manchester, stabbing Rhyan to death on an Urmston Street, Rhyan had been stabbed nine times.

Rhyan's parents were not told about their son's death for eight hours despite going to the scene of the murder and to the hospital where their son had been taken. They were left to find out about their son's death online.

I was alerted to Rhyan's murder and the police failings over the weekend. I had a high profile in the media and was not shy in speaking on issues involving race and injustice. I went around to the family address only to find that I knew Rhyan's family particularly, his father who grew up in the same area that I had, he recognised me instantly. Rhyan's family were devastated, not only by their son's death but by their treatment at the hands of the police.

From Rhyan's family home, I contacted the head of MIT who was Detective Superintendent Peter Jackson. Peter and I had known each other for many years as we had worked on homicide investigations where our paths crossed. Although I did not agree with Peter politically, I found him to be an honest man who wanted to do the right thing. Peter was not one of those ambitious incompetents who towed the party line to curry favour with command and to snake their way up the ladder. He was not pissed on power, a quality that I admired. He arranged for a Chief Officer to attend Rhyan's family home to explain what had gone so badly wrong. I had bridged the gap between GMP and the family.

Rhyan's murder was reported in the local and national press. The police failing was a story in its own right. One local headline read;

'Rhyan Wilson's family not told of his death for eight hours'

I was quoted in the article;

> 'Det Con Paul Bailey, Chair of GMP's BAPA said; "Full transparency is needed and a full review of the officer's actions should be published. There are similarities between what happened here and in the Stephen Lawrence case, such as when he was fatally stabbed in the street and witnesses were treated poorly. Rhyan Wilson's family were treated very poorly"

ACC Garry Shewan is also quoted;

> '…We are making no attempt to shy away from the mistakes that we made that night, which led to a heart-breaking delay in informing the family that Rhyan had died, for which we

have personally apologised to the family. GMP failed the family at the worst possible moment and these failings led to increased anguish and pain for Rhyan's family. Nothing we say or do can rectify that…'

Rhyan's murder had more than shades of Stephen Lawrence – all the talk we had from command about the progress GMP had made since the Stephen Lawrence Inquiry had been blown away in an instant. Rhyan's family put out a statement;

'It is our desire to see a full and transparent review of the police actions as we do not want to see any other family go through the terrible ordeal that we suffered during the morning of Saturday 16th August, a day that we will never forget.

In addition, we would like to see changes in police policy and practice that prevent the police or the NHS dealing with bereaved families in the same manner that we were treated, race and colour should not be a factor.

We would like to thank all those who have supported us; they have been both generous and kind.'

In October, I left the country on holiday, I returned to find that the BME staff referred to in the dossier had been contacted by GMP and actively encouraged to make a complaint about me. I believed that the force had embarked on an exercise to intimidate any relevant witness and frustrate any subsequent investigation. I felt that the conduct of DCC Hopkins and ACC Copley was not only gross misconduct but a criminal offence – that their actions had been an attempt to pervert the course of justice.

I contacted DCC Hopkins to seek confirmation from him as to whether I was under investigation, and if so the nature and purpose of the investigation. On 3rd November 2014, DCC Hopkins wrote an email stating that I was not under investigation.

In September, November, and one day in January 2015, employment tribunal four was held in Manchester. It was interesting to see those who had power in GMP, be powerless whilst giving their evidence in court. Chief Superintendent Caroline Ball was particularly entertaining as she had drunk her clear plastic bottle dry and then kept trying to drink from it.

ACC Steve Heywood's name came up in conversation a lot but he was not a witness. It was clear to me that he was the senior officer involved in my abrupt return to GMP. I recalled writing to him before employment tribunals one to three. After hearing the evidence, the court would reserve its judgement which was expected in February 2015.

[During the Anthony Grainger public inquiry in 2017, Steve Heywood would be forced to make a cowering apology when his testimony was ripped to shreds by counsel. He said; "I apologise unreservedly, sir, if I have given the impression of being unhelpful or, even worse, misleading. I have got an unblemished 28-year police career, sir, and I would never knowingly mislead a court of inquiry." Mr Heywood would never return to policing]

Revenge Is A Dish Best Served Cold

2015.

[All I do Is Win – D J Khaled]

19th January 2015.

After all of the evidence had been heard by the court for employment tribunal four on January 19th 2015 I was called into CID headquarters, Nexus House, where I was served with gross misconduct papers. The Appropriate Authority, the person ultimately in charge of the investigation, was ACC Dawn Copley who had been named in my dossier. Gross misconduct papers meant that I was under threat of losing my job and potentially my pension. I considered this to be an act of victimisation. This was the second time that I had been turned from complainant to suspect – could there be anything more sinister?

The gross misconduct papers related to a complaint that had been made by two former police officers of GMP, one who had resigned following allegations of criminal conduct and misconduct, the other had been sacked as a result of such allegations. These Ex-police officers, who were clearly not credible, raised concerns that an article had been printed about them in the Manchester Evening News and that the article must have been written following or as a result of information leaked by GMP or a member of GMP staff. These complaints were made in January 2014 – DCC Hopkins had told me that I was not under investigation on 3rd November 2014 over nine months later. At no point was I named or my identity alluded to in their complaints. I did not know who these officers were, I don't believe that I had ever met either of them. Once again, I found myself at the centre of an investigation where the complainant was not known to me.

The regulation papers that were served on me were vague and an embarrassment to GMP and West Yorkshire Police. The officers were named in the notice but their Names were later redacted during the subsequent hearings – the misconduct papers read,

> 'Following an article published in the Manchester Evening News dated 25th January 2014, an investigation has commenced into public complaints made against Greater Manchester Police by two former officers X1 and X2.
>
> This investigation has identified information that points towards you accessing a confidential discipline file that related to a Professional Standards investigation named Operation Atticus. Specifically, that you accessed with the assistance of Sergeant Tom Elliott [Retired] from Greater Manchester Police Federation, the discipline file relating to X2 between 1st November 2013 and 17th December 2013.
>
> It is believed at the time that you neither had the consent of X2 or that you were not acting in the proper course of your police duties.
>
> The Standards of Professional Behaviour identifies an officer's responsibilities under 'Confidentiality'. This sates that Police Officers treat information with respect and access or disclose it only in the proper course of their police duties. An unauthorised access to X2's discipline file may constitute a breach of the Standards of Professional Behaviour.'

What complete hogwash, the notice started by stating that the investigation was as a result of an article in the Manchester Evening

News on 25th January 2014 but then does not even allege that I passed information to that paper. Then it used vague terminology such as 'that points towards,' it did not use words such as 'evidence'. What the notice missed was that Sgt Elliott had formally stated that he had not given the discipline file to me. It was clear to me that this was a poorly disguised witch-hunt.

Four Police Federation officers had provided statements supporting the investigation against me. Their statements were dated in January or February 2014 and contained no evidence that I had done anything wrong. It was also entirely possible that the Manchester Evening News article could have been put together using information already in the public domain. I was not convinced that any leak of information had ever occurred.

2nd February 2015.

During 2015, I continued to represent black and minority ethnic officers and staff in addition to my full-time job as a detective.

One of the staff who I represented was a young Asian man who had been dismissed from GMP. At the hearing I argued that his dismissal was unfair not only because the process adopted by GMP amounted to bullying but that GMP had not considered the Equality Act when the decision to dismiss the Operational Support Officer was made. The Chair accepted that the member of staff had been treated unfairly and reinstated him with immediate effect.

9th February 2015.

The employment tribunal of Inspector Scott Winters, a GMP police officer, started in Manchester. I had known Scott for some time, he was a very intelligent and articulate man and a skilled orator. I had relied on Scott as he was strong-willed, fearless and pretty much unbeatable with a pen or a keyboard. He didn't suffer fools gladly, a man after my own heart, and would not be intimidated by anyone's rank or supposed standing in the organisation. He was like Karin but on nitrous oxide. As a black man he had suffered racism and like me would not be a subservient victim. If GMP thought that they had made a mistake taking me on, then they had certainly made a mistake taking Scott on.

In March 2013, Scott was involved in an 'altercation' with a junior officer in a custody office. This incident led to Scott being pursued under misconduct. This was yet another example of GMP pursuing a black officer and where their strict interpretation of Section 22 of the Police Reform Act would not be that strict. When they wanted to pursue you then they did. I openly supported Scott at the hearing that did not get passed Scott's opening evidence. GMP would later settle the case out of court.

10th February 2015.

On 10th February, I learned that I had won employment tribunal four. The court found that I had suffered race discrimination and victimisation. I believe that cases like these are one-sided against the claimant. The Chief Constable has the services of the force at his disposal, the claimant does not. The Chief Constable also has funds at his disposal, albeit public funds; the claimant does not always have the support of a trade union that will fund the cost of the hearing – Shazia Awan for example.

15th February 2015.

The tribunal's verdict for tribunal four was reported in the local media under the title,

'Tribunal finds GMP victimised black police officer, leading to fresh claims of institutional racism.'

Charles Crichlow is quoted in the article;

> 'GMP is still institutionally racist. Paul Bailey was discriminated against on the grounds of his race. This is the 50th anniversary of the first race relations legislation in the UK. GMP is supposed to be celebrating that as a progressive organisation.
>
> But to be found guilty of racism like this is problematic. People should be disciplined for this.'

Deputy Chief Constable Ian Hopkins is quoted in the article;

> 'Greater Manchester Police acknowledges the judgment made by the employment tribunal with regard to Detective Constable Paul Bailey.
>
> We agree with the ruling of the tribunal that DC Bailey's return to Greater Manchester Police following his secondment was managed badly but did not amount to direct discrimination. We accept the findings of the tribunal that the force's actions amounted to victimisation because of a previous agreement made with DC Bailey.
>
> We also accept the findings of the tribunal that the force should have referred DC Bailey's complaint about his treatment to PSB (GMP's Professional Standards Branch) and that our failure to do so amounted to discrimination and victimisation. This is something we as a force take extremely seriously.
>
> The organisation will always try to resolve workplace complaints in the most appropriate forum and this issue, together with the other important lessons the tribunal identified, is something we will look to learn from as we move forward.'

Ian Hopkins accepted the findings of the tribunal – his words were clear. This was little comfort to me less than a month after being served yet another set of misconduct papers. Charles Crichlow called for people to be disciplined, but that didn't happen, I was the one in GMP's crosshairs.

17th February 2015.

The local media reported on Dannall Dunkley being convicted of the murder of Rhyan Wilson. I was in Manchester Crown Court when Mr Dunkley apologised to Rhyan's family saying that he was truly sorry for what he had done. Mr Dunkley was sentenced to life imprisonment, he must serve at least fifteen years and nine months before being eligible to apply for parole.

I continued to work as the Disclosure Officer on the OP Holly investigation. I had not been removed from my post; I believed that this was due to my previous tribunal claims where GMP had capitulated. GMP had painted itself into a corner. The money laundering investigation had stalled as the prosecution Barrister, Ian Unsworth QC, would not move forward with giving authority to charge the suspects in the case whilst I was still in post. The service of papers on me had bitten GMP in the arse. I had been in post for years, and to replace me meant that all the work I had done would have to be done again by a different disclosure officer. Paul Massey was one of the suspects in the case, he had been arrested in 2011 and had been on police bail ever since. His bail was cancelled during the debate over my status in OP Holly.

19th March 2015.

A local paper reported on Paul Massey's bail being cancelled. Mr Massey is quoted in the article;

> 'It has been a long time for anyone to be on bail. I have never known of anyone being on bail for that length of time before.

When I was arrested my wife was arrested too. She was put through hell. It was a terrifying experience for her. I am confident that there is no case to answer.'

Mr Massey remained a suspect in the investigation.

18th May 2015.

I met Detective Inspector Tim Dean, the Senior Investigating Officer for OP Holly, and Russ Jackson who was now Detective Chief Superintendent in charge of CID operations, at Nexus House. I was told that on the advice of Counsel, I was being removed as the Disclosure Officer from OP Holly with immediate effect. I asked to see the advice from Counsel.

22nd May 2015.

I went to TITAN's offices where I met Tim Dean. Tim had been given the nickname 'Dark Cloud' by his staff in the Financial Investigation Unit. I had not initially understood why he was called this, it did not take long to figure out. The man seemed to carry the troubles of the world on his shoulders. I found him to be a weak man who would be ignored if it was not for his rank. I never trusted him as I had made him for a company man literally from the first moment that I met him.

When I met with Tim, he allowed me to view Ian Unsworth's advice, but I was not allowed to copy or record it. The advice was based on two main premises – the first being that I had taken my employer (GMP) to an employment tribunal and won and as such I would make a poor witness for the prosecution as I would speak 'truthfully' about my trust in GMP and as such it was not felt that I would speak favourably about GMP under cross-examination. Taking that slowly, I was removed from being a disclosure officer as it was thought that I 'would' tell the truth in court.

The second premise was that as Disclosure Officer I would have to disclose [on] myself. This is total tripe as police officers disclose themselves all the time and, in any event, I had not been found guilty of anything. Before leaving TITAN's offices, a woman who I used to work with saw me, we spoke for a short while. She said that she and others from my old unit wanted to buy me a leaving present but they realised that they did not know anything about me. Even though I had worked there for years and hadn't shied away from conversation.

This made her laugh she said, "We are not sure if your name is really Paul" – I was the 'Grey Man.' Black officers had adopted the grey man for a long time. Whilst our white counterparts spoke openly about their personal lives some black officers like me never did. This is a protection mechanism, if they don't know anything about you then they cannot use it against you.

29th May 2015.

On the 29th, Russ Jackson, without any input from me, posted me to GMP's Major Incident Team. The man who had removed me in 2007 under restricted duties returned me there eight years and three months later, I told him I'd be back! For clarity, I could not work on a money laundering investigation, but homicide investigations were OK – I laughed. I downloaded a picture of Lester Freamon from the television series 'The Wire,' framed it and placed it on my desk at MIT. Lester Freamon was a black homicide detective who was transferred out of the department as a punishment – he spent thirteen years and four months away before being brought back. The image of Freamon had the words '*All the pieces matter*' written along the bottom edge. The picture would remain there until my last day in GMP.

1st June 2015.

Even though I had been removed as the disclosure officer from OP Holly as my position was untenable,' according to TITAN. TITAN still wanted to use my assessment of the material I had reviewed whilst on OP Holly. I had compiled a 'List of Issues' that TITAN wanted. I resisted this in an email on June 1st.

> 'I discharged the role of Disclosure Officer on OP Holly from March 2012 until May 2015. During that time, I compiled a list of issues that I believed, as the disclosure officer at that time, had the potential to 'impact' on any case should one be brought to trial. I did this beyond my role which was to assess the unused material that was presented to me. There was no requirement for me to do this nor was I instructed to do this by any supervisor. I did it to assist my role post charge.
>
> When I took on the role of disclosure officer I did not rely upon the assessment(s) of the previous post holder; I assessed all of the information. The list was shaped by my assessment. This is subjective i.e. what I believe is an issue, you may not...'

If there was any intention to use my assessments to move OP Holly on quickly after my departure, this email outlining my position put an end to that. Another disclosure officer would need to reassess all of the material for themselves. I was so concerned that there would be a re-branding of my work that I compiled a statement of evidence detailing these concerns before sending the statement to the Crown Prosecution Service. Both the CPS and the Police Service had been put on notice; I would be watching any development in OP Holly. I cannot imagine that they thought that I would react in such a way, they had misjudged me, hugely.

7th June 2015.

Dominic Doyle was found injured after a disturbance on a street in Denton. Mr Doyle was taken to hospital where he later died from his injuries; he had been stabbed. This was my first murder investigation after my enforced hiatus of eight years and three months. Whilst I'd been away, I had some great experiences.

I had welcomed the departure from the politics found in other areas of GMP, particularly at force headquarters. And I had enjoyed not being surrounded by self-centred sycophants trying to climb the greasy pole of promotion.

Russ Jackson had posted me to MIT syndicate 3 – Yep, syndicate 3. It would be funny if it wasn't so sad. Within weeks of returning to MIT duties, I felt like I had not been away. The syndicate had a new look and new location, but homicide investigations still required the same skills and I had those. It was like inter-house school basketball all over again.

In the Dominic Doyle murder investigation six people would later be sentenced for the attack including Colin McDonald. Mr McDonald had been previously convicted of manslaughter in 1997 and for causing death by dangerous driving in 2011. He was found guilty of manslaughter and sentenced to serve a minimum of fifteen years in prison. Richard Linehan pleaded guilty to the murder of Dominic Doyle, he was sentenced to life imprisonment with a minimum of fourteen years and two months before being eligible to apply for parole.

26th July 2015.

Paul Massey was shot and killed outside of his home in Clifton, Salford. It was thought that he was shot with a machine gun. Mr Massey was still a suspect in the OP Holly investigation at the time of his death. Mark Fellows would be eventually convicted of Paul Massey's murder, receiving a whole life sentence. Where would Paul

Massey have been on July 26th if the investigation had not been delayed?

14th August 2015.

On the 14th August police patrols chased a blue Nissan car in Rochdale. The boot of the car held the body of a woman who had been murdered by one of the car's occupants, Lee Nolan. Mr Nolan and another man were arrested but the woman had not been identified. This was only the second murder investigation in my career where the investigation team did not know the identity of the victim, the other being the Amanda Hardwick investigation.

I had returned to a role in the major incident room - MIR, showing my versatility in being able to carry out multiple roles in homicide investigations. It also cemented the fact that I had not suffered from my time away from MIT.

The victim in this case was identified as Katelyn Parker a young woman who suffered from learning difficulties. Lee Nolan had strangled Katelyn, placed her in the boot of his car and boasted to others about what he had done. The second man arrested was released without charge, but Lee Nolan was convicted on murder with a minimum tariff of eighteen years.

20th August 2015.

I met ACC Garry Shewan. Garry had been referred to on social media as 'Honest Garry,' this was not a compliment. He was referred to as 'honest' in the same way that an obese person would be called 'slim' or a tall person 'shorty.' I didn't need to be reminded of this as I had seen honest Garry in action years earlier when he was caught out by the notes of Judge Franey. If I said that I did not trust Garry that would have been an understatement. Garry Shewan told me there was no case to answer and the case against me had been discontinued. I had not even been interviewed concerning the misconduct papers that I had been served. Due to the three months less one day rule, I lodged a further two employment tribunals, five and six, that covered the decision to investigate me and the decision to remove me as disclosure officer. I waited for confirmation from Honest Garry in writing for obvious reasons. Let's just say I didn't want his memory to fail him.

October 2015.

In October, Ian Hopkins succeeded Sir Peter Fahy as Chief Constable of GMP. He had joined GMP as an Assistant Chief Constable in 2008 and had now taken over the top job at one of Britain's largest forces. I can state without any doubt that I found him to be the most inept, unethical and disingenuous person in GMP and probably outside of it.

20th and 21st October.

I sat through the GMP appeal to their loss in tribunal four. The appellant or person appealing the conviction was none other than the Chief Constable of GMP, Ian Hopkins himself. Hopkins was the person who said after the tribunal had handed down its verdict in February;

> 'Greater Manchester Police acknowledges the judgment made by the employment tribunal with regard to Detective Constable Paul Bailey...We accept the findings of the tribunal that the force's actions amounted to victimisation because of a previous agreement made with DC Bailey.
>
> We also accept the findings of the tribunal that the force should have referred DC Bailey's complaint about his treatment to PSB (GMP's Professional Standards Branch) and that our failure to do so amounted to discrimination and

victimisation.'

This was not true as he did not accept the verdict and now, with a cost that probably ran into tens of thousands of pounds, he was appealing it. He was a liar and completely unethical, yet he was not taken to task over it by the Police and Crime Commissioner or to my knowledge anyone else. If a junior officer had so blatantly lied in the course of their employment, I had no doubt that they would be disciplined and would face the most severe sanction. In Ian Hopkins' case, nothing.

In addition to the barrister who had defended the Chief Constable in the lower court and lost, Ian Hopkins had now enlisted the help of Simon Gorton QC – how much did he cost per day? Two barristers representing the Chief Constable; I thought Hopkins was prepared to do everything he could to redeem himself yet sadly, for him, he could never do that as all the fancy trickery in the world would not reverse the minds of the people who had seen the original judgment. Hopkins was in that spiral of diminishing returns, he could never get back to square one – unethical and disingenuous he was.

When I arrived at the court and was in the process of booking in one of the staff said, "I know who you are Mr Bailey, I followed the case," Win or lose the most important thing is the fight. People are drawn to David versus Goliath because they want to hear the story of the little man taking on the brute, in my case taking on injustice. It is the fight, courage and determination that is inspiring. I don't think people like Hopkins will ever understand that.

It was the first time that I saw or even heard of Simon Gorton. It didn't take me long to get his number. I saw him as Ian Hopkins' Johnnie Cochran, in fact, I cannot even think of Gorton's name and not hear 'If the glove doesn't fit, you must acquit.' At least Johnnie was charismatic and had a modicum of decency, I couldn't see either in Gorton who reminded me of a salesman flogging second-hand cars that would be better off in the scrapyard than on a garage forecourt.

The court process was strange as my barrister was there to defend the Judgment of the lower court. That being the case why wasn't the judge who handed down that verdict present defending himself? Surely, he was the best person to speak on the judgment – his judgment. Gorton wafted around the court like a vampire and seemed to argue every point. It became tedious watching and listening to his monochromatic drawl, after a while I found myself drifting away mentally imagining the Justice slapping Gorton across the face and telling him to get on with it. My barrister was Miss Assunta Del Priore, who had represented me at the lower court and who had skilfully won the case. Even Assunta looked fed up with Gorton and interrupted him to add clarity to the proceedings. After two days in the High Court in Salisbury Square, London, it was over. The Honourable Mrs Justice Elisabeth Laing DBE would deliver her judgement in December.

During 2015, I wrote a number of articles for BAPA's quarterly newsletters. One article was titled;

'When GMP says that it has learned lessons we should all be frightened.'

And read.

> 'We are continually told as far as race and discrimination are concerned GMP has moved on greatly since the Stephen Lawrence Inquiry in 1998 and the inquiry report of 1999.
>
> "There are two ways to be fooled, one is to believe what isn't true, the other is to refuse to accept what is true" – Soren Kierkegaard.
>
> The reality is that the issues that minority groups complained about in the 1990s are the very same issues that are being complained of today. Despite several false starts such as 'Operation Catalyst' [Stephen Lawrence] and the 'Respect Programme' [The Secret Policeman] GMP has continued to

allow discrimination and corruption within its ranks. Those who stand against this corruption or who speak out about corruption become targets or 'Public Enemies' dodging criminal and misconduct investigations intended to silence or disgrace them.

The term 'We have learned lessons' has become a euphemism for 'Nothing has changed or nothing to see here.' When we hear this term, we should all be afraid, very afraid. What will it take to Change GMP?

Focused on defending the reputation of individuals at all costs.

"What I have learned is that a whole lot of people with degrees don't know a damn thing, and a lot of people with no degrees are brilliant" – John Henrik Clarke.

We are constantly told that GMP actions are intended to protect the reputation of the force, but what does that mean or look like in reality? In a time of austerity and instant global media it is apparent to me that what GMP are actually doing is protecting individuals within the force, the higher the rank the greater the protection. The reputation of the force has nothing to do with it whatsoever. If it did then why are we continually subjected to the types of negative media reporting that leave so many of us flabbergasted and exhausted.

The ultimate measure of how GMP treats its staff is when staff members take the force to court, either through civil court or via an employment tribunal. Both of these processes cost the taxpayer huge amounts of money as these actions are costly to instigate and defend. I am not advocating that the force admits wrongdoing if no wrongdoing occurs, the problem here is that GMP never admits wrongdoing, even when faced with overwhelming evidence.

The consequence of this approach is that the force has no credibility in the community or within sections of its workforce or legal system.

There are other consequences, the impact that these actions have on the plaintiff [person bringing the action] is neither acknowledged nor appreciated by the force.

They are expected to be productive members of the force once the action is over; the alternative is leaving the force completely.

Rather than improve the systems within GMP, a claim that I am sure the force will make, in reality, GMP are making it more difficult for those subject to discrimination to have their complaints investigated. New policies lean towards mediation allowing discriminators to go unpunished and protected from any type of sanction.

At a time when GMP wants to recruit a more diverse workforce the outlook for those within the force from BME backgrounds – at best uncertain, at worst bleak.'

3rd December 2015.

Mrs Justice Elisabeth Lang handed down her judgement. Justice Lang dismissed Hopkins' appeal. It was as simple as that. Hopkins' attempt to overturn the lower court's ruling that I had been racially discriminated against and victimised had failed. I was annoyed at Hopkins' lies. He said one thing and then did the opposite – he was immoral. In spite of hiring two barristers, one being Queens Counsel, he had still lost. More importantly, his spiral downwards was accelerating. There was no blaming anyone else, he was the Chief Constable and therefore the buck stopped with him. The High Court's judgment was reported in the media;

'High Court judge throws out GMP appeal to overturn ruling it racially discriminated against black detective.'

I was quoted in the article;

'The force had a QC and other counsel as well as their own solicitors. The investigation into me must have cost hundreds of thousands of pounds. GMP blames austerity for a lack of investigation into public complaints but there seems to be no limit to how much they spend on defending internal complaints and that must be wrong.'

Lights-Camera-Action

2016.

[Pop Ya Collar – Usher]

I was working in the MIT office at Chadderton when I overheard a conversation between some of my colleagues. They were talking about a detective who had been diagnosed with cancer. They spoke about the detective in glowing terms, describing him as brilliantly old school. I heard them use the name 'Barney' several times then it occurred to me who Barney was. I turned to them and shouted across the office "You don't mean Chris Barnes, do you?" – "Yes" was the reply, "Do you know him." When I picked up my mobile and called Chris, they got their answer.

I drove around to Chris' house and sat with him in one of the rear rooms that overlooked his beautifully manicured garden. Chris had been diagnosed with prostate cancer. He had ignored the symptoms for a while but had been persuaded to see a doctor by his partner Heather. Heather and Chris had been together for many years. Heather had two boys, who Chris loved and cared for. Chris looked well and was in good spirits, he had a positive attitude about his illness and was in no doubt that he would recover and return to work.

I visited Chris at home over the weeks and saw his ups and downs. He battled on with his treatment. Like Karin before him when we were together, he wanted to speak about anything other than cancer.

Daniel Smith was a young man who had drifted from city to city. He had found himself living rough in Manchester and socialised with other homeless people around the city centre, collectively they used a disused workshop under the railway arches at Gore Street near Salford Central Railway Station. On the 19th of January, Daniel was attacked by two men, Adam Acton and Luke Benson – who bore a grudge against him. One of the men knocked Daniel out, then he was punched and kicked as he lay unconscious. Daniel was attacked further with a rounders bat and a hammer. Daniel lay helpless in a tent, after his death Benson set the tent alight and fled. This shocking murder was featured in the BBC Two documentary The Detectives: Murder on the Streets.

Although my syndicate had not been assigned this murder, a number of my syndicate were allocated suspects arrested in connection with Daniel's murder and who needed to be interviewed. Detective Constable Rob Kitchen and I were asked to interview Amanda Briggs, who was the girlfriend of Acton, and who was present during the attack.

I had known Rob for many years, he was a young detective at Wigan CID when I spent time there. Rob was a thoughtful and keen young man with strong ethics and a desire to do well. Rob led the interview, and between us, we were able to break Amanda Briggs down who eventually gave vital information for the investigation team. This interview is featured in the episode but Rob and I cannot be seen as we both refused to give our consent. I refused to take part in the episode at all as I believed the documentary was nothing more than a PR exercise used by command officers to further their careers. When the programme aired, the BBC had managed to crop Rob and I out of the footage and limited my voice to only one line. Luke Benson and Adam Acton were convicted of Daniel's murder being sentenced to life imprisonment with tariffs of twenty-one and twenty-two years respectively.

On January 17th 2016, BBC Radio aired a programme called

Bent Cops? I was one of those interviewed by the BBC during the making of the 'File on Four' programme, when it was aired, I didn't have to wait long to hear my voice.

> "I am Paul Bailey, I'm a serving Detective Constable with Greater Manchester Police and I investigate murders, serious and organised crime, money laundering, the most serious criminality that occurs…"

> Narrator – 'A serving detective accuses his own police force of criminal behaviour'

> "I have come to speak to you today because no investigation has taken place and I've literally been stonewalled – the public needs to know what's going on."

> Narrator – He says that he's gathered evidence alleging corruption and victimisation by a unit within the force against other police officers. He's not alone, other officers say they've been unfairly targeted ending up sacked or in jail.

The programme introduced John Buttress, an ex-GMP Chief Inspector who was sacked after a disciplinary hearing where it was found that he had breached the standards of professional behaviour over his mortgage. Mr Buttress launched an employment tribunal claiming that he had been wrongfully dismissed, he accused GMP of conducting a witch hunt. His case also appeared on the BBC's 'Inside Out' programme, the segment on John Buttress even I found alarming. John Buttress had made an allegation of bullying by his supervisor after GMP cleared the supervisor of any wrongdoing John found himself and his finances under investigation – same old party trick.

John and I had run a similar path. Like John I had been taken to a misconduct hearing but in my case GMP were unable to hang anything substantial on me. I walked away with my career and pension intact. John was not so fortunate – he faced a fraud case where he was cleared by a jury in under an hour. He had faced two charges but days before his court appearance the Crown Prosecution Service or CPS disclosed a page of vital evidence that led to the first charge being dropped. Had this page not been found at the 11th hour John potentially could have been found guilty. John did not fare so well when left at the mercy of GMP in a misconduct hearing. John subsequently made eleven criminal complaints against senior officers in GMP. The BBC had revealed that I was not alone in my assessment of corruption within GMP, John Buttress said;

> "I choose my words carefully; I believe there was corrupt police practice in targeting me. And I'm saying that sitting here in a police uniform in a BBC studio, I shouldn't have to be doing this but I am."

I was certain that there would be a price to pay for my appearance on the BBC. I had seen GMP in action too many times before. If anyone had thought that there was no risk in what I had done or that there was no consequence to my actions then John Buttress stood as a stark reminder of the perilous road that I had committed to. In the same programme Ian Hopkins said;

> "Would your listeners want an officer who has influence in this organisation who is deliberately dishonest to be serving as a police officer? I don't think they would."

This must be the only thing that Hopkins had ever said that I was in complete agreement with. But what if that deliberately dishonest officer was the Chief Constable?

Andy Burnham also appears in the programme. At the time he was the Labour MP for Leigh and the Shadow Home Secretary. Burnham says that one of the cases highlighted in the programme, that of ex-GMP Police Inspector Mohammed Razaq, did not add up. Burnham said;

> "The suggestion is that some of the evidence in his case was

not safe so, that is why I will support Mo Razaq in taking his case to the Criminal Cases Review Commission because I have concerns about his case."

Andy Burnham placed himself on the record that if there were concerns about the evidence in a case then it should be investigated. In Mohammed Razaq's case, to the Criminal Case Review Commission. Surely, if Burnham became the Mayor of Manchester, he would not forget the position that he took in 2016. Burnham continued;

> "Other people have come to me, including constituents, who've said there's a similar pattern of events here. Now that's one side of the story so, I can't say that that proves something against Greater Manchester Police. What is being said to me is that charges are brought very zealously against individuals for reasons that I'm not certain about and there are of course the legal costs that accrue to those kinds of investigations.
>
> So, the question I've got to ask is – is it in the public interest that those cases have been brought, I'm aware that there are cases where those charges ultimately have been dropped, it is my job then to ask some questions about whether or not the Greater Manchester Police is going about these concerns in the right way"

On February 9th, Sebastian Zuchlinski, a 39-year-old amateur cage fighter, was attacked on a street in Bolton. Despite the efforts of the emergency services and the general public, Sebastian died at the scene of the attack; he had suffered multiple stab wounds and died from his injuries. I was at a Manchester primary and junior school giving a talk to a group of children when I learned that my syndicate was going to investigate Mr Zuchlinski's murder. Alan Greene's wife was a teacher at the school and had invited me to speak there. Over the years, since the week-long misconduct hearing in 2009, Alan and

I became friends. He told me how he felt about GMP and their efforts to sanction me for complaining about discrimination and racism in the force. He said that he thought that the proceedings against me were unfair and inappropriate. He did not believe that I should face any sanction and therefore he would not agree to it. Fortunately, for me I suppose, a second-panel member agreed with Alan – I got a flashback to Superintendent David Hull, throwing his pen down and pushing his chair back. Alan never said who the other panel member was but he didn't have to. Alan had become disenfranchised from GMP. He was fed up with the antics, corruption and duplicity of the command team. He would later write an article entitled 'Senior Officer Behaviour in Policing' that I would publish in full in one of BAPA's quarterly newsletters.

I finished my talk with the children at school, said goodbye to Alan's wife, and made my way to the incident room. During this investigation I interviewed one of the main witnesses to the attack on Sebastian, the interview was video recorded. I also interviewed one of the suspects with the use of an interpreter. Through this interview, the suspect maintained that he did not speak English, but this fell apart when he described how he had watched a movie at a local cinema. He then described the plot of the movie to me perfectly, when I asked in the movie was in English, he realised his faux pas and shrugged his shoulders. Tomasz Bubrowski was later convicted of Sebastian Zuchlinski's murder. He was sentenced to life imprisonment with a minimum of thirty-one years.

Tommy Fung became a neighbourhood Police Constable after his departure from Wigan CID. He was a very proactive officer who targeted criminals and drug dealers in his area – he reminded me of me, albeit a much younger me. Tommy then became the target of a vile and racist hate campaign; 'PC Fung U Chinese dirtball' was daubed on a wall. That was followed by 'PC Fung chink boy.' Tommy continued to target the drug dealers executing warrants at addresses, recovering drugs and charging several suspects.

I Did That

Numerous racist Twitter posts were identified;

> 'Fuck the CHINK al send him on his way the little shit,'

And

> 'IS PC TOM FUNG (AKA CHINK) OUT TO NIGHT HARD patrolling our hoodd?? Well tell him banged out!'

And

> 'pc tom fung (AKA CHINK) is about in your hood tonight so don't be scard people.'

[The posts are verbatim – clearly all Mensa candidates]. Tommy was disappointed the racist crimes were not being investigated by GMP. Naturally, Tommy received public complaints, but he did not pay much attention to them until one of the complaints came from a colleague in GMP. Tommy's college complained that 'PC Fung caused the suspect to be racist towards himself.' I have been the victim of nonsensical complaints but none as stupid as this. Tommy was now the cause of the racism that he suffered.

Tommy arrested a suspect on suspicion of committing a public order offence. The suspect told Tommy to go back to his own country and spat in his face. Tommy took decisive action to stop the suspect from spitting again. A complaint from the suspect resulted in Tommy being placed on restricted duties, for six months, pending the outcome of a Professional Standards Branch investigation. Whilst on restricted duties, GMP received information that threats towards Tommy and his family home had been made but as far as Tommy was aware GMP decided that no action was needed as he was on restricted duties. Tommy later transferred to another division and actively decided not to be proactive at work. These are Tommy's words;

> 'No one from the Salford Division Senior Leadership Team (SLT) came to speak with me. My Fed Rep did his best for

me. But it was DC Paul Bailey (Chair of BAPA) who really helped me, AGAIN.'

Such was the work that I undertook in BAPA day to day. Little did Tommy know that I had suffered in the same way that he had so, I had at least some idea of how he felt throughout his ordeal.

On June 28th, Atatürk Airport in Istanbul was the scene of a terrorist attack. Gunmen, who were armed with automatic weapons and who were wearing explosive belts attacked the international terminal. Three attackers and forty-five people were killed with more than two hundred and thirty injured. As terrible as this tragedy was it was not going to stop me. Three days later, Clare and I flew out to Istanbul.

When we landed at the airport, there was a memorial to the dead in the terminal building. Workers busied themselves repairing the damage and replacing broken windows. I was amazed at the speed of the recovery; I thought that in the UK we would still be sifting through the debris for clues. We carried on visiting all the sites that Istanbul had to offer. I am sure that the Sultan Ahmed Mosque, also known as the Blue Mosque, would normally rate as number one on most traveller's list. For me it was a boat trip across the Bosphorus to the Asian part of Istanbul followed by a delicious lunch at Mr Hassan's; this stole first prize. A few days later we left Istanbul for a more relaxing leg of the trip, Beirut.

A faction of the Turkish armed forces attempted a coup d'état on July 15th. We had left for Beirut before the coup began. Chris had taken to calling me on my work mobile number, I didn't have that with me during the trip. I returned to the UK to find that knowing that I was going to Istanbul he had called and messaged me trying to make sure that we were OK. When I next saw him, we laughed – I thought it was a great holiday. He said, "Let me get this straight so, you went to Istanbul after the terrorist attack and left before the coup." I suppose my timing was impeccable.

I Did That

Chris had been treated for prostate cancer and was in remission. I was unable to describe how happy I was to hear the news. Chris had decided to retire from GMP as he was now old enough to do so and having looked at his finances, he thought that the time was right. He sent out an email informing every one of his plans but sent this private email to me before he left;

1st September 2016,

Bails, You will have received an email from me saying goodbye. However, I wanted to send a personal one to special people, you being one!

It has been a pleasure and a privilege to have known you all these years. I admire your moral courage (possibly not always the way you go about it tho!!). You are by far one of the best detectives I've ever worked with and someone I am proud to call a friend.

Thanks for your support over the last year. All the best for the future brother, Chester.

PS Try and keep your head down!!

If You Can't Beat Them, Cheat.

2016.

[Stronger – Kanye West]

Richard Pendlebury was a GMP Police Sergeant who was charged with shoplifting from a local superstore. He was suspended from work whilst he awaited trial. I had never heard of PS Pendlebury and to this day, I have never met him. I was aware of his case as I had met with Chief Inspector Clara Williams who had sought my advice. Clara had become embroiled in PS Pendlebury's case, she had been accused of covering up for him.

In February 2016, I attended a Continuing Professional Development seminar at GMP's training school, Sedgley Park. I attended this seminar in line with my duties as a Major Incident Detective and I was on duty throughout, in fact, the seminar was classed as a tour of duty. There were possibly a hundred or more detectives at the event.

During the seminar one of the presenters, Steve Retford, who was employed by GMP, made comments about a live case – that of PS Pendlebury's. I thought that the comments made by Steve Retford were inappropriate. I openly challenged Steve's conduct in front of the whole audience. I stated that it was completely inappropriate to speak about this case during his presentation. He asked me if I knew the case, I confirmed that I had and questioned how many other people present at the seminar had knowledge of it also. Steve apologised for his conduct, stating that he wanted to speak about the case for learning.

By the 22nd of September 2016, Paul Pendlebury, Richard's father appeared on the ITV news. Richard had been cleared by a jury of shoplifting but he was told that he would face an internal investigation and would remain suspended on full pay.

In October 2016, I was approached by Detective Inspector Melani Hall of the Professional Standards Branch. Hall stated that she had been tasked with investigating a complaint about Steve Retford. There was no file reference number attached to her email, a sign to me that this was a whitewashing exercise. At no time was there any suggestion that I had done anything wrong in challenging Steve Retford's conduct. The College of Policing Code of Ethics and GMP's own doctrine expect inappropriate behaviour to be challenged. I provided PSB with a statement of the events in February.

Chief Superintendent Lee Bruckshaw was another who became embroiled in the PS Pendlebury case. Lee had been my divisional commander during my time at Wigan CID where he had given me a commendation for my work. Lee was accused of Perverting the Course of Justice. The criminal investigation was later dropped; the misconduct hearing against him was called off. Lee appeared on BBC television where he spoke out calling the investigation into him an 'Expensive Shambles.' Lee's appearance on the BBC was a very public resignation from the police, he claimed that GMP had wasted half a million pounds of public money investigating allegations that he considered to be trumped up. Lee said that Ian Hopkins was at the heart of the [investigation] "The whole thing was a shambles."

2017.

By January 11th 2017, Chief Inspector Clara Williams had made the local paper;

> 'Police Chief 'considered killing herself' as she was being investigated tribunal hears'

Clara had taken GMP to an employment tribunal alleging that she had been unfairly brought into a criminal investigation only because she had blown the whistle on the conduct of the Superintendent over his decision relating to a detained person. Clara was one of three officers who faced a criminal investigation following the arrest of PS Pendlebury. Partway through the tribunal, GMP agreed to settle Clara's case. The local media continued their reporting on Clara's Tribunal and on 15th January 2017 wrote an article titled;

> GMP settles case brought by senior cop who claimed she was 'fitted up'

In this article the Deputy Chief Constable of GMP Ian Pilling is quoted;

> 'We accept that some elements of the IPCC managed investigation were not carried out in the effective manner that we always aspire to and it took too long to reach the final conclusion. However, we maintain that the investigation was one which needed to be carried out. The public rightfully expects the highest possible standards from the police when a report of officer misconduct is received, it is only right that the case is thoroughly investigated.'

[At this point I invite you to read the Court of Appeal – Case Number A2/2015/4355 especially paragraph 87 and the conclusion in paragraph 100 onwards. Around the time that DCC Pilling was quoted making these comments you will be able to read for yourself what Ian Hopkins and GMP were arguing in the Court of Appeal]

March 2017.

[Iconic – Madonna]

As Chair of BAPA, I pushed for the contributions of black staff to be recognised and memorialised by the force. I was infuriated that in one article black contribution to GMP was limited to Sandra Douglas winning a bronze medal in the 4x400 metres relay at the 1992 Barcelona Olympics. Don't get me wrong, this was a fabulous achievement for Sandra, who I knew and who I had worked with, but a bronze medal at the Olympics was not the limit of black achievement. I thought that Karin Mulligan, my friend and mentor, should be properly remembered. Through Claire Light, GMP had agreed to place a memorial in the foyer at police headquarters. The memorial was to be unveiled at a ceremony on 14th March 2017.

On the 17th, I spoke at the ceremony before an audience of Karin's family, friends, and colleagues. Hopkins was present, I did not doubt that he saw an opportunity for himself in the event. He stood alongside me trying to give the impression of a united front. I thought that he was a snake and I would weave that into my speech. During my speech, I praised Karin's achievements and contributions to GMP. I finished each paragraph with "She was a much better person than me." Not that I had a speech written out, I didn't and never did. I found read speeches cold and uninspiring. I thought that I'd leave the lacklustre performance to Hopkins – I thought that he was good at that.

In my speech, I told a story of a young girl, a BME girl, who whilst walking through the woods one day found a snake dying in the grass. Against her better judgment, she picked the dying snake up and took it home. There, over the following weeks and months, she nursed the snake back to life. She played with the snake, fed it, and went out for walks with it. The snake and the girl had become the best of friends. When the snake was in full health the girl let her guard down, the snake bit her. She was horrified and writhed with pain from the snake's bite. As she lay there she said to the snake "How could you do this to me after all that I have done for you," the snake turned to the girl and said, "Yes but you always knew that I was a snake, didn't you?"

You see being black and surviving in GMP was like living in a snake pit. I never forgot who I was dealing with, Fahy, Shewan, Burnham and Hopkins were people who I could never trust even though I could exist alongside them. I got the impression that Hopkins understood the moral of the story. I knew people like him and what they are capable of. 'When you understand the nature of a thing, you know what it is capable of.' – Blade.

The memorial to Karin read;

> Throughout her service distinguished herself as an excellent Police Officer and advocate of equality and social justice.
>
> Karin dedicated enormous energy and experienced significant prejudice moving GMP forward on equality and diversity issues.
>
> She was instrumental in the formation of BAPA and its national networks.
>
> She became the first black woman in the UK to reach the rank of Chief Inspector and Temporary Superintendent.
>
> In the varied roles and responsibilities, she held throughout her career until her untimely passing in 2009, she held to the simple principle that
>
> "You can't make a rainbow with just one colour"

I wrote a tribute to Karin in the BAPA newsletter. It is still as fitting as it was when I wrote it;

> 'For Karin,

I Did That

A memorial for Karin Mulligan has been unveiled at Force Headquarters. Karin reached the substantive rank of Chief Inspector and at one time was the highest-ranking women from a minority ethnic background in the country.

I would like to thank Karin's family for allowing this memorial to be placed within GMP premises. I can only imagine the emotional struggle of this decision especially when one considers the prejudice and discrimination (double discrimination) that Karin suffered whilst serving in the force.

We often hear eulogies that do not reflect the person's life or how they lived. On this occasion every positive thing written about Karin is true. She was a remarkable person who was ahead of her time.

She taught me so many things about the police and how to survive the police; it was only much later in life that I realised and understood fully the special gift that Karin had.

The timing of this memorial means different things to different people. To me, it is the first permanent reminder of the contribution that people from black or minority ethnic backgrounds have made within GMP. The fact that it has taken until 2017 for this to happen, eight years after Karin's passing, is an indication of how far we have to go.

This memorial is not just about Karin's amazing contribution to the police service but for all BAPA's contributions to policing that have been ignored, undermined, re-written and removed. There are people within GMP who did not want this memorial and, like deceitful cowards, worked in the shadows against me and BAPA.

I am pleased that for once decency prevailed.

Over the years I have written a number of articles that paid tribute to Karin, I am sure that this will not be my last. She was an inspiration to me and to so many people; we should unashamedly continue to say her name and speak about the things that she did.

In 2015, I used a quote by Ralph Waldo Emerson that summed up Karin's contribution to BAPA, to policing and to a great many people. Do not go where the path may lead, go instead where there is no path and leave a trail.'

22nd March.

I attended the Court of Appeal as Ian Hopkins was appealing tribunal four for a second time having lost at the Employment Appeals Tribunal. There seemed to be a bottomless pit of public money available to GMP. My barrister, Miss Assunta Del Priore, felt that Queens Counsel should appear in front of the Court of Appeal so briefed Paul Gilroy QC to represent me. I was more than happy with Assunta, who had won at the lower court and the EAT, but if she thought that I was best served by Paul Gilroy I was not going to argue with her. My reservation with Paul was that he had not lived the case and therefore was susceptible to error.

Clare and I found our way to the court through what felt like a never-ending maze of ornate corridors. There we sat at the back listening to arguments about the Police Reform Act 2002 and Police Conduct Regulations 2012. My issue with the Police Reform Act dated back to 2008. Karin had written to ACC Terry Sweeney asking GMP to acknowledge what I had achieved with the IPCC. GMP had done nothing to advance my work back then and Honest Garry never did get back to me. I was also disappointed with Paul Gilroy's depth of knowledge of the case; I hoped that he had not left me exposed. Partway through the hearing the court stopped proceedings momentarily before declaring that there had been an attack in London. They did not give any more details – or at least I do not recall any further details about it. The Court of Appeal would hand down their decision at a later date.

When we left the Court of Appeal, London looked like a scene from a zombie apocalypse movie. Not that there were hordes of the undead walking streets no, the streets outside were empty. We went into a pub to learn that a terror attack had occurred outside of the Palace of Westminster. Khalid Masood, a British national, drove a car into pedestrians on Westminster Bridge killing four and injuring dozens more. He was shot and killed by an armed police officer

I was subsequently approached by solicitors acting on behalf of PS Pendlebury. PS Pendlebury claimed that Steve Retford breached data protection when delivering his presentation. The defendant in PS Pendlebury's action was the Chief Constable of GMP who was Ian Hopkins. I provided PS Pendlebury's solicitor with a copy of the statement that I had given to PSB. My statement recorded the facts of the incident that also supported PS Pendlebury's claim. The case of Richard Pendlebury v The Chief Constable of Greater Manchester Police was placed before the County Court. GMP submitted a defence to PS Pendlebury's claim that contained a declaration a 'Statement of Truth' signed by Catherine Shackleton, a solicitor working in GMP's Legal Services Department:

5th May 2017.

>The Statement of Truth

>'The Defendant believes that the facts stated in this Defence are true, I am authorised by the defendant to sign this statement.'

>Within the statement of truth, the defendant admits;

'On 11th February 2016, Mr Stephen Retford, acting in the service of the Defendant, delivered continuing professional training to the Defendant's detectives.'

Referring to DC Paul Bailey.

'His intervention amounted to further disclosure of information concerning the Claimant.'

'Any identification of the claimant by any other person present after DC Bailey's intervention was a result of additional information given by him.'

'At no material time was DC Bailey acting under the Defendant's direction or control.'

The statement of truth was simply not true. Hopkins was willing to tell the court that Steve Retford was acting in his service but I, a serving detective on duty, on police premises, at a seminar provided by GMP was not. Hopkins was also willing to say that I had disclosed information, which I had not – there had never been any suggestion that I had done anything wrong. The statement of truth was signed on 5th May 2017 the very day that Andy Burnham took office as Mayor of Manchester.

On May 11th 2017, I reported conduct matters, relating to the Chief Constable's statement of truth, to Deputy Chief Constable Ian Pilling. I was in no doubt that the submission of the statement to the court was a criminal offence – an offence of Perverting or Conspiring to Pervert the Course of Justice. DCC Pilling was the Appropriate Authority or person in charge of misconduct investigations for the force. I recalled Ian Hopkins' words when he was interviewed by the BBC – he said;

"Would your listeners want an officer who has influence in this organisation who is deliberately dishonest to be serving as a police officer? I don't think they would.'

Ian Hopkins

Despite, DCC Pilling's comments after Clara Williams' employment tribunal, no investigation into Catherine Shackleton or Ian Hopkins took place. So, when Pilling is quoted saying;

> 'The public rightfully expects the highest possible standards from the police when a report of officer misconduct is received, it is only right that the case is thoroughly investigated.'
>
> Ian Pilling

This is nothing other than bullshit.

21st May 2017.

The BBC File on Four team released another programme featuring GMP. In this episode entitled 'Policing the Police' the BBC examined the police complaints system that some saw as corrupt, others saw as broken. Dame Anne Owers, the then Chair of The Independent Police Complaints Commission, accepted that the police were not always as open as they could be. She stated that there was sometimes resistance to scrutiny and resistance to accountability in forces. She went on to say that some forces did not always deal with investigations in the right way. The IPCC found that in cases where the complainant had appealed to the IPCC, four out of ten police investigations were flawed. She said that in some police investigations; all lines of investigations were not followed, police evidence wasn't sufficiently challenged, that there was not a sufficiently robust investigation, or the police had not applied the proper tests when looking at cases.

Inspector Scott Winters appeared on the programme, I mentioned Scott and his case in less detail earlier in this book. The full details of his case were laid bare by the BBC. In 2013, Scott had been pursued for misconduct after a minor disagreement with a junior officer in a custody office. Scott was served regulation papers – a formal disciplinary notice, he was accused of intimidating and threatening conduct and assault. The subsequent investigation involved nineteen officers and lasted for almost a year. Scott took GMP to an employment tribunal as he felt that he had been treated less favourably and disproportionately because he was black. In February 2015, during his cross-examination, Scott was asked about an incident that the force claimed occurred eighteen years previously, it was alleged that Scott had grabbed a female colleague by the throat. Scott denied vehemently that the incident ever happened he described the allegation as a fantasy.

I also appeared on the BBC programme. This was my second time on 'File on Four.' I was in court when the allegation of assault was put to Scott. On the programme, I described that from my point of view, GMP had tried to portray Scott as the stereotypical angry, aggressive, black man. I was no stranger to this as in 2009 GMP had tried to portray me in the same light, using Rebekah Sutcliffe as their star witness. The PSB investigation into me had gone back years in an attempt to bolster the evidence against me. Scott said that the alleged incident did not happen, I had no reason to disbelieve him especially when the Chief Constable, Ian Hopkins, folded and settled Scott's case out of court. Scott later asked GMP to record a crime of Perverting the Course of Justice in relation to the allegation of assault on the female officer that was placed before the employment tribunal. GMP referred Scott's complaint to the IPCC but the subsequent IPCC inquiry stalled as GMP refused to co-operate with an investigation that they had initiated. The IPCC referred Scott's complaint back to GMP who, after an internal investigation, found that there was no case to answer. This is what I said to the BBC;

> "It's ridiculous that the IPCC can be stonewalled by any force or any person within that force who just decides that they are

not going to give any information. If the IPCC don't have the power to obtain that information then what is the point to them? I think it's utterly ridiculous and I think that it is for the IPCC and GMP to explain how this situation could arise."

Following immediately on from my comment the BBC put to Dame Anne Owers that being forced to hand the investigation back to GMP, after they had refused to co- operate, made a mockery of the IPCC, she responded;

"Well, it does but fortunately it is rare."

Chris Barnes had found a Job at the IPCC – he was good but not even he could save this bunch. He had settled into his new role and appeared to be enjoying it. On a personal front, he had received some bad news that he was still trying to come to terms with. Chris' cancer had returned and had metastasised. He was the same old Chris trying to keep a positive outlook, but I could see that the return of the cancer had hit him hard. It wasn't long before Chris was not well enough to work, he was faced with more home care. I tried to go around to see him whenever I could. Sometimes I would stay fifteen minutes or so, sometimes much longer. It really depended on how Chris was feeling on the day. The cancer the second time around was more aggressive and had moved to his back making it difficult for him to climb the stairs or even climb out of his seat. The nurse made her home visits to do what she could for him, but he was struggling. It pained me to see him this way.

14th June 2017.

The Court of Appeal handed down its Approved Judgment. The appeal was upheld. I read the judgment with different eyes that day. Two courts had previously found in my favour, the third had not and I was back to square one. As a black man in Britain and as a Police Officer, a Police Detective no less, I had lost faith in the judicial process. For me, it had become a pantomime where the real issue of race and discrimination, something that Britain has yet to face, has become a secondary consideration. Andy Burnham gave a speech in the House of Commons after the Hillsborough verdict.

He complained about the police;

"A police force which had consistently put protecting itself against, over and above protecting people harmed by Hillsborough."

He complained about the judicial system;

"A flawed judicial system that gives the upper hand to those in authority over and above ordinary people."

"Why should the authorities be able to spend public money like water to protect themselves when families have no such help"

Andy Burnham was the Mayor of Manchester at the time of this judgment. He did not contact me about it or try to discuss it with me in any way. What was even more shocking was that I was one of those constituents who went to see him and who he referred to in the BBC File on Four – Bent Cops Programme. I look back at that speech now and in my view, it is total bunkum. A light show to gain Burnham's attention and fame.

16th June 2017.

I reported the conduct matters, relating to the Chief Constable's statement of truth, to Andy Burnham. I made it clear that Burnham should consider offences of Conspiracy to Pervert the Course of Justice and Corrupt or other Improper Exercise of Police Powers and Privileges that fell under Section 26, Criminal Justice and Courts Act 2015. I spelt the offences out for Burnham as he was not a police officer, I believed that both of these offences had been made out. I heard what Burnham had said to the BBC during the 'File on Four' programme 'Bent Cops?' now was the time for him to put his money where his mouth was.

On July 17th, having had no response from Burnham I emailed the complaint to Dame Anne Owers who appeared with me on the 'Policing the Police' BBC broadcast. GMP ultimately dropped its defence to PS Pendlebury's case and paid him compensation, a small victory for Rick. Only a blind man could not see why there was this sudden change of heart by the Chief Constable – the defence was not truthful and I had found out about it. Hopkins would later be known as 'Half-Truth' Hopkins on social media, I thought that this title was generous.

On the 16th, Ellen Higginbottom, an eighteen-year-old student was reported missing by her father after she had failed to return home. The police found her body in Orrell Water Park, in the early hours of the following morning.

On Saturday 17th June 2017, I was on duty with my MIT syndicate when we received the call to attend this incident. Ellen had suffered severe wounds to her neck which would later be recorded as the cause of her death. The scene where Ellen's body was found revealed evidence of an attempt to conceal her. The incident felt extraordinary to me despite my years of investigating homicides. Whoever was responsible for murdering Ellen, needed to be traced, and fast. During the subsequent fast-moving investigation, Mark Buckley, a fifty-two-year-old man with links to Orrell, was identified as a suspect. He was quickly arrested. I was tasked with interviewing Buckley with DC John Crook.

I had known John since returning to MIT. John was around my age and had joined GMP twelve months before me. Being that bit older than the rest of the syndicate John was more measured in his responses and his actions. Maybe that was just his way or maybe John was acutely aware of how close he was to retirement and did not want to do anything to fuck that up. In any event, he was a calming force who I could have an adult conversation with. We had become the elder statesmen of the syndicate and were both well-trained and experienced interviewers.

Forensic Psychologist Dr Adrian West was called in to assist with the murder investigation. Adrian was regarded as one of the most eminent criminal psychologists in Britain, and years earlier had assisted with the investigation into the murder of five women in Ipswich. John and I sat with Adrian, we discussed strategy and how to get the most out of Buckley during the interview. The circumstances of the murder indicated to me that Buckley was potentially a very dangerous man, I needed to bring my 'A' game to this interview.

Buckley had his consultation with his solicitor then it was time for him to be questioned. I led the interview and therefore would speak first from the police's point of view. The questioning was down-streamed, which meant that others could watch the live interview from another location. I started with introductions and rules. I wanted to take my time and ensure that there could be no challenges to the conduct of the interview later on. I have always been an advocate of the first question in any suspect interview being "Did you do it." I saw little point in going around the houses with questions only for the suspect to admit the offence without any resistance. I had had suspects admit to committing murders previously; John Rao admitted killing his mother and sister by way of example of this. Surely Buckley would not admit such a heinous act to me.

The first question I asked Buckley was whether he had murdered Ellen. Buckley admitted the murder straight away, then described what he did. It was chilling to hear Buckley's account; I was determined not to look shocked or react in any way. After a short while, I became inured to Buckley's admissions and descriptions – but I have never forgotten them. Many officers think that interviewing a suspect starts in the interview room, it doesn't. It starts from the very moment that you meet them in the custody office or the moment you arrest them. It has everything to do with how you treat them irrespective of what they are accused of. It is how you comport yourself. If you are an arse, they will see you as such and you will get nowhere, and it is about how you present the evidence to them. Clear and concise not convoluted and judgemental. The number of confessions that suspects made to me in my career, even to the most serious offences, was not an accident.

Buckley was charged with Ellen's murder. During the trial the prosecutor said;

"Mark Buckley went out that day equipped with a knife to carry out a violent assault. We believe he selected his victim at random, and Ellen Higginbottom was simply walking through the park at the time he chose to attack, with tragic consequences"

The judge said;

"She simply did not stand a chance. What must have been going through her mind is beyond imagining."

Mark Buckley was sentenced to life imprisonment; he must serve a minimum of thirty-one years.

30th July 2017.

The body of a man was found in a flat in Oldham. He was later identified as Jonathan Herd, aged 44, who had been stabbed to death. Jonathan had sustained over a hundred injuries. Michael Pickering was arrested on suspicion of Jonathan's murder; DC John Crook and I were tasked with interviewing Pickering whilst he was in custody. The second murder interview for John and me in the space of a few weeks. We interviewed Michael Pickering who struggled to control his emotions under questioning. He definitely would not have made a good poker player as I suspected that if he was dealt a poor hand it would be written all over his face. The evidence against Pickering was solid enough for him to be charged. He was later found guilty of torturing and murdering Jonathan Herd receiving a life sentence with a minimum of thirty-six years. Michael Pickering would not be the last suspected murderer that John and I would interview together.

31st July 2017.

Dame Anne Owers responded to my complaint about the 'Statement of Truth' that had been filed for the Chief Constable in the PS Pendlebury County Court case. Her reply boils down to this one line.

> 'Currently, the IPCC cannot investigate a matter without a referral from the relevant force.'

I questioned the point of the IPCC on the BBC – Policing the Police programme, but I still had not found an answer. I had complained to Burnham and would therefore have to wait for his reply.

September 2017.

The first two weeks in September saw employment tribunal five, named the OP Holly tribunal, get underway in Manchester. GMP, now happy to pay for Queens Counsel in the lower court, was represented by Simon Gorton. It amazed me how someone in such a position could look so dishevelled. He always looked to me as though he had bought a suit from Oxfam the day before and slept in it overnight. This tribunal was regarding my removal as disclosure officer from OP Holly, a North West Regional Organised Crime Unit investigation. My removal had not happened when I was served with the regulation papers or disciplinary notice, but months later after Ian Unsworth QC had delayed making a charging decision and wrote a report about why he considered I could no longer carry out that role. My previous employment tribunals were very much on his mind.

The Chief Constable of GMP's defence was that the decision to remove me was that of Dermot Horrigan, a Lancashire Constabulary Police Officer, and as such I could not seek a remedy through an employment tribunal because Horrigan worked for a different force to me. They also stated that my removal had nothing to do with any protected act that I had made or my previous tribunals.

Unlike their witnesses' comical performances in tribunal four, their witnesses this time seemed to have their accounts together – these accounts felt rehearsed. The redaction of documents during the disclosure phase left me scratching my head, Ian Unsworth's report had been heavily redacted which came as no surprise to me. Andy Burnham's speech about level playing fields after the Hillsborough verdicts was a dim and distant memory. My confidence in the judicial process was at rock bottom. Looking on the bright side, my confidence could not get any lower. Gorton did his usual thing, defragmenting everything until he got an answer that he could use later on. The public purse had a hole burnt through it. The circus was definitely in town.

Tribunal five was still being heard when I was approached by Peter Jackson. Peter, who retired from GMP in February 2017, had been a Detective Superintendent in GMP and at one time headed MIT. He told me that he had significant information about my tribunal.

He had been approached by a former colleague who told him that they had had a conversation, with DI Tim Dean, the Senior Investigating Officer on the OP Holly investigation, and witness for GMP at the tribunal. During the conversation Dean said that he was very angry at GMP and their approach to the tribunal. He said that his statement for the tribunal had been prepared by GMP solicitor Laura Shuttleworth and that she had included information that was not accurate or truthful. Dean told Shuttleworth that he was not happy with the content of the statement which subsequently resulted in several versions being re-written and passed back and forth via email before Dean agreed to sign it. He said that Shuttleworth had then added an additional paragraph which was not truthful or accurate. Dean objected to this which prompted a heated exchange between Dean and Shuttleworth with Shuttleworth saying words to the effect "If GMP lose this case then it will be on your head."

Dean was angry that he was being asked to sign something that was not true and felt GMP were trying to make him a scapegoat. He firmly blamed GMP for the situation and there had been a breakdown of relations between GMP and NWROCU. The former colleague that had given Peter this account was DS Julie Barnes, the Deputy SIO on the OP Holly investigation. Julie was fearful that if she came forward, she would be victimised by senior officers inside and outside of GMP. Julie has since retired from GMP and I have no misgivings about naming her here.

Peter regarded the conduct of Laura Shuttleworth as the potential criminal offence of Attempting to Pervert the Course of Justice. He also regarded it as serious misconduct and a serious breach of professional behaviour. He thought that if Shuttleworth had taken this approach with one witness then she may have taken the same approach with other witnesses. In the interest of fairness and justice, he wanted the Employment Tribunal to be provided with the information. When Peter told me, I was in no doubt that criminal offences had taken place. I ensured that Peter informed my legal representatives which he did immediately on 10th September. It was hard to list the number of breaches in legislation and process that had occurred, but it was all too late for these proceedings. Peter would subsequently report the matter to The Solicitors Regulatory Authority on 4th October 2017, to the IPCC on 17th October 2017 and on 14th November 2017 to Andy Burnham. No formal investigation has taken place to my knowledge.

28th December 2017

>Dear Mr Jackson,

>>Complaint against Police Staff (Laura Shuttleworth) I refer to your complaint to the IPCC dated 17th October 2017 and received by us on 21st December 2017 regarding the above.

>>I am writing to clarify the situation about who can complain against the police under the provisions of the Police Reform Act 2002.

>>The four categories of persons who can make a complaint in relation to these allegations are;

- Those personally aggrieved by the alleged conduct
- Witnesses to the alleged conduct
- Adversely affected by association with the aggrieved
- Acting on behalf of an aggrieved.

>>Please see Section 12(1)(b) Part 2, Police Reform Act 2002 Writing about an incident in which you are not personally involved does not qualify you to make a complaint against the police. From the information you have provided, it appears you were not present or witnessed the incident at the time and were not directly affected.

>>In the circumstances and in the absence of a complaint from

anyone who does qualify to complain, I am not recording this as a conduct complaint against police.

If you are unhappy with this decision you can appeal direct to the IPCC within 28 days from the day following the date of this letter.

Michael Thornton
Complaints Manager
Appropriate Authority
Professional Standards Branch Investigations

I doubt that in the face of a criminal complaint, from a member of the public, there could be an obscener reply from GMP. Two solicitors from the Legal Services Department with allegations of corruption against them in two court proceedings where I am concerned. What did DCC Ian Pilling say again about reports of misconduct?

> 'The public rightfully expect the highest possible standards from the police when a report of officer misconduct is received, it is only right that the case is thoroughly investigated.'

What did Ian Hopkins say to the BBC;

> 'Would your listeners want an officer who has influence in this organisation who is deliberately dishonest to be serving as a police officer. I don't think they would.'

What did Andy Burnham say to Parliament after the Hillsborough verdict;

> 'A police force which had consistently put protecting itself against, over and above protecting people harmed by Hillsborough. A flawed judicial system that gives the upper hand to those in authority over and above ordinary people. Why should the authorities be able to spend public money

like water to protect themselves when families have no such help.'

What did Professor John Grieve write in his review of the Karin Mulligan employment tribunal before his finding that GMP was racist;

> 'This review holds it as fundamental that serious allegations by one officer against another should be investigated and that all officers should cooperate. The statutory test and the experience of numerous concerns raised by Chief Inspector Mulligan and not acted upon leads to a finding of incompetence, racism and sexism.'

How did Sir William Macpherson define institutional racism in the Stephen Lawrence Inquiry;

> 'The collective failure of an organisation to provide an appropriate and professional service to people because of their colour, culture or ethnic origin.'

16th September 2017.

[See You Again – Wiz Khalifa]

It was a Saturday morning, Clare and I had gone out shopping earlier than usual that day, I don't know why that happened. When we returned home, I checked my work mobile phone. When I checked my phone there was a message from Chris, he had been admitted to a hospice. He also said that he was getting married and he would like me to be there. I looked at my watch, the wedding was in five minutes, the hospice was at least a ten-minute drive from my house. Clare and I left the shopping where it lay and got into the car; there was no time for getting changed into clothing more suited for a wedding. I drove to the hospice, using driving skills that Sir Lewis Hamilton would envy, arriving at the hospice's reception on time.

There were a few people already there, I assumed that they had had more than five minutes' notice. We went into the chapel and took our seats. Chris was brought into the chapel in a wheelchair. He was smartly dressed wearing a suit and looked well-groomed. I sat down next to Chris and took his hand. After explaining my appearance Chris told me that the pain had got so bad that he could no longer stay at home. With a tear in his eye, he said that he had had enough and wanted it all to end. I tried to hold back my tears, a futile effort as my cheeks were sopping wet. I was lost for words.

There were a few other work colleagues there, a handful, who took pictures with Chris. I did not want to do that, not because I was self-conscious in any way but because I did not want to remember Chris that way. I had known him since 1989 – a lifetime.

Heather came into the chapel looking radiant, the ceremony was the nicest and the saddest thing all at the same time. Chris and Heather were married, they held a reception afterwards where everyone celebrated their union. Chris was given oral morphine whilst trying to enjoy his new status as a married man. I recall Detective Inspector Carl Jones leaving the reception. Chris, Carl and I had served together on the Trafford Division early in our careers. As Carl said his goodbyes he burst into tears and left. Clare and I stayed for a while before it was our turn to leave. I hugged Heather and then Chris and said goodbye. Whilst walking out of the hospice I knew that I would not see Chris again, I suppose Carl had thought the same when he was leaving. During the following week, Heather contacted me to say that Chris had gotten into a state of 'Terminal Agitation,' I couldn't bear to see him this way.

It was the following Saturday after Chris and Heather's wedding. Heather sent me a message; Chris had died.

6th October 2017.

The court handed down its judgment in tribunal five and agreed with the defence submission. They agreed that Dermot Horrigan had decided to remove me as disclosure officer from OP Holly, that he had done so alone and that my previous employment tribunals were not a factor in his mind. The court did say that if they were wrong about Mr Horrigan's motivation then I was not able to claim against him as he worked for a different force and the law didn't allow for this. This being the case I question why officers were allowed to work for NWROCU in the first instance.

13th October 2017.

Chris was cremated at Altrincham. I carried his coffin with his family. It was the second time in my life and in my police career that I had been asked to carry a dear friend's coffin at their funeral. Once again, I was honoured and proud to do this and once again there was an honour guard at the entrance. The crematorium was packed; some people had to stand outside in the car park during the service. It showed me how well-loved Chris was. The service was a celebration of Chris' life and like him, it was amusing and touching. I knew that I would miss him.

[The Climb – Miley Cyrus]

The National Black Police Association annual conference was held in Cheshire in the City of Chester. I intended to spend both days at the conference as Chester was only a hop, skip and a jump away from my home. I was nearing the end of my career and believed that this conference would probably be my last. On the first day, I took the train to Chester as Clare was coming to the dinner that was held on the first night and we didn't need both cars there. These conferences hadn't changed over the years for me. It was attended by those who believed in the struggle and wanted to be part of that fight, and those who thought that there was something in it for them, that being part of the NBPA was a means of getting something better for themselves. The first day of the conference wasn't remarkable for me. A few speeches intended to inspire the audience punctuated by seminars intended to do the same.

There was an Assistant Chief Constable from Cheshire Constabulary at the event, he was called Nick Bailey. Nick and I went to Stretford Grammar School together. At school, Nick and his brother Phil were the second pair of Bailey brothers, the distinguishing feature being that my brother Andrew and I were black. Nick was nearing retirement also, and we discussed what we intended to do post the police. People looked at my jovial conversation with Nick, I had not mentioned the fact that I had known him since aged eleven as I did not want his association with me to be a hindrance to his upward progression. That did not seem to bother Nick as he declared that we were friends from school to a PC who was earwigging our conversation. My Employment Solicitor Juliette Franklyn was at the conference, I had not known that she was going to be there, but it gave us a chance to catch up with my tribunals.

That evening Clare and I attended the dinner with a few other members of BAPA. During the evening, there was an award ceremony where the NBPA honoured people for their contribution to the NBPA and, I suppose, the wider police service. I sat at our table enjoying the evening and listening to the presentations. One of the presentations was the lifetime achievement award. I sat there listening to the description of the person who was going to receive it, about three sentences in I realised that they were talking about me – I think it was the line about challenging anyone that did it. There was rapturous applause from the audience as I got up to receive my award. It was humbling to be honoured in this way by so many people. Not only that but the recognition of a lifetime of struggle and achievement, a lifetime of ups and downs and a lifetime of sacrifice warmed my heart. There was only one way to celebrate – to the bar, a bottle of fizz. Nick came over to me with his mobile in his hand. He took a selfie of us. I understand that he tweeted the photo congratulating me. It was a very pleasant night indeed.

[In The Air Tonight – Phil Collins]

At the beginning of day two Nick gave a speech to the audience where he declared to everyone that he and I had gone to school together. The length of time that we knew each other and our association was out there, there was no putting the genie back into the bottle. I just hoped that he had not harmed himself in any way.

I later went to a seminar hosted by Dr Angela Herbert MBE. I had always found her fascinating and entertaining. She always caught my attention as her message was always something I could use or consider. Dr Herbert provided life coaching to several Greater Manchester Police employees. I was instrumental in this service and knew that anyone who I referred to Dr Angela would be much better off for the experience. After a slow start, it turned out to be a very eventful conference after all.

15th December 2017.

Dear Mr Bailey,

I refer to the allegations which appear to relate to the Chief Constable of Greater Manchester Police (GMP), which were forwarded to my office by GMP Professional Standards Branch.

In the exercise of his duties as the Police and Crime Commissioner (PCC) for Greater Manchester, the Mayor of Greater Manchester is the appropriate authority to consider complaints and allegations made against the Chief Constable.

Part of the PCC role is to ensure the Chief Constable's actions are consistent with the 'Standards of Professional Behaviour'.

The College of Policing has produced a Code of Ethics, which applies to all police officers. Paragraphs 1.4.3 and 1.4.5 set out what is expected of chief officers and leaders in the service.

The Standards of Professional Behaviour and the Code of Ethics are both in the public domain. They can be found on the College of Policing internet site. Section 3.11 of the Independent Police Complaints Commission (IPCC) statutory guidance to the police service on the handling of complaints includes:

The following persons cannot make a complaint under the Police Reform Act 2002;

- A person who at the time of the alleged conduct was under the direction and control of the same chief officer whose conduct it was; or

- A person serving with the police, a member of staff of the

Serious Organised Crime Agency or the National Policing Improvement Agency or a person on relevant service (falling within the meaning of section 97(1)(a) or (d) of the Police Act 1996) if he or she was on duty at the time that;

- The conduct took place in relation to him or her; or
- He or she was adversely affected by it; or
- He or she witnessed it.

Source; section 29(4) of the Police Reform Act 2002 The mayor has reviewed your allegations against the Chief Constable. In accordance with section 3.11 of the IPCC guidance; and section 29(4) of the Police Reform Act 2002, he does not consider you are a person who is eligible to make a complaint against the police under the Police Reform Act 2002.

Therefore, he will not record the matters you raise as conduct complaints.

I refer to sections 6.4 and 6.5 of the IPCC guidance:

Conduct matters may come to light where a person who is prevented from being a complainant by the Police Reform Act 2002 raises issues that satisfy the definition of a conduct matter. The person raising the issues may be treated as an interested person if the matter is treated as a recordable conduct matter.

'Recording' in this context means that a record is made of the conduct matter giving it formal status under the Police Reform Act 2002. This means that it has to be handled formally in accordance with the Police Reform Act 2002 and this guidance.

He has considered whether or not your allegations fall into

the category of recordable conduct for the Chief Constable. Section 6.2 of the IPCC Guidance defines 'conduct' matters:

Subject to some limited exceptions a conduct matter about which there is not or has not been a complaint, where there is an indication (whether from the circumstance or otherwise) that a person serving with the police may have committed a criminal offence or behaved in a manner which would justify disciplinary proceedings.

(Section 12, Police Reform Act 2002)

There is no indication that the Chief Constable was involved, directly or otherwise, in any of the matters referred to the Mayor of Greater Manchester Police. There is no right to appeal against the Mayor's decision to treat/not treat allegations as recordable conduct matters.

You may appeal against the Mayor's decision not to record your allegations as a complaint to the IPCC. Your appeal must be received by the IPCC within 28 days of the day following the date of this letter, which indicate the final date for you to submit an appeal is 12th January 2018. The address for the IPCC is:

Independent Police Complaints Commission
PO Box 473
Sale
Manchester
M33 0BW

Baroness Beverley Hughes
Deputy Mayor of Greater Manchester
Policing, Crime and Criminal Justice.

Beverley Hughes wrote about Andy Burnham's decision as

Mayor in this letter. So, to be clear, Burnham was using the Police Reform Act not to investigate or even record an allegation of criminal conduct against Ian Hopkins as the Chief Constable of GMP. Furthermore, Burnham considered that the Chief Constable's 'Statement of Truth' in the County Court Proceedings with PS Pendlebury had nothing to do with the Chief Constable. The untruthful statement submitted to the court was allowed to stand.

Retired Detective Superintendent Peter Jackson had been informed by GMP PSB that he could not complain, as the victim nor could I. What are the comments made by Burnham, Hopkins and Pilling to the media and parliament if not lies?

As for the IPCC, on 18th December 2017 the IPCC Contact Centre wrote;

> 'After reviewing the correspondence. The issues that you have raised within your letters have been dealt with by the IPCC as far as we can under relevant legislation. Therefore, we will not be taking any further action with your correspondence.'

I could see no point in the IPCC. Dame Anne Owers was wrong about one thing when she said, "Well, it does but fortunately it is rare." It wasn't that rare.

19th December 2017.

On Tuesday, The Times newspaper, in the opinion of many the country's premier newspaper, published an article on the front page entitled;

Police 'took Bribes from organised crime gang'

The article reported on the collapse of a £3.5 million-pound investigation into a notorious organised crime gang. It revealed that police officers from GMP were accused of taking bribes from associates of Paul Massey and that the allegations emerged during a five-year inquiry into money laundering, fraud and tax offences. The Times had blown the lid off the collapse of Operation Holly. The piece written by Fiona Hamilton, the paper's Crime Editor, described how GMP faced serious questions after The Times had exposed the corruption allegations and established that GMP had failed to investigate these allegations. 'This was a factor in a decision by prosecutors in June not to bring charges against Massey's alleged associates, it is understood.'

This didn't work out too well for OP Holly, TITAN and GMP, after they had removed me, had it! My immediate reaction was to laugh out loud, which I did. GMP had wasted £3.5 million pounds of taxpayer's money, had been called out on corruption and had had its pants pulled down in the national media, with Burnham and Hopkins at the helm. I had originally put a great deal of work into OP Holly and should have been sad that it failed, but I wasn't. The fact that the investigation had been burned down over disclosure was equally amusing. Pursuing me on some trumped-up allegation that was never even proven to have happened had ended with abject failure. I hoped that someone was going to be held accountable for this mammoth disaster.

Interlude

Late 2010's.

[Across 110th Street – Bobby Womack]

In the years after finding out about my son, I had made the child support payments each month without fail but had had no relationship with him whatsoever, his mother had made sure of that.

I had become accustomed to this status quo and saw little point in troubling my mother, sister, or brother with news of a relative that they would have no relationship with. I had only told my wife at the time. The years had quickly passed by and the boy had become a man – a man in his late twenties.

The Brexit referendum meant that the United Kingdom would leave the European Union on 31st December 2020. UK nationals would lose the right to freedom of movement and employment across the EU, some found ways to remain European. My son had traced me, I suppose that wasn't a difficult task considering my media profile, as he wanted to apply for an Irish passport to be able to continue working for his international company. He needed information about me to satisfy the application process. Although, being a complete stranger to me, I did not want to do him any harm and therefore gladly gave him the information that he needed. I had never met him.

My mother was an elderly woman by now living alone in the same Victorian terrace in Old Trafford. My father's son and granddaughter appearing at the front door unexpectedly in the 1960s was a distant memory by this time.

One day, equipped with the new information that I had given him, my son appeared at the front door of my mother's house, papers in hand – 'Hi, I'm your grandson' was the last thing that she had expected to hear when she answered the door. I had some explaining to do for sure. 'The apple does not fall far from the tree,' never a truer phrase spoken.

I Did That

History Repeating

2018.

[Express Yourself – Charles Wright]

I continued as Chair of BAPA and continued to challenge and scrutinise GMP wherever the need arose. I had a high media profile and gave many radio interviews on a local inner-city radio station. I was amazed to learn that there was an entire web page dedicated to my radio interviews. I hoped that my contribution to the community was well received, welcomed and of some use. The listeners could be assured of two things, what I said would be real and unfiltered.

As I neared the end of my police career, I became conscious that there needed to be a succession plan for BAPA, especially for the role of Chair. When I took over the role of Chair BAPA was insignificant and unattractive. By 2018 it had become very desirable again. The time was right for me to step down, I had enough service left to act in an advisory capacity to the new Chair and to be a point of contact for the new Executive Committee. I was proud not to have left the association in a worse condition than I found it.

On the 2nd of February 2018, I stood down as Chair of BAPA. I had been the association's first Chair in 1999 and came back for a second stint that had lasted six years. I had been elected and re-elected at that time without anyone coming close to matching my performance, dedication or output. So many people came to my farewell speech, some brought me gifts that I greatly appreciated and will always remember. After standing down, I received many tributes, here are a few:

> 'Your influence will be missed. "The lived experience" continues…'

West Yorkshire Police Black Police Association.

> 'Bro Paul, you have been & will remain one of the most influential Race and Equality activists within the criminal justice system. You have my utmost respect for maintaining a stance that has exuded ethics & integrity no matter the hurdles that you have faced.'

Ruwan

> 'Alone, but not alone. We stand with you Paul.'

NBPA UK.

March 2018.

[Shout – Tears For Fears]

Employment Tribunal six was heard in Manchester on dates from December to 23rd March 2018. The Chief Constable was represented in the lower court by Simon Gorton QC. Gorton had again been enlisted by Hopkins with apparently no expense spared. I could only imagine the hourly and daily rates that Gorton was charging GMP – money that was ultimately coming out of the public purse under Andy Burnham's watch. Despite the complaints of attempting to Pervert the Course of Justice and professional misconduct made by retired Detective Superintendent Peter Jackson in tribunal five, Laura Shuttleworth was again in court representing the Chief Constable. It was clear to me that she was acting with the consent of the Chief Constable whether that consent was express of tacit. Her being in the court was like hiring Jimmy Savile to babysit – after the allegations of child abuse.

This tribunal was in relation to the misconduct investigation itself and the service of the disciplinary notice on me in January 2015. The Chief Constable's defence was that the investigation had been launched on the back of decisions made by West Yorkshire Police claiming that it was WYP who were the decision makers and not GMP or GMP's Appropriate Authority who at that time was ACC Dawn Copley. West Yorkshire Police again, how many secret reports could I look forward to this time around? So, GMP had argued that the decision to remove me from post in tribunal five was made by Lancashire Constabulary Police Officer Dermot Horrigan. Now, in tribunal six, they claimed that the decision to investigate me was made by officers of the West Yorkshire Police. Who were they going to blame next – Santa Claus?

It was the most appalling court hearing that I had ever seen. It made the court scenes in the movie My Cousin Vinnie look competent. The judge gave an oral verdict finding in GMP's favour and accepting GMP's defence. Whilst giving the oral judgement the judge shook uncontrollably and even knocked over her glass. I thought that she was having a seizure or a stroke of some kind. The written judgment was requested later, it does not cover all the things that the judge said orally. I got the impression that the judge never wanted the judgement to be written down as it would be available for scrutiny.

First things first, the court maintained the ridiculous charade of referring to the two ex-GMP officers, who had made the complaint that their details had been leaked to the Manchester Evening News, by pseudonyms X1 and X2. This was nonsense as far as I was concerned as the whole basis of their complaint was that their details had been published by the paper. Anyone could read the article that was published on 25th January 2014 under the heading *'Police Officer Sacked after GMP secrets leaked to drug dealer'* and see that their names were PC Anthony Kokuciak and PC James Parkinson. If the title of the MEN article catches your eye well it did mine also. Parkinson resigned and Kockuciak was sacked after a gross misconduct hearing in relation to police information being leaked to a drug dealer. Apparently, Parkinson admitted to four counts of obtaining personal data without consent. Now they were complaining about the leak of their information – please, and these complaints were credible?

The disciplinary notice that I was served read;

> 'Following an article published in the Manchester Evening News dated 25th January 2014, an investigation has commenced into public complaints made against Greater Manchester Police by two former officers James Parkinson and Anthony Kockuciak.
>
> This investigation has identified information that points towards you accessing a confidential discipline file that related to a Professional Standards investigation named Operation Atticus. Specifically, you accessed with the assistance of Sergeant Tom Elliott [Retired] from Greater Manchester Police Federation, the discipline file relating to Anthony Kockuciak between 1st November 2013 and 17th December 2013. It is believed at the time that you neither had the consent of Anthony Kockuciak or that you were not acting in the proper course of your police duties.'

The court understood that I had worked on Operation Holly the court judgment reads;

> 'Operation Holly gave rise to another operation called Atticus which was an investigation into allegations of corruption by two police officers who had worked on Holly (referred to in the hearing before us as X1 and X2). One was dismissed and the other resigned. There was a criminal trial which (as we understood it) did not lead to the conviction of

X1 or X2.'

This is paragraph 2 of the judgement under 'Background and Issues.' Operation Holly started in 2012. The GMP investigation that proceeded was called OP Goldfinch. The Manchester Evening News article published on 25th January 2014, which is at the very centre of the case, being fundamental to the case, reported;

Chief Superintendent Paul Rumney, of GMP's Professional Standards Branch, said:

> "Operation Atticus was an investigation led by GMP Counter Corruption Unit from 2010 into the disclosure of police intelligence to a male suspected of being concerned in the unlawful supply of drugs."

According to GMP Operation Atticus started in 2010. OP Holly, which started in 2012, could not have given rise to OP Atticus which predated it. The court was fundamentally wrong on the facts of the case and that's according to GMP.

In any event, if the court understood that I was the disclosure officer for OP Holly that 'Gave Rise' to OP Atticus; Atticus being an investigation into allegations of corruption against Parkinson and Kockuciak 'Who had worked on Holly' then I would absolutely have the right to see and disclose those disciplinary cases to the CPS – that would be the very definition of my role. The disciplinary notice served on me would therefore be complete nonsense and unjustified. The court's understanding of this case was in my view completely flawed from the outset. I was only on paragraph two. I had not seen or sought any discipline files connected to either man and did not know who Parkinson or Kockuciak were.

The Chief Constable's witnesses were accepted by the court as straightforward and truthful. During the West Yorkshire Police investigation, they interviewed retired GMP Police Detective and Police Federation representative Aidan Kielty who has since spoken about his interactions with WYP;

> "I was interviewed twice by WYP on behalf of GMP. It would have been around the same time. WYP wanted me to implicate Paul Bailey and/or Charles Crichlow. This was despite me saying that it was neither of them who telephoned me."
>
> Aidan Kielty

Aidan Keilty was not called as a witness by GMP's Chief Constable, Aidan's subsequent statement explains why and would have clearly undermined the Chief Constable's case. The judge described their witnesses as straightforward and truthful – really?

On the other hand, I was attacked by Gorton whilst giving my evidence. Gorton, not happy with the attack on me in the witness box continued his attacks on me in his skeleton argument. This even found its way into the judgment. So now the court was attacking me. I thought that Gorton's and the court's actions were despicable, no other victim would have been treated this way in court. But you can be when you have made a claim about discrimination or victimisation. On page 23 of the judgment the Judge wrote;

> 'In summary, the claimant's evidence demonstrated a tendency to exaggerate and to make the most serious allegations with no factual basis for them.'

I was asked by Gorton what I 'thought' of DI Flindle, from GMP's Professional Standards Branch. My reply highlighted by the judge was "Absolutely thought he was corrupt." I was then attacked for making an allegation. Allegation? – I told the court what I thought of Flindle in response to a question. Now this had been regarded as an allegation for which I did not have evidence. I was not allowed to have thoughts or opinions in the judge's eyes, and this was a stick to beat me with. Anyway, what does what I thought of Flindle have to do with anything?

If I thought that Flindle was a crossdressing, devil worshipping, juggler from Coventry, what relevance would that have had?

The judge goes further with her attack on me, she writes;

> 'There was a further troubling exchange in relation to the letter from his solicitor dated 1st April 2015 which alleged bias by DCC Hopkins and ACC Copley. The claimant replied that he had not made the allegations – his solicitor, Mr Kumar had. He eventually conceded that he must have agreed to the content of the letter, as Mr Kumar would not have made such allegations unless instructed to.'

First of all, Solicitor Mandip Kumar sent an email on April 1st 2015, not a letter as written in the judgment. I'm a firm believer that if you are going to make a judgment then at least get the facts straight, especially, when you are attacking the victim in the case. The judgment was unable to get even minor details correct. This is a flavour of what Mandip Kumar wrote;

> Dear DI Ryan
>
> My Client: DC Paul Bailey
>
> I write to confirm that I have been instructed by the Police Federation of England and Wales to advise my above-named client.
>
> The purpose of this letter is to advise you of the serious concerns that I have about the conduct of the Appropriate Authority in serving the Regulation 16 Notice on my client on 19/1/2015 under the Police (Complaints & Misconduct) Regulations 2012.
>
> My concern is that there appears to be an appearance of bias as to the legal basis upon which the complaint has been recorded and an abuse of the Police Regulations to subject my client to a misconduct investigation. I am concerned that due to my

client's previous history and current complaints against officers from GMP, he has been subjected to a misconduct investigation.

I would invite you to please provide a full response to the points raised below. I am placing you on notice that I am currently considering whether we should seek a Judicial Review against the decision of the Appropriate Authority to serve a Regulation 16 Notice. In addition to this, my client will be seeking further legal advice from his employment lawyers about him being victimised...'

A solicitor with no prior knowledge of this case raises concerns about the entire process. He writes that they are his concerns, he could not have been any clearer, yet this is used to attack my evidence. Mr Kumar wasn't instructed to come to his conclusions or his concerns they were his and he says this, and of course, I knew that he'd sent the email.

Then the judge attacked the skeleton argument submitted by my counsel, Mr Searle. I found the judge's view both misleading and duplicitous. Skeleton arguments are written by legal professionals on behalf of their client's case. Counsel makes the argument using their knowledge of the law. That is the whole purpose of hiring a barrister to represent you in court. No one buys a dog and barks themselves. The client reads the skeleton but it is written by counsel, what legal professional would submit a demonstrably wrong argument or one that they did not agree with? The judge makes assumptions and seeks to absolve Mr Searle in one sentence on page 24;

A further example of this, was certain statements made (no doubt on instructions) in Mr Searle's skeleton argument.

What did the judge know of the instructions that Mr Searle may or may not have had? The simple answer is nothing. The judge, in my view, was a disaster who gave herself away. Finally, in the last paragraph, where it is evident that she did not want to see any further litigation in court. I do not think that that was her place and there is no limit on how many times a person can turn to litigation. [Case No. 2405789/2015]

But my experience was not the only time that a black police officer, who had previously taken the police service to court, found the tribunal experience very different the second time around.

In 2014, PC Carol Howard, a black police officer in the Metropolitan Police took the Met to an employment tribunal. She claimed that she was subjected to a 'vindictive and spiteful' campaign of discrimination and smears. She won in court with the court ordering the Met to pay her a reported £37,000 in damages. She did not remain in the Met so thirty-seven large did not seem enough. Carol went to work for the IPCC, a mistake in itself if you ask me, later taking the IPCC to tribunal accusing the IPCC of discrimination and harassment. Carol lost the case with the judge's comments reported in the media;

> 'The judge described the former officer as "misguided" and said that her "lack of perspective is astonishing". In a damning ruling the judge suggested a £37,000 pay-out in a previous legal action against the Metropolitan Police four years ago lay behind her claim against the IPCC.'

Can anyone imagine a defendant being indicted and on trial for rape in a criminal court and the victim being described by the presiding judge as 'misguided,' the Judge then suggesting that the victim had made the allegations up? – neither can I. Whether it was intentional or not the employment tribunal service was sending a clear message to black police officers claiming discrimination more than once. Carol would later face allegations from the IPCC that she leaked 101 work related emails.

Carol had saved the emails to preserve evidence in a whistleblowing case that she was building. A jury acquitted Carol of unlawfully obtaining personal information under the Data Protection Act. This is what I had come to expect from establishments like the police service or the IPCC – victim turned suspect. Carol and I had walked similar paths, yet I had fared better than her. I had at least emerged unscathed professionally. I had no doubt that if I was not an exceptional police officer and detective then I would have succumbed.

ACC Dawn Copley did not appear as a witness in tribunal six. In April 2016 she had to step down from the role of acting Chief Constable of South Yorkshire Police, after only 48 hours, as it emerged that she had been appointed despite having declared that she was the subject of a misconduct investigation. The allegation of 'Corrupt practice' had been made against Copley by John Buttress. These allegations were independent of the concerns raised by Mandip Kumar in my case. The ignominious fall of Copley turned a frown upside-down.

6th June 2018.

[Liar, Liar Remix – MoStack]

The Times Newspaper published an article about Ian Hopkins entitled;

> 'Manchester Police Chief who used watchdog to defend force said that it wasn't up to job'

Basically, Hopkins had used an IPCC investigation and findings to defend GMP's handling of a surveillance incident, where a senior police officer allowed a boy to be left alone in the home of a suspected paedophile and organised crime group member for over an hour. Despite junior officers raising concerns about the boy's welfare, the boy was allowed to remain in the house. However, a 2013 recording of Hopkins describing the IPCC as being unable to investigate misconduct emerged highlighting the duplicity of Hopkins about the IPCC. The recording revealed Hopkins' speaking about an earlier IPCC investigation into the fatal shooting of Anthony Grainger where the IPCC were critical of GMP, he said;

> "I don't think that will do any of us any favours because yet again the IPCC report is abysmal.
>
> So, I think, the wider issue is you know the IPCC and their inability to investigate things, timely, thoroughly etc."

The emergence of the recording was an embarrassment for Hopkins, who had been called out by The Times in the most public of fashions. There was a rumour circulating around GMP that at the time of the publication Hopkins was furious and that he wanted an investigation into who had 'leaked' the recording to the paper. For me, the issue was not that there was a recording, or even that The Times had obtained a copy of it, the issue was one of the 'honesty and integrity' of the Chief Constable, saying one thing publicly and another privately. It was like investigating the person who took the Rodney King video but not the conduct of the officers recorded on the footage. Hopkins had been caught. As far as I was concerned the person who made that recording was a hero and deserved a pat on the back for destroying Hopkins so easily.

6th August 2018.

Margaret Oliver is a former GMP Detective Constable who exposed GMP's poor handling of child sex abuse investigations in Rochdale. In 2013, Maggie resigned from her post in GMP in response to Rochdale but had never given up the fight for justice for the victims of sexual abuse. The BBC produced 'Three Girls' which was a dramatized version of the events surrounding the Rochdale child sex abuse ring. The three-part drama was aired in May 2017; Lesley Sharp played Maggie Oliver in the series – for the keen-eyed, Lesley Sharp was one of the main characters in 'Scott and Bailey.'

On the 6th of August, Peter Jackson, Maggie Oliver, and I, visited Andy Burnham and his Deputy, Beverley Hughes, at Burnham's offices. Pete had managed to get an audience with Burnham, but Burnham did not expect Maggie and I to arrive at Pete's side reminiscent of the British light cavalry. We had a whole host of issues, concerns or complaints that needed to be addressed by Burnham. He looked like a cat caught in the headlights. He could not say that he didn't know of some of the issues as I had visited him at his constituency offices whilst he was a sitting Labour MP. In this meeting, he looked at his most uncomfortable.

Pete had written a statement of evidence concerning Laura Shuttleworth's actions in my employment tribunal. I had written a statement about the Chief Constable's 'Statement of Truth' submitted to the County Court in the PS Pendlebury case. The statements that Peter and I submitted to Burnham met with Criminal Procedure Rules, met with the Criminal Justice Act 1967 and met with the Magistrates' Court Act 1980. These types of signed sworn statements are used in practically every criminal prosecution in England and Wales. Burnham had been cornered and caught out.

15th August 2018.

Keith Harris was stabbed to death in a Premier Shop in Radcliffe. He died from his injuries in this seemingly unprovoked attack, he died from a stab wound to the chest. Michael Long had been arrested near the scene of the murder after crashing his Citroen into a number of parked cars. John Crook and I interviewed Long who stated that he was under the influence of drugs and alcohol at the time of the attack but accepted that he must have been responsible for Mr Harris' injuries when faced with our questioning. Michael Long was later convicted of Keith Harris' murder. receiving a life sentence with a minimum of twenty-five years.

7th December 2018.

[Don't Mess With Me – Brody Dalle]

'How can the same shit happen to the same guy twice' –

John McClane

Clare and I walked along Canal Street in Manchester City Centre having just been to a local hotel bar. I had had a meeting with Judith Moritz from the BBC.

Judith was interested in doing another article on GMP. The forecast had been for rain when Clare and I left the house, so I had a large BMW umbrella with me – not that the make of the umbrella had any bearing on the story. As we approached Canal Street's junction with Princess Street Clare said "Paul, they're stealing that bike." I looked to the junction where there were two mopeds parked next to a small row of unattended motorcycles. There was a male sat on one of the mopeds. I could not see his face as he was wearing a full-face motorcycle helmet, but he was definitely male from his shape and build.

The second moped was stood on its stand whilst two other males, also wearing full-face motorcycle helmets were in the process of cutting a chain off a rather expensive-looking motorcycle that had been secured to a post. One of these males was using a pair of bolt cutters that must have been close to a metre long; the other had a battery-powered angle grinder. There was only Clare and I there in addition to these would-be motorcycle thieves and it was dark. I immediately pushed my way in between the motorcycle and the males as they struggled to cut through the security chain. They looked at me and then shouted at me to move out of the way – yeah like that was going to happen. One swung the bolt cutters at me, but he did not want to get too close to me as I suspect he feared an arse kicking if caught. The second held the angle grinder towards me with the blade making a high-pitched whistle as it rotated. Clare shouted at me to watch out, but I wasn't going to let these stooges get the better of me. I moved forward forcing them to retreat. I had not even swung my umbrella once, if truth be known I didn't want to break it. These guys were punching above their weight, it just took a little time for them to realise this.

Several passers-by had stopped and were now recording the encounter on their mobile phones, we had become a spectacle. One of the men got too close to me, I grabbed him with one arm still holding the umbrella in the other. I recognised the danger that I was in by grabbing him as I was left vulnerable to the other two so, I let go. He tried to get onto the second moped, but I grabbed him and the moped dragging them to the ground in one movement, the moped smashed into the tarmac, his coat and bolt cutters lay on the ground. These three thieves had arrived on two mopeds expecting to leave with their mopeds and a newly acquired motorcycle. Now, I had stopped them from stealing the motorcycle, had commandeered one of their mopeds, had one of their coats and their bolt cutters. I looked around, the street was filled with people, and even the old warehouse building windows were crammed with people watching the scene unfold.

One of the men pulled his helmet off and started posturing as though he was going to attack me – not a good move as we can now see your face dickhead. He had youth on his side; he was about a hundred pounds too light though and was close to an arse whooping. The three men looked at each other for inspiration. The tide had turned and they were now not foolish enough to get anywhere near me. One of them said "Can I have my bike back," like a ten-year-old who had been naughty. He wasn't getting it back, he was a thief, technically a robber as soon as he used or threatened force. One of the women who had stopped shouted at the men, "You are being recorded why don't you fuck off." This wasn't enough to make them leave but the sound of police sirens and flashing lights seconds later did. The police cars rolled down the one-way street like an invading force, a scene worthy of the finale in 'Bad Boys'.

A Police Sergeant who had recognised me as a police officer from the moment he arrived said, "You are on the job, aren't you, where's the gun." Gun? – I hadn't seen a gun but if I had this whole scenario would have played out very differently. As it turned out several people had called the police, at least this time I wasn't considered a suspect. As people dispersed several shook my hand or waved to me. One older and more distinguished gentleman approached me and said that the police had his details. He gently patted me on the back, he didn't say anything at this point the look of admiration said it all. A younger woman thanked me and asked how I had managed to stay so calm. That was it, Clare and I walked away unmarked. I was pleased about that because I had a five-hundred-pound coat on, hers was three times that price. Ironically, my coat was made by 'Belstaff' famed for motorcycling apparel. To the bar, where we had a G&T or two and wondered how we had escaped.

Ordinarily, a police officer who did anything like this especially whilst off duty would have been commended to the highest level. GMP did not even acknowledge that the incident happened. This came as no surprise as after my Lifetime Achievement Award and after being pressured, GMP begrudgingly put out an acknowledgement on the force intranet system that had missed out my rank.

[Paper Gangsta – Lady Gaga]

If there had been any doubt about the environment - the police environment - that I had survived, and in some instances thrived during my three decades-long tenure as a police officer then this event that took place in 2018 will leave you in no doubt.

I hadn't intended to mention this incident, in fact, I had made no mention of it in the first draft of this book. Please do not misinterpret this as an oversight on my part as this certainly is not the case; the reason for the omission in the first draft is that I did not want to mention a particular Inspector as I believe him to be utterly insignificant and did not want to afford him any level of fame or notoriety. Now; after some consideration, he will be mentioned but not by name – a compromise that my conscience is happy to live with. Instead let us call him Inspector 'C'.

Inspector C - Shall we shorten it further to just 'C' – had knocked around the uniform ranks for some time. I had never heard of him until he arrived at my syndicate at Chadderton Police Station. I hadn't formed any in-depth opinion of him for the first few months other than that he was aspirational, clearly looking to be promoted to the next rank. In time, after observing him at arms-length, it was apparent to me that this guy was a total and complete incompetent arsehole. Sir Arthur Conan Doyle brought us the fictional character of Detective Inspector G Lestrade who appeared in several Sherlock Holmes stories. Lestrade, an incompetent of the first order, was happy to reap the rewards of Holmes' superb investigations. Inspector C made Lestrade look like a fucking genius. C was clearly not a detective; most scratched their heads as to how he managed to become a police officer in the first instance. C had no investigative ability to speak of and, from what I could see of him, lacked any investigative experience. He had a list of 'things to do' or ask when he took briefings – he literally read instructions from a sheet. 'Colour by Numbers' is a method of creating a picture by filling in sections that are marked out in advance and that are numbered according to the colour to be used. This may be acceptable for wannabe artists but does not work in homicide investigations. We deserve detectives who can display original thoughts and creativity.

I Did That

Colour by numbers is not the reason C is called C.

C was married to a children's entertainer who performed at parties. When I first heard that I laughed for about a week; C was married to a clown. A clown married to a clown – that one never gets old. Not content with the clowning around at home C's car was seen outside the private home address of a young single female member of the syndicate. When confronted with this he came up with the highly believable story that he was returning a scarf. The serious issue here was that C became a liability and a serious blackmail risk. I suppose the biggest problem C had was me. I wouldn't subscribe to his bullshit or allow his shenanigans to pass unchallenged.

In April 2018, C, during an impromptu meeting – the fact that the meeting was unrehearsed and improvised would lead to C's undoing. During the meeting C in an attempt to undermine me publicly said,

"You are monkeying about."

It is a well-established racist trope to refer to black people or people of African-Caribbean descent as monkeys. Throughout the ages, in the United Kingdom, it was not uncommon to see black people depicted as monkeys, referred to as monkeys or for black athletes to have bananas thrown at them. For some reason, racists believe monkeys only eat bananas. In this case, C had revealed himself; it would not end there. C's manager would not record a formal complaint stating that the Police Reform Act (2002) did not allow for it – total nonsense. As I wasn't going to allow C to get away with his racist remark, I referred C to the Professional Standards Department and had C's comments recorded as a hate incident. Unfortunately for C, the assessing officer was a black Detective Chief Inspector who thought that C's conduct should be formally recorded; C was given 'Management Action'.

Now anyone would think that after C's racist comments were exposed GMP would not consider him for promotion. After this incident C was promoted to Detective Chief Inspector; A telling-off followed by a promotion, increased pay and a larger pension. In the fictional series Line of Duty, Detective Superintendent (DSU) Ian Buckells turned out to be the incompetent who spectacularly failed upward becoming the mysterious H. I do not doubt that C would give H a run for his money.

Everything That Has A Beginning

2010.

[In The End – Linkin Park]

2019 marked the last year of my service in GMP. I had made it through a turbulent number of years with significant events stacking up one after the other, I felt as though I had lived through a Michael Bay movie or at least a Robert Zemeckis film. There were so many others who had taken on GMP and lost more than they could have ever imagined.

John Buttress had been sacked, despite the noises made by Andy Burnham initially, he had no one in authority to back him. Mo Razaq had been sacked and found himself in prison with his pension being in real jeopardy. Rick Pendlebury had also been dismissed from GMP even after he had been acquitted by a criminal court. Shazia Awan had suffered heart attacks and finally left GMP as she could not remain with the organisation any longer. Maggie Oliver resigned early because of the issues she had with GMP. She would have to make a living elsewhere. Pete Jackson had retired earlier than he wanted as he could no longer work alongside many in GMP. Karin Mulligan had passed away before she reached the end of her service and would not enjoy a well- deserved retirement. Yet I was still there having not taken a single day's sick leave for nineteen years. I realised that my continued presence in GMP irritated some but was celebrated by so many more. I was like an immovable object. Credit to Scott Winters who had also fought the good fight and made it into retirement under his own terms. He and I were two inner city kids who did not suffer fools gladly, trusted no one in the organisation and had the intellect to see the backs of so many who would have revelled in our demise.

It had taken Andy Burnham until April 30th to provide any meaningful response to the meeting where Pete, Maggie and I had cornered him in his own building. He wrote,

> 30th April 2019 Dear Paul,
>
> I refer to the various documents you provided at our meeting on 6 August.
>
> We recognise that it has taken some time to reply to you but you will understand that when we met many issues were raised which wanted to examine carefully before responding to you and Mr Jackson. This was particularly true for the concerns that were raised about Operation Augusta. The independent review will report shortly.
>
> As you know, the legislative framework that relates to the police complaints system limits my involvement in complaints regarding the Chief Constable. You are aware that the Police Reform Act 2002 does not allow an officer to make a complaint about another officer under the direction and control of the same chief officer. I did, however, undertake to review the documents you provided and respond to you with my thoughts and intentions.

Burnham then attempted to confuse and convolute very simple issues concerning the attempt to pervert the course of justice complaint that had been made about Laura Shuttleworth during my ET, as evidenced by Pete Jackson. Instead of referring this complaint for an investigation, Burnham tried to become the investigator asking for evidence from the other witness. This was not his role, Burnham had a complaint, and even more than that he had evidence in the form of a sworn witness statement from a retired

Detective Superintendent and former head of MIT. Burnham was not there to investigate but to refer complaints for investigation. Burnham had no skill or track record in investigating serious allegations of corruption or criminality like this.

He then stated that he considered the false statement submitted by Catherine Shackleton for the Chief Constable in the PS Pendlebury County court case to be an employment issue. Again, this was a clear criminal complaint. It was clear to me that Burnham was completely untrustworthy and had no intention of ever holding Chief Constable Ian Hopkins to account. Burnham misinterpreted legislation when it suited him and had a predilection for pious people instead of those who challenged him. He had been provided with evidence of crimes yet had done nothing to have those crimes investigated. He was in my view disingenuous and dangerous. His attempted trickery fell well short for me and I'm sure fell short for Maggie and Pete also. I thought and think that Andy Burnham is a disgrace to the office of the Mayor of Manchester.

18th May 2019.

Tommy Robinson visited a predominantly white housing estate in Oldham during his campaign to become a North West MEP. Robinson, whose real name is Stephen Yaxley-Lennon, had links to the English Defence League and was outspoken about Islam and Pakistani grooming gangs. He visited the estate to deliver a speech to the residents and no doubt drum up support for his campaign. A counterdemonstration by the 'Muslim Defence League' took place at the Tommy Robinson rally. The result was the eruption of serious disorder where missiles were thrown into crowds, police vehicles damaged, and fireworks set off in occupied streets. Fortunately, no one was seriously injured.

I was one of two MIT Detectives sent to an inquiry team who

would investigate the incident, the other MIT officer was my old friend DC Chris Gill. I thought of the investigation as a gentle route into retirement, but I still took the inquiry seriously. I had been allocated the main suspect from the Muslim Defence League, but first Gilly and I travelled to Bedfordshire to interview Robinson.

The journey to Luton gave Gilly and I time to catch up. It had been years since we last worked together and even longer since we had travelled and spent the night away on an inquiry. The last time we were away was on 14th February 2006. On the evening of the 14th, we went out for a meal and drinks at a restaurant. During the meal, a young woman came up to me asking if I wanted to buy Gilly a rose. "A rose?" I asked, "why would I want to buy him a rose," "Aren't you a couple?" she inquired, "No what makes you think that?" I replied. "Well, it's Valentine's night, you are having a candlelit dinner for two with wine," – She had a point. Gilly embellishes that story every time he tells it. The last version had him sitting on my knee with a rose in his hair.

We met Tommy Robinson at Luton Police Station where we had booked an interview room. I wasn't an ardent follower of Robinson by any stretch of imagination, but I knew who he was and was aware of his reputation. He obviously left that reputation at the police station door as he was meek and polite. Apart from his incessant fondling of his mobile phone, he was just an ordinary man. If he was using his mobile to record the conversation covertly then the recording would have made dismal listening. Gilly and I were business-like and to the point.

This was my last trip away in the police. I had travelled far and wide over the years and had had some great experiences and memories. The last trip was not overseas or anywhere exotic but was memorable for a different reason.

BAPA had slipped back into obscurity, the new chair was not a go-getter. The BAPA website had disappeared, so had the association's Twitter history. The Chair's explanation for this was less than convincing. I was in no doubt that BAPA was doing Hopkins' bidding and becoming the very thing that the founder members fought to prevent – BAPA had become a tool of command. With key people in the association assured in comfortable roles, I found it necessary to distance myself from them. I had been in the trenches for years, I had done my time, there was nothing more that I could do for them.

My last police raid was on 27th November 2019, the week before my last working day. A colleague and I travelled to West Yorkshire where we arrested and interviewed the head of the Muslim Defence League. I couldn't help but feel sorry for the poor chap. Enthused with a desire to fight the right wing of the political spectrum, he was ill-equipped and overmatched for the fight in every way. He admitted what he had done even if he did not appreciate the trouble that he was in. He was the last suspect that I interviewed. Twenty people were later charged in connection with the incident.

29th November 2019.

Usman Khan stabbed five people in what was described as a terror attack in the London Bridge area of the capital. Two of the people who were stabbed during the attack died from their injuries. The attacker was shot dead by the police after being held down by members of the public. One of the members of the public who had tackled Khan was John Crilly. John Crilly and David Flynn had been convicted of the murder of Augustine Maduemezia in 2005. I had predicted that the offender was white after he had mistaken a plantain – a food used in Africa, Asia and the Caribbean, for a banana. By now you have Googled this case and discovered that Crilly and Flynn were white. Crilly had his murder conviction reduced to manslaughter due to a change in the interpretation of 'joint enterprise.' He was heralded as a hero for his actions on London Bridge when he confronted Khan.

I could not believe the story when I saw it in the news, the murderer turned hero. I cannot pretend that it did not turn my stomach or leave a bitter taste in my mouth. How fickle society is.

5th December 2019.

[Keep On Singin' My Song – Christina Aguilera]

It was my last working day at GMP. No rush to get up as I was taking Clare to work first. The only emotion that I was full of that day was relief. I knew that I would not have to make that journey to the other side of the county again, nor would I have to endure the leadership of the force that in my view had fallen into disrepair and into disrepute.

I could not believe that I had made it to the end, my service was not exactly without incident. Some say remarkable, I say memorable. Despite the best efforts, of many, I was still standing, I had seen them off and survived to tell the story. Scott Winters said that he was not amazed by my resilience or that I had made it into retirement. "People like us, always make it to the end," he said. I have to agree with him. If Scott and I were on the Titanic I have do not doubt that we would have found a set of double doors to use as a makeshift life raft. My thoughts were with Karin and Sue and Chester who were no longer with us, I would have a drink to them later.

Remarkably, I received an email from Ian Hopkins. That man was the epitome of two-faced the very personification of insincerity. After all of the things that he had put me through, the misconduct investigations, the court hearings, the high court hearings, the reported criminal offences within those court hearings – he had the gall to send me this;

    4th December 2019
    Dear Paul,

    Each month I receive a list of those retiring from GMP and I saw your last day is 14th January 2020. However, I have been told that your last working day is actually tomorrow.

I just wanted to wish you well in retirement and to thank you for your service.

I know that your role as Chair of BAPA GM often put you in a difficult place with the organisation. I also remember the really constructive role you played when we started to seriously to (sic) look at improving representation with the Force around 2014. The work we did then is the bedrock for the progress we are now making.

Once every 6 weeks or so I do an awards ceremony for commendations, long service recipients and retiring colleagues. You will receive an invitation in the New Year. It would be good if you were able to attend and receive your certificate of service in person.

Best Wishes for the future, Ian Hopkins
Chief Constable
Greater Manchester Police

Did he have no shame? If he thought so highly of me then he had a funny way of showing it. Liars flatter and deceive; I was having none of it. [And if anyone feels that this was sincere consider this – despite holding attestation ceremonies during the Covid-19 pandemic, my commendation ceremony was cancelled – twice. I got a bent certificate, disguised as a printed piece of paper, through the post.]

My colleagues had clubbed together and bought me a number of gifts that all turned out to be bottles of Champagne, some with champagne glasses. They had worked out that I liked proper fizz, possibly the only thing that they knew about me. My favourite was a bottle of 'Veuve Clicquot' that had 'Paul Bailey 7826 From All Your Friends' inscribed on the tin. I was grateful for the gifts and Detective Chief Inspector Gary McIntyre's humorous farewell speech.

I picked up my Lester Freamon picture and that was it. I walked out of the front door, head held high, without a mark on me. Thank you, Karen, for walking with me x.

> Dear Clare,
>
> Thank you for your love and support over the years. You made the whole ordeal manageable. You held my hand through the darkest times and picked me up when I was down. I don't know what I would have done without you. Thank you for travelling the world with me, 116 countries and counting; but that sounds like a whole new story x.
>
> [Picture Me Rollin' – 2Pac]

Acknowledgments

I would like to thank my mother and father for their selfless determination, courage, resilience and will, the will to carry on regardless of the hurdles placed before them.

Without them, I would not have enjoyed the opportunities that I had, opportunities that they did not enjoy for themselves. Despite the events described in this book, I truly believe that I will never fully understand the bravery of their decision to move from the warm, sunny, idyllic island of Jamaica in the West Indies to a cold island in the North Atlantic; a place that they had never visited before. The term hero is used regularly in today's society, some may say overused. I am proud to state that my parents are heroes, my heroes even if that was not their intention when they embarked upon their journey to the United Kingdom.

My parents were part of the Windrush Generation. After the second world war, a huge part of Europe and Britain itself was left in ruin. In addition to the physical damage to property, Britain was faced with labour shortages. It was essential that the gap in labour was plugged. The British Nationality Act of 1948 gave citizens of British colonies overseas the right of settlement in the United Kingdom. In addition to the Act the British government encouraged citizens from British colonies to migrate to the United Kingdom. Between 1948 and 1970 nearly half a million people moved from the Caribbean to Britain. My parents were two of those pioneering West Indians who answered the call from Britain in its time of need. This story may seem romantic on the surface but the reality of what my parents embarked upon could only be described as a living nightmare. They recall stories of how Britain was sold as a magical place, not quite the story that the streets were paved with gold – that would be ridiculous, but that their lives would be enhanced if they moved to Britain. They arrived in Britain with the belief that they would work hard, raise a family and have productive and peaceful lives. At least this is the illusion that they were sold. What they found in short was racism.

In those days there were still signs in the windows that said 'No Irish, No Blacks, No Dogs.' In some of the signs displayed, no dogs came before no blacks. This signified the order of things. Black people were seen to be lower than a dog. I can say without hesitation or doubt in my mind that one of two things would have happened to me if I had been faced with the level of discrimination that my parents faced. Either I would have saved enough money to get the next boat back to Jamaica writing off my time in Britain as an experiment that went badly wrong, or I fear that I would have reacted in a way that would have landed me in prison. The fact that my parents did neither of these things choosing to persevere in a hostile environment is a credit to them and to all of the Windrush generation whose shoulders I was allowed to stand on.

I Did That

References

MLA style: "Gina Adair had wild sex with 28 men while Johnny was in prison; NEW BOOK REVEALS THE SECRET, KINKY PRIVATE LIFE OF LOYALIST TERROR LEADER..." The Free Library. 2003 MGN
LTD 07th Jan.
2021https://www.thefreelibrary.com/Gina+Adair+had+wild+sex+with+28+men+while+Johnny+was+in+prison%3b+NEW...-a0108768546

Bolton Evening News: "Shots were fired at the Horwich House where the family of Irish Terrorist, Johnny "Mad Dog" Adair is seeking refuge. 30th April 2003 Gunman fires at terror chief's house | The Bolton News

Wikipedia: "Johnny Adair" 2020
https://en.wikipedia.org/wiki/Johnny_Adair

The Guardian: "Five-year-old stabbed 52 times by mother was 'let down' by health service 14th January 2010
https://www.theguardian.com/society/2010/jan/14/chloe-fahey-report

Wikipedia: "Windrush Scandal" 2020
https://en.wikipedia.org/wiki/Windrush_scandal

Wikipedia: "1983-84 National Basketball League season" 2020
https://en.wikipedia.org/wiki/1983%E2%80%9384_National_Basketball_League_season

BBC News: "Leroy Logan: Who is the Met Police officer in Steve McQueen's Red, White and Blue?" 29th November 2020
https://www.bbc.com/news/uk-55109363

I Did That

LA Times: "Player with Heart Problems Dies in Game"

Feb 28th, 1990

https://www.latimes.com/archives/la-xpm-1990-02-28-sp-1745-story.html

Wikipedia: "The Secret Policeman" 2020

https://en.wikipedia.org/wiki/The_Secret_Policeman

Wikipedia: "Murder of Stephen Lawrence" 2020

https://en.wikipedia.org/wiki/Murder_of_Stephen_Lawrce

Manchester Evening News: "Victim of the ritual killer mum" 13th August 2004 updated 18th January 2013

https://www.manchestereveningnews.co.uk/news/greater-manchester-news/victim-of-the-ritual-killer-mum- 1098806

Manchester Evening News: "Posters going out in Mandy murder hunt" 28th May 2005 updated 21st January 2013

https://www.manchestereveningnews.co.uk/news/local- news/posters-going-out-in-mandy-murder-1097811

BBC News: "Kalvinder Singh murder: Man held over 2004 takeaway attack" 29th May 2015

https://www.bbc.co.uk/news/uk-england-manchester- 32929723

Manchester Evening News: "Shots fired at Adair family hideaway" 10th August 2004, updated 12th January 2013

https://www.manchestereveningnews.co.uk/news/greater-manchester-news/shots-fired-at-adair-family-hideaway- 1143288

The Irish Times: "Loyalists fire shots at Adair house" May 1st 2003

https://www.irishtimes.com/news/loyalists- fire-shots-at-adair-house-1.357455

Manchester Evening News: "The wild-west shooting at Salford's Brass Handles pub that sent shockwaves through the underworld" 10th December 2017, updated 11th December 2017 https://www.manchestereveningnews.co.uk/news/greater-manchester-news/wild-west-shooting-salfords-brass- 14014355

Lancashire Telegraph: "Police target the racists" 27th August 1999 https://www.lancashiretelegraph.co.uk/news/6112248.poli ce-target-racists/

Manchester Evening News: "Revealed: GMP ordered report on police discrimination – then ordered a rewrite to dilute it" 28th January 2014 https://www.manchestereveningnews.co.uk/news/greater-manchester-news/revealed-greater-manchester-police-ordered-6636459

Manchester Evening News: "Life for junkies who beat tribal chief to death" 17th December 2005, updated 17th January 2013 https://www.manchestereveningnews.co.uk/news/greater-manchester-news/life-for-junkies-who-beat-tribal- 1095719

Independent: "Black policeman was passed over for promotion 5 times" 1st April 1997 https://www.independent.co.uk/news/black-policeman-was-passed-over-for-promotion-56-times-1264675.html

Manchester Evening News: "Top officer accuses GMP of race bias" 13th August 2004, updated 18th January 2013 https://www.manchestereveningnews.co.uk/news/greater-manchester-news/top-officer-accuses-gmp-of-race- 1106399

Personnel Today: "Manchester Police pay out to settle race and sex discrimination case" 21st October 2004 https://www.personneltoday.com/hr/manchester-police-pay-out-to-settle-race-and-sex- discrimination-case/

Independent: "Police chief admits to racism in ranks" 23rd October 2011
https://www.independent.co.uk/news/police-chief-admits-to-racism-in-ranks-1178083.html

Manchester Evening News: "Sir David Wilmot dies: Tributes paid after death of former Greater Manchester Police Chief Constable" 15th June 2015
https://www.manchestereveningnews.co.uk/news/greater-manchester-news/sir-david-wilmot-dies-tributes-9457916

Wikipedia: "Michael J Todd" 2020
https://en.wikipedia.org/wiki/Michael_J._Todd

Wikipedia: "Pirates of the Caribbean: The Curse of the Black Pearl" 2020
https://en.wikipedia.org/wiki/Pirates_of_the_Caribbean:_The_Curse_of_the_Black_Pearl

Manchester Evening News: "Sad end to sweet dreamer" 19th April 2010, updated 12th January 2013
https://www.manchestereveningnews.co.uk/news/greater-manchester-news/sad-end-to-sweet-dreamer-907421

Independent: "Gangland feud fear as drug dealer is shot dead" 23rd October 2011
https://www.independent.co.uk/news/gangland-feud-fear-drug-dealer-shot-dead-1597381.html

Wikipedia: "Metropolitan Borough of Wigan" 2020
https://en.wikipedia.org/wiki/Metropolitan_Borough_of_ Wigan

Oxford Academic: Dale R Wagner, Vivian H Heyward "Measures of body composition in blacks and whites: a comparative review" June 2000, pages 1392 – 1402 Abstract
https://academic.oup.com/ajcn/article/71/6/1392/4729362

Wikipedia: "Rodney King" 2020
https://en.wikipedia.org/wiki/Rodney_King

Wikipedia: "1992 Los Angeles riots" 2020
https://en.wikipedia.org/wiki/1992_Los_Angeles_riots

BBC News: "Stephen Lawrence murder: A timeline of how the story unfolded" 13th April 2018
http://www.bbc.com/news/uk-26465916

VOA News: "Black Police Officers Conference Focuses on Better Service – 2001- 08-15" 28th October 2009
https://www.voanews.com/archive/black-police-officers-conference-focuses-better-service-2001-08-15

Manchester Evening News: "GMP failed to record 80,000 crimes in 12-months and people are being 'denied justice', says blistering report" 10th December 2020
https://www.manchestereveningnews.co.uk/news/greater-manchester-news/greater-manchester-police-failing- record-19430359

The Guardian: "The Macpherson report: summary" 24th February 1999
https://www.theguardian.com/uk/1999/feb/24/lawrence.uk crime12

Manchester Evening News: "Race re-jig" 14th August 2007, updated 21st January 2013
https://www.manchestereveningnews.co.uk/news/local-news/race-re-jig-1124304

Manchester Evening News: "Teen murders mum's partner" 7th December 2006, updated 12th January 2013
https://www.manchestereveningnews.co.uk/news/local-news/teen-murders-mums-partner-1052518

Manchester Evening News: "Mayor's office fails to state confidence in Greater Manchester Police's Chief Constable after damning report" 10th December 2020
https://www.manchestereveningnews.co.uk/news/greater-manchester-news/mayors-office-fails-state-confidence- 19437433

Manchester Evening News: "Home Secretary Priti Patel writes to Andy Burnham over 'deeply concerning' GMP inspection report" 11th December 2020
https://www.manchestereveningnews.co.uk/news/greater-manchester-news/home-secretary-priti-patel-writes- 19439700

The Bolton News: "Man found guilty of murder gets life" 21st October 2003 https://www.theboltonnews.co.uk/news/5876150.man-found-guilty-of-murder-gets-life/

Wikipedia: "National Black Police Association (United States)" 2020
https://en.wikipedia.org/wiki/National_Black_Police_Association_(United_States)

Manchester Evening News: "I had a bad life, I've changed: Killer John Crilly made a vow after being released… 12 months later he defended people against a terrorist on London Bridge 6th December 2019 https://www.manchestereveningnews.co.uk/news/uk-news/how-london-bridge-killer-freed-17373720

BBC News: "Pensioner's killers get life term" 16th December 2005 http://news.bbc.co.uk/1/hi/england/manchester/4535120.st

Wikipedia: "Johnny Adair" 2020
https://en.wikipedia.org/wiki/Johnny_Adair

Mirror: "So charming… but he hid a sinister secret" 3rd June 2005, updated 21st February 2012
https://www.mirror.co.uk/lifestyle/sexrelationships/charming-hid-sinister-secret-695814

BBC News: "Man left murdered girl in street" 25th April 2005 http://news.bbc.co.uk/1/hi/england/manchester/4482791.

Manchester Evening News: "Shamed 'boobgate' cop Rebekah Sutcliffe resigns from force but lands '£122,000 job' at Oldham Council 21st February 2019
https://www.manchestereveningnews.co.uk/news/greater-manchester-news/shamed-boobgate-cop-rebekahsutcliffe- 15853402

Daily Mail Online: "Shamed ex-Assistant Chief constable, 49, found guilty of gross misconduct for baring her breast in drunken Rant at hotel bash quits force for "122,000 job at local council" 21st February 2019, updated 22nd February 2019
https://www.dailymail.co.uk/news/article6729225/Police- officer-bared-breast-drunken-rant-quits-122-000-job.html

Grimsby Live: "Former police chief Justine Curran blasts crime commissioner in first interview since her sudden exit" 28th August 2017 https://www.grimsbytelegraph.co.uk/news/former-police- chief-justine-curran-390005

Manchester Evening News: "The strong, long arm of the law" 28th May 1993

Manchester Evening News: "Away from 'king of the North', why policing could be Andy Burnham's biggest weakness 15th December 2020
https://www.manchestereveningnews.co.uk/news/greater-manchester-news/away-king-north-policing-could- 19465029

BBC News: "John Rao admits killing mum and sister in Wigan" 16th July 2012
https://www.bbc.co.uk/news/uk-england-manchester- 18853343

Manchester Evening News: "Schizophrenic killed sister" 28th August 2009, updated 18th January 2013
https://www.manchestereveningnews.co.uk/news/local-

news/schizophrenic-killed-sister-928496

Daily Mail Online: "Man who battered Alzheimer's wife to death weeks before golden wedding anniversary walks free from court" 19th December 2008 https://www.dailymail.co.uk/news/article-1098542/Man-battered-Alzheimers-wife-death-weeks-golden-wedding-anniversary-walks-free-court.html

Manchester Evening News: "Pensioner charged with wife's murder" 18th April 2010, updated 21st January 2013 https://www.manchestereveningnews.co.uk/news/greater-manchester-news/pensioner-charged-with-wifes-murder- 955964

Employment Tribunals: Case Number 240250/2007 **Employment Tribunals:** Case Number 2402742/2008 **Employment Tribunals:** Case Number 2407164/2008

Employment Tribunals: Case Number 2405789/2015 – 3rd July 2018

Employment Tribunals: Case Number 2407913/15 – 6th October 2017

Employment Tribunals: Case Number 2402005/2013 – 10th February 2015

Employment Appeals Tribunal: – Appeal Number UKEAT/0166/15/DA

Court of Appeal: – Case Number A2/2015/4355 – 14th June 2017

BBC News: "Widow forgives dead police chief" 6th October 2008 http://news.bbc.co.uk/1/hi/wales/7655611.stm

Rochdale Online: "Top police woman dies at 45" 1st April 2009 http://rochdaleonline.co.uk/news-features/2/news headlines/22307/top-police-woman-dies-at-45

BBC News: "Tributes paid to female officer" 3rd April 2009
http://rochdaleonline.co.uk/news-features/2/news-headlines/22307/top-police-woman-dies-at-45

Manchester Evening News: "Greater Manchester Police to be placed into special measures after damning inspection report" 17th December 2020, updated 18th December 2020
https://www.manchestereveningnews.co.uk/news/greater-manchester-news/breaking-greater-manchester-police- placed-19478035

BBC News: "Greater Manchester Police failings: Andy Burnham 'should resign' 18th December 2020
https://www.bbc.co.uk/news/uk-england-manchester- 55361452

The Guardian: "Acting South Yorkshire police chief steps down over conduct questions 28th April 2016
https://www.theguardian.com/uk-news/2016/apr/28/new- south-yorkshire-police-chief-hillsborough-dawn-copley- offers-resign-over-conduct

Wikiwand: "List of Olympic Games scandals and controversies" 2020
https://www.wikiwand.com/en/List_of_Olympic_Games_ scandals_and_controversies

Wikipedia: "Daniel Sickles" 2020
https://en.wikipedia.org/wiki/Daniel_Sickles

Wikipedia: "Cruella de Vil" 2020
https://en.wikipedia.org/wiki/Cruella_de_Vil

JSTOR Daily: Kimberly Fain "The Devastation of Black Wall Street" 5th July 2017 https://daily.jstor.org/the- devastation-of-black-wall-street/

Manchester Evening News: "Top PCSO fell seriously ill after battle with bosses over 'coconut' slur 31st March 2014, updated 13th April 2014
https://www.manchestereveningnews.co.uk/news/greater-manchester-news/greater-manchester-police-pcso-fell- 6895495

Neil Wilby: "Catalogue of policing scandals that shame the two-faced Mayor of Manchester" 2015-2019
https://neilwilby.com/2019/08/12/catalogue-of-policing-scandals-that-shame-the-two-faced-mayor-of-manchester/

Wikipedia: "2001 Oldham Riots" 2020
https://en.wikipedia.org/wiki/2001_Oldham_riots

Wikipedia: "Manchester Town Hall" 2020
https://en.wikipedia.org/wiki/Manchester_Town_Hall

The Times: "Police 'took bribes from organised crime gang'" 19th December 2017
https://www.thetimes.co.uk/article/greater-manchester-police-took-bribes-from-organised-crime-gang- nvnm5h9nw

Manchester Evening News: "Family of Denton stabbing victim Dominic Doyle reveal tragic last Facebook post" 8th Jun 2015
https://www.manchestereveningnews.co.uk/news/family-denton-stabbing-victim-dominic-9414542

The Guardian: "Man charged with murder after woman's body fund in car boot" 16th August 2015
https://www.theguardian.com/uk-news/2015/aug/16/man-charged-murder-womans-body- found-car-boot-heywood

Manchester Evening News: "Murder investigation launched after man stabbed in shop in Radcliffe – latest updates" 15th August 2018
https://www.manchestereveningnews.co.uk/news/greater-

manchester-news/premier-shop-radcliffe-man-stabbed- 15031600

BBC News: "Ellen Higginbottom murder: Police search delayed by four hours" 5th April 2018
http://www.bbc.com/news/uk-england-manchester 43656388

BBC News: "Man, 36, jailed for Radcliffe shop stab murder" 19th June 2019
http://www.bbc.com/news/uk-england-manchester- 43656388

Employment Cases Update +The Competent Lawyer: "Greater Manchester Police v Bailey [2017] EWCA Civ 425"
https://www.employmentcasesupdate.co.uk/site.aspx?i=ed 35570

Planet (Hits) Radio Manchester: "Man admits murdering Ellen Higginbottom" 4th September 2017
https://www.employmentcasesupdate.co.uk/site.aspx?i=ed 35570

Neil Wilby: "Mystery of the 'missing' peer review" 2015- 2019
https://neilwilby.com/tag/john-buttress-paul-bailey/

Manchester Evening News: "Two men jailed for life for beating homeless man to death and then setting his tent on fire" 11th August 2016, updated 12th August 2016
https://www.manchestereveningnews.co.uk/news/greater-manchester-news/daniel-smith-sentencing-murder-jailed- 11737708

Manchester Evening News: "High Court Throws out GMP appeal to overturn ruling it racially discriminated against black detective" 11th December 2015
https://www.manchestereveningnews.co.uk/news/greater-manchester-news/police-paul-bailey-racial-discrimination-10583608

Manchester Evening News: "Tribunal finds GMP victimised black police officer, leading to fresh claims of 'institutional racism'" 15th February 2015
https://www.manchestereveningnews.co.uk/news/greater-

manchester-news/black-gmp-police-officer-wins-8649071

The Times: "Manchester police chief who used watchdog to defend force said it wasn't up to job" 26th June 2018
https://www.thetimes.co.uk/article/manchester-police-chief-ian-hopkins-who-used-watchdog-to-defend-force-said-it-wasn-t-up-to-job-708505f92

The Times: "Police chief 'misled public' over boy in abuser's lair" 15th October 2015
https://www.thetimes.co.uk/article/police-chief-misled-public-over-boy-in-abusers-lair-grvxljv3t

Neil Wilby: "Hidden in plain sight" 2015-2019
https://neilwilby.com/tag/dcc-ian-pilling/

BBC Radio 4: File on 4, "Bent Cops?"
https://www.bbc.co.uk/programmes/b06vkg22

Wikipedia: "Battle of Isandlwana" 2020
https://en.wikipedia.org/wiki/Battle_of_Isandlwana

Wikipedia: "Battle of Rorke's Drift" 2020
https://en.wikipedia.org/wiki/Battle_of_Rorke%27s_Drift

Manchester Evening News: "The rise and excruciating fall of Steve Heywood, the police officer who was shamed in the Anthony Grainger shooting inquiry" 3rd June 2020
https://www.manchestereveningnews.co.uk/news/greater-manchester-news/rise-excruciating-fall-steve-heywood-18352855

Manchester Evening News: "Killer of Rhyan Wilson gives tearful apology to victim's family as he is jailed for life over Urmston stabbing" 17th February 2015
https://www.manchestereveningnews.co.uk/news/greater-manchester-news/rhyan-wilson-killer-apology-family-8663679

Manchester Evening News: "Rhyan Wilson's family not told of his death for eight hours" 25th August 2014
https://www.manchestereveningnews.co.uk/news/greater-manchester-news/rhyan-wilsons-family-not-told-7666131

Daily Mail Online: "Woman, 25, arrested on suspicion of murder after teenager, 18, was 'stabbed to death in a fight which spilled out from a pub'" 16th August 2014, updated 17th August 2014
https://www.dailymail.co.uk/news/article2726611/Woman-25-arrested-suspicion-murder-teenager-18-stabbed- death-fight-spilled-pub.html

Wikipedia: "Lester Freamon" 2020
https://en.wikipedia.org/wiki/Lester_Freamon

Manchester Evening News: "Paul Massey murder trial: All the evidence heard by the jury day-by-day" 17th January 2019, updated 18th January 2019
https://www.manchestereveningnews.co.uk/news/greater-manchester-news/paul-massey-murder-trial-evidence- 15677944

BBC News: "Dominic Doyle: Double-killer Colin McDonald jailed for manslaughter" 29th February 2016
http://www.bbc.com/news/uk-england-manchester- 35691640

Manchester Evening News: "Lee Nolan jailed for life for murder of Katelyn Parker whose body was found in boot of car in Heywood" 9th February 2016
https://www.manchestereveningnews.co.uk/news/greater-manchester-news/katelyn-parker-murder-lee-nolan- 10862867

Wikipedia: "2016 Turkish coup d'état attempt" 2020
https://en.wikipedia.org/wiki/2016_Turkish_coup_d%27%C3%A9tat_attempt

I Did That

Wikipedia: "Terrorism in Turkey" 2020
https://en.wikipedia.org/wiki/Terrorism_in_Turkey

Manchester Evening News: "Man charged with murder of amateur Bolton cage- fighter Sebastian Zuchlinski" 14th February 2016
https://www.manchestereveningnews.co.uk/news/greater-manchester-news/man-charged-murder-amateur-bolton- 10891688

Manchester Evening News: "Much-loved nursery manager Chrissy Kendal strangled to death by controlling husband when she said she was leaving" 21st February 2017
https://www.manchestereveningnews.co.uk/news/greater-manchester-news/chrissy-kendall-husband-murder-jailed- 12925174

BBC News: "Sacked officer: Police admit hacking phone of ex-partner" 25th July 2016
http://www.bbc.com/news/uk-england-manchester 36883167

BBC Northwest: "The Case of Chief Inspector John Buttress of Greater Manchester Police" 2016 https://youtu.be/HQcbfCKe_1g

Manchester Evening News: "Greater Manchester Police inspector found guilty of fraud for making false mortgage claims" 1st June 2013
https://www.manchestereveningnews.co.uk/news/greater-manchester-news/greater-manchester-police-inspector-found-4036147

Manchester Evening News: "Family of homeless man Daniel Smith who was burned to death in a tent speak out for the first time #TheDetectives" 27th September 2017
https://www.manchestereveningnews.co.uk/news/greater-manchester-news/family-homeless-man-daniel-smith- 13681892

ITV News: "Police officer cleared of shoplifting at home on full pay" 22nd September 2016
https://www.itv.com/news/granada/update/2016-09- 22/police-officer-cleared-of-shoplifting-at-home-on-full- pay/

BBC Northwest: "Ch Supt Lee Bruckshaw criticises Greater Manchester Police" 2016
https://youtu.be/liQg6j8ojlM

Manchester Evening News: "GMP settles case brought by senior cop who claimed she was 'Fitted up'" 15th January 2017, updated 16th January 2017
https://www.manchestereveningnews.co.uk/news/greater-manchester-news/gmp-admits-mistakes-settles-tribunal- 12458786

Manchester Evening News: "Police Chief 'considered killing herself' as she was being investigated" 11th January 2017
https://www.manchestereveningnews.co.uk/news/greater-manchester-news/police-chief-considered-killing-herself- 12439928

Wikipedia: "Atatürk Airport attack" 2020
https://en.wikipedia.org/wiki/2016_Atat%C3%BCrk_Airp ort_attack

Wikipedia: "2017 Westminster attack" 2020
https://en.wikipedia.org/wiki/2017_Westminster_attack

Manchester Evening News: "Police 'Keeping an open mind' after man's bod was found in Oldham" 30th July 2017, updated 31st July 2017
https://www.manchestereveningnews.co.uk/news/greater-manchester-news/police-keeping-open-mind-after- 13407687

BBC News: "Oldham murder: Two more men arrested over stab death" 1st August 2017
http://www.bbc.com/news/uk-england-manchester- 40797292

Manchester Evening News: "Sadistic killer tortured and brutally murdered man in his own home – before trying to sell his belongings" 1st February 2018
https://www.manchestereveningnews.co.uk/news/greater-manchester-news/sadistic-killer-tortured-brutally-murdered-14235720

BBC Radio 4: File on Four "Policing the Police" 21st May 2017
https://www.bbc.co.uk/programmes/b08q60pp

Manchester Evening News: "Police officer sacked after GMP secrets leaked to drug dealer" 25th January 2014
https://www.manchestereveningnews.co.uk/news/greater-manchester-news/police-officer-anthony-kokuciak- sacked-6593034

Lancashire Telegraph: "Psychologist on case is 'the best'" 26th December 2006
https://www.lancashiretelegraph.co.uk/news/1090222.psy chologist-case-the-best/

BBC News: "Ellen Higginbottom murder: Mark Buckley jailed for a minimum of 31 years" 14th September 2017
http://www.bbc.com/news/uk-england-manchester- 41264245

Wikipedia: "Margaret Oliver" 2020
https://en.wikipedia.org/wiki/Margaret_Oliver

Evening Standard: "Ex-Met poster girl cleared in leak case tells of 'horrific trial'" 3rd March 2020
https://www.standard.co.uk/news/london/exmet-poster- girl-cleared-in-leak-case-tells-of-horrific-trial- a4376811.html

Evening Standard: "Met Police 'poster girl' loses £144,00 claim for damages from watchdog" 11th May 2018
https://www.standard.co.uk/news/london/met-s-poster-girl-loses-ps144-000-claim-for-damages-from-police- watchdog-a3836761.html

Wikipedia: "Margaret Oliver" 2020
https://en.wikipedia.org/wiki/Three_Girls_(miniseries)

Manchester Evening News: "Twenty people charged after violence erupted in Tommy Robinson's visit to Oldham" 3rd March 2020
https://www.manchestereveningnews.co.uk/news/greater-

manchester-news/twenty-charged-tommy-robinson-oldham-17853287

Manchester Evening News: "Police want to speak to these 26 people over violence when Tommy Robinson visited Oldham"
https://www.manchestereveningnews.co.uk/news/greater-manchester-news/tommy-robinson-violence-police-appeal-17324138

Wikipedia: "2019 London Bridge stabbing" 2020
https://en.wikipedia.org/wiki/2019_London_Bridge_stabbing

BBC News: "London Bridge: What we know about the attack" 3rd December 2019 https://www.bbc.co.uk/news/uk-50594810

www.ingramcontent.com/pod-product-compliance
Lightning Source LLC
Chambersburg PA
CBHW061733070526
44585CB00024B/2658